Finding a Life of Harmony and Balance

A Taoist Master's Path to Wisdom

Chen Kaiguo and Zheng Shunchao

Translated and with an introduction by
Thomas Cleary

TUTTLE Publishing
Tokyo | Rutland, Vermont | Singapore

Published by Tuttle Publishing, an imprint of Periplus Editions (HK) Ltd.
www.tuttlepublishing.com

Library of Congress publication data is in progress.

ISBN: 978-0-8048-5274-6

Printed in Malaysia   2004VP

23 22 21 20   10 9 8 7 6 5 4 3 2 1

Distributed by
North America, Latin America & Europe
Tuttle Publishing
364 Innovation Drive
North Clarendon, VT 05759-9436 U.S.A.
Tel: (802) 773-8930; Fax: (802) 773-6993
info@tuttlepublishing.com
www.tuttlepublishing.com

Japan
Tuttle Publishing
Yaekari Building, 3rd Floor
5-4-12 Osaki, Shinagawa-ku, Tokyo 141 0032
Tel: (81) 3 5437-0171; Fax: (81) 3 5437-0755
sales@tuttle.co.jp; www.tuttle.co.jp

Asia Pacific
Berkeley Books Pte. Ltd.
3 Kallang Sector
#04-01, Singapore 349278
Tel: (65) 6741-2178; Fax: (65) 6741-2179
inquiries@periplus.com.sg
www.tuttlepublishing.com

CONTENTS

Translator's Introduction

This book is a translation of the authorized biography of Wang Liping, a living Taoist master, written by two of his longtime disciples. Wang Liping is an eighteenth-generation Transmitter of the Longmen or Dragon Gate branch of Taoism, which traces its spiritual lineage back over eight hundred years. In his childhood, Wang Liping was chosen for special training as a Transmitter by three elderly masters of Dragon Gate Taoism.

The practice of bringing up specially chosen individuals as holders and Transmitters of esoteric teachings is practiced by Tibetan Buddhists and Khajagan Sufis as well as Dragon Gate Taoists.

After being located by the elderly Dragon Gate masters, Wang Liping was subsequently educated and trained in Taoist practices for a period of fifteen years. Now he is himself a teacher. This is the story of his early life and esoteric training, based on his own recollections.

The Dragon Gate branch is a sect of the powerful Complete Reality school of Taoism, which integrated Buddhism and Confucianism into a comprehensive new form of Taoism. Complete Reality Taoism eventually spread all over China during the Middle Ages, and still continues in existence today. Numerous classics and texts of this school have been translated into English over the last ten years.

Complete Reality Taoism is generally divided into two main traditions, Southern and Northern. The somewhat older Southern tradition is rooted in the work of Zhang Boduan (Chang Po-tuan, 983–1082), whose masterpiece *Understanding Reality* is considered one of the classics of Taoist Spiritual alchemy and is also studied by Taoists of the Northern tradition. Another work on spiritual alchemy by this same master, *Four Hundred Character Treatise on the Gold Elixir*, is also widely esteemed and studied by Taoists of both Southern and Northern traditions.

The Northern tradition of Complete Reality Taoism is rooted in the work of Wang Chongyang (Wang Che, 1113–1171), particularly his *Fifteen Statements on the Establishment of a Teaching.* Wang is believed to have learned from Lu Dongbin (Lu Tung-pin n.d.), the great master known as Ancestor Lu. This Ancestor Lu is associated with the integration of Buddhism and Confucianism with ancient Taoism to produce the germ of the new spiritual alchemy of Complete Reality Taoism. Wang Chongyang is also believed to have studied from Lu's own teacher; later he himself taught a number of famous figures in Taoist tradition.

English versions of works by and about Ancestor Lu, Wang Chongyang, Zhang Boduan, and other adepts of Complete Reality Taoism can be found in *Understanding Reality; Inner Teachings of Taoism; Vitality, Energy and Spirit; The Spirit of the Tao; Immortal Sisters; The Book of Balance and Harmony,* and *The Secret of the Golden Flower.*

The Dragon Gate sect of Taoism, of which Wang Liping is an heir, was an offshoot of the Northern tradition of the Complete Reality school. Its spiritual descent is traced to the thirteenth-century master Chang-chun, who was one of the great disciples of Wang Chongyang. Chang-chun, the Master of Eternal Spring, was one of the sages who advised Genghis Khan to preserve the ancient civilization of China after the Mongolian conquest, over eight hundred years ago. Genghis Khan appointed Chang-chun overseer of religions in China, and the Dragon Gate sect thus played a critical role in the conservation of Chinese culture.

Taoists attribute to Chang-chun the core of the work known as *Journey to the West,* a symbolic story encapsulating Taoist, Buddhist, and Confucian teachings. *Journey to the West* was popularized in drama during the Yuan dynasty (1277–1367) and later elaborated during the Ming dynasty (1368–1644) into one of the most famous and most popular novels of Chinese literature. Comments on the interior spiritual significance of *Journey to the West,* written by Liu I-ming, an eleventh-generation master of the Dragon Gate sect, can be found translated into English in *Vitality, Energy, Spirit.*

A living survivor of the tumultuous era of the Great Cultural Revolution, Wang Liping is reputed to be master of a very unusual range of knowledge and capacities. As a specially trained Transmitter, he continues the Dragon Gate tradition of maintaining and updating Taoist sciences. In addition to his teaching and healing activities and work on recompiling the Taoist canon, Wang Liping also serves as an advisor to numerous official committees devoted to research on Chinese medicine, diet, and other elements of Chinese culture traditionally subtended by Taoism. He is also a husband and father.

Over the ages, it has been customary for Taoists to design and employ different educational formats, in accordance with original principles of flexibility enunciated in the ancient classic Lao-tzu, or Tao Te Ching. For the purposes of modern projection of the Dragon Gate teaching, Master Wang Liping presents a new philosophical framework, referred to as the Triple World.

The first level of the triple world consists of three realms; people, events, and things. This is the level of experience that has both form and substance, that which is accessible to ordinary human senses and the scientific instruments that have been invented to extend and augment the range of these senses.

The middle level of the triple world consists of the three realms of heaven, earth, and humanity. This level of experience includes that which has form but no substance, and that which has substance but no form. This is already beyond the domain of ordinary understanding. That which has form but no substance is like dreams; that which has substance but no form is called vitality, energy, and spirit.

The highest level of the triple world consists of the three realms of the universe, time, and space. These terms, as used here in the Taoist context, do not have exactly the same meanings as ordinarily understood. Said to be the domain of that which has neither form nor substance, the upper three realms, as experienced through Taoist practice, are found to be even vaster and richer than what are ordinarily experienced by the senses as the universe, time, and space. This is the realm of the Tao.

As is the case with all working Taoist frameworks, this philosophical system is not for the purpose of doctrinaire conditioning or abstract conceptualization, but rather is designed as an expedient means of structuring knowledge, practice, and experience. Special cultivation of the faculties is necessary even to perceive what is beyond ordinary conception; so orientation requires some way of hinting at what cannot be exactly described.

As will be seen in this book, describing outstanding events in the course of Master Wang Liping's training, each level of the system corresponds to certain Taoist exercises, levels of perception, and modes of self-cultivation. Thus the system leads the mind from the realm of the known into the realm of the unknown, by development and refinement of capacities that ordinarily lie dormant in the uncultivated state.

This book illustrates something of the possibilities of Taoism hinted at in the classics, through the remarkable story of a modern wizard of the tradition. Along the way, the book describes conditions in China past and present, outstanding personalities of yesteryear, principles and practices of Taoist immortals, the origins of the Dragon Gate teachings, and new visions of human potential and the possibilities of the future.

Part I

ENTERING THE WAY

1

The Teachers' Search

In the year 1960, one of the most momentous events in the secret history of China took place one night on a sacred mountain crag, unknown to all the world. The night was brightly lit by the moon from above and pleasantly refreshed by an ocean breeze from below. Three old men, lonely heirs to an ancient knowledge, sat outside a secret cave on holy Mount Lao, deep in meditation.

Mount Lao, or Lao Shan in Chinese, is not well known to many people outside of China. To lay people there, it is the source of most excellent water; to initiates and pilgrims, it is one of the sacred sites of Taoism, China's original wisdom tradition, the world's oldest science. Mount Lao faces the sea on two sides, east and south; steep and imposing, it seems to rise from the very ocean floor. The mountain is scattered with enormous boulders and huge rocks and covered with all sorts of plants and trees. The waves of the sea roar at its feet, white clouds encircle its waist. When you sit on the mountainside gazing at the sea as the sun rises, you feel an enormous sense of transcendence beyond the ordinary world. Thus Mount Lao came to be treasured by Taoist seekers as a place to cultivate realization and develop their essential nature.

Over the centuries, many famous Taoist masters have practiced their secret lore on Mount Lao. Through the years, many Taoist cloisters were built on the mountain; there are also many secret caves in the defiles, covered by foliage and vines, extremely difficult of access and known only to a few.

The three old men sitting on the mountainside that moonlit night in 1960 were masters of the Dragon Gate sect of the Complete Reality school of Taoism, holders of secrets and capacities long believed legendary.

Zhang Hodao, Wayfarer of the Infinite, was the sixteenth-generation

Transmitter of the Dragon Gate sect. Eighty-two years old at the time, he had once been the grand physician of the Imperial court of the Qing dynasty (1644–1911). This wayfarer was popularly called the Uncanny Physician.

Wang Jiaoming, Wayfarer of Pure Serenity, was a seventeenth-generation Transmitter of the Dragon Gate sect. A disciple of the Grand Master Zhang Hodao, he was seventy-two years old at the time. Formerly an instructor at Huangbu Military Academy, he was an advanced expert in martial arts. He was also an expert at the abacus, and was known as the Uncanny Calculator.

Gu Jiaoyi, Wayfarer of Pure Emptiness, was another disciple of Zhang Hodao, and also chosen as a seventeenth-generation Transmitter of the Dragon Gate sect. He had a unique method of curing illness by acupuncture without actually inserting needles into the body; because of this, he was popularly known as the Infinite Acupuncturist.

Over the preceding year, the three Taoist masters had been engrossed in secret consultations about a matter of utmost importance, not only to them, but to the world at large. Advanced in age, they were trying to find a successor, an individual who would bear the knowledge that would enable him to become the eighteenth-generation Transmitter of Dragon Gate Taoism.

The Taoist school of Complete Reality was founded nine centuries ago, when northern China, the ancient homeland and cultural center of the Chinese people, was overrun by mounted warriors of the steppes. The mission of the school during this crisis was to preserve not only the inner teachings of Taoism, but also the inner teachings of Buddhism and Confucianism as well.

Taoists of the Complete Reality school look upon five people as the Five Northern Ancestors: Wang Xuanbu, Zhongli Quan, Lu Dongbin, Liu Haizhan, and Wang Chongyang. Seven outstanding disciples of the last-named master Wang are known as the Seven Realized Ones of the North.

Among those seven was Qiu Chuji, more generally known as Changchun, or the Real Man of Eternal Spring. He was the founder of the Dragon Gate sect eight hundred years ago. Such was the spiritual repute of the Real Man of Eternal Spring that Genghis Khan called him to Central Asia and appointed him head of all religions in China under the Khan.

Secrets inconceivable even to other Chinese, let alone people of the

West, are still held within the Dragon Gate, even to this very day. Such is the power of the inner teachings that the three elder masters of the sixteenth and seventeenth generations spent countless hours in deep meditation on the problem of finding an heir to this knowledge.

Part of the secret lore of the Dragon Gate is a special book of symbolic patterns, known as Figuring the Backbone. Once used to analyze trends and forecast events, this special book was deliberately scrambled over six hundred years ago by covert Imperial design, as part of a broad campaign to keep the populace in ignorance and in thrall. Fortunately, the original integrity of the book was kept intact within the Dragon Gate sect of Taoism, in accord with its mission of preserving esoteric knowledge.

The new Transmitter the elders sought turned out to be a youth named Wang Liping, who was eleven years old in 1960. Wang Liping was born in 1949, precisely in the middle of the lunar year. People who know him say he was different even as a child. He could always locate misplaced articles around the house and never failed to find his playmates at hide-and-seek, no matter how well they were hidden.

Wang Liping was born in a large city in northeastern China, then later moved with his parents to an ancient fortress town near the famous Everwhite Mountain, Changbai Shan. Through the district of the fortress town cuts Yongding, the Turbid River, which has its source in the depths of Everwhite Mountain. Backed by a mountain and facing a river, the fortress town has an extraordinary energetic force in its atmosphere. With "black gold" in the ground, it is called Coal City, and has thrived all the more in modern times. This new city in an ancient fortress town is where Wang Liping has lived most of his life.

The Wang families were an important clan in the region, one whose ancestors had once been distinguished. In the time of Wang Liping's father, his family was not as it had once been, but he still managed to graduate from Fengtian Industrial College, which was considered no mean feat in those days.

Mother Wang was a good-natured, kindly woman. She gave birth to four sons and two daughters, all lively and robust except for the second son, Liping, who was slight and weakly. When Liping was one year old, there was a fire in the Wang house. Lost in the commotion, baby Liping got burned on the head. Although the burn healed all right, after that the child continued to suffer from headaches, and his eyesight was also affected. To his mother's dismay, furthermore, none of the doctors they consulted were able to help the boy.

The Wang family had many children, and back then in the late 1950s and early 1960s everyday life in China was hard. Even from childhood little Liping was kind and dutiful, mannerly and deferential, so naturally he was protective of his younger brothers and sisters. He was even that way with his neighborhood friends and playmates. Whenever another child wanted anything and Wang Liping happened to have it, he would give it away freely.

One day in the autumn of 1962, as the Wangs were eating their noon meal, they suddenly heard a loud call at the door: "A mouthful of food, please!" Now life had been very difficult for the past few years, so there were many people fleeing destitution and seeking food all the way from the central plains to the northeast. Whenever people came to the door begging, Mother Wang would gladly give something to help out.

This time it was Liping who was the first to get up on hearing the beggar's cry at the door. Before his mother could rise from the table, he had already grabbed a few vegetable dumplings and was on his way to the door with them. When he opened the door, Liping was startled by what he saw. There were three old men standing there. They looked quite different from the sorts of people who usually came begging. These old men looked kindly and benevolent, and though their clothes were worn and tattered they stood erect like strong young men, their bearing firm and steady, their presence projecting an air of vigor and strength.

The three old men reached for the dumplings Liping had brought. Gobbling them down at once, without a word the old men extended their hands again, as if to ask for more.

Somewhat disconcerted, Liping went inside without ado and fetched more dumplings for the old men. After they had eaten these, the old men exchanged glances and set off in high spirits. Mulling over the oddness of the event, when Liping looked up, the three old men had already disappeared without a trace.

Although he didn't know it at the time, young Wang Liping had good reason to be disconcerted by this encounter. As it turned out, the three old men were not ordinary people, but Taoist wizards who had long been living in hiding in mountain caves practicing secret arts. In reality, they had not come down from the mountains to beg for food, but to find the heir to their knowledge.

Taoism is the native religion of China. Its most direct and universal functions for people in the ordinary world are recognition of natural laws, promotion of health, prevention of illness, prolongation of life, and stimulation of the development of culture and civilization based on successful cooperation between humanity and nature, and between the individual and society as a whole.

The three Taoist masters who came to find Wang Liping had spent many years in mountain caves cultivating themselves. They had already reached the highest realms of attainment in both inner and outer exercises, far beyond the scope of ordinary Taoists.

In order to find a successor, they had used their inner vision, as well as the special prognostication book handed on in their sect. Arriving at the conclusion that the individual they were looking for had already been in the world for over ten years, they made preparations to leave the mountain to find him.

Their journey to meet their heir took over two months, with more time taken healing and helping local people along the way than in traveling. Charity and service are part of Taoist tradition, whether practiced openly or in secret.

After the three wizards had reached the home of Wang Liping that day and found their spiritual heir, the hardships of the road seemed to vanish into thin air. They talked and laughed on the way back to the abandoned building where they had taken up lodging. Shaking the dust off themselves, they sat back to wait for Wang Liping to come looking for them.

As for the youth, after his first encounter with the three wizards that day, Liping couldn't shake the urge to go looking for them. A fifth grader at the time, he was in a daze all that afternoon at school. After classes, instead of walking home with his classmates as usual, he found himself absentmindedly wandering around, ultimately wending his way toward the place where the masters had pitched camp.

Wang Liping found the old men sitting in a shed, talking and laughing among themselves. Mesmerized, he sat down to listen to them.

The teachers had found their disciple. And the future Transmitter of Dragon Gate Taoism had found his guides. So in the autumn of 1962 Wang Liping began a course of apprenticeship in Taoist wizardry that was to last for fifteen years.

2

Refining the Mind

Even though the three Taoist wizards sat and talked among themselves, appearing to ignore the young visitor, they were covertly examining him with their inner perceptions. Ascertaining that the boy suffered from chronic migraine and eye trouble, the old masters set about curing him without making any overt indication of what they were doing.

In a gradual manner, Wang Liping became aware of an exceptional clarity of mind, and his eyesight also cleared. Now he knew those three old men were most certainly not ordinary people.

For their part, once the old masters had gotten a good look at Wang Liping, they realized he was indeed the one they had been seeing in their visions over the last three years, the one they had been looking for. Wang Liping was destined to become the eighteenth-generation Transmitter of Dragon Gate Taoism.

The eldest of the three men sat quietly for a while with his eyes closed. Then he slowly opened his eyes and turned his gaze to young Liping. "Hey there, schoolboy! It's getting late, and you're a long way from home! Aren't you afraid of walking back in the dark?"

Without thinking the youth replied, "Afraid of what? When I play hide-and-seek with my friends, the darker it gets the more fun it is! What's there to be afraid of?"

The three elders were delighted. Gu Jiaoyi pulled Wang Liping to him and said, "Come on, play hide-and-seek with us!" Taking him outside to a graveyard not far away, the men challenged the boy to a game of hide-and-seek, telling him they'd consider him the winner if he found even one of them out there in the darkness.

Liping readily accepted the challenge. He passed by there every day and knew every detail of the terrain; he thought there was no way the old men could hide from him.

The boy covered his eyes and began to count, waiting for the old men to hide. But Zhang Hodao pulled him over and said, "No need for that. Just stand here with your eyes open and watch us go hide. Watch carefully—we won't go far!"

But the elders just stood there, so Liping urged them to go hide. They still didn't move, but a voice said, "Better take a close look—we've already hidden!"

Hearing this, Liping strained his eyes to look, but couldn't find a trace of the old men. How could they have disappeared even as they were speaking? Why didn't their footsteps make any sound? Liping began to look all over the area, searching every nook and cranny, anywhere that someone could hide. Nothing. Not a sound. The whole place was deserted. Thoroughly stumped, after nearly an hour the boy returned to the tree where the game had started. There the old men suddenly appeared before him, inviting him to admit defeat! In reality, the wizards had never gone anywhere. They'd been there all the time, exercising the art of disappearance. These Taoist masters didn't even need the cover of darkness; they knew how to disappear from the sight of ordinary people even in broad daylight. This is an art attained only in the middle range of realization.

Wang Liping knew nothing of this; he only knew his astonishment and growing awe of the three ancients. They told him to go home and come back after school the next day; and to tell no one what he had witnessed.

When Liping got home that night, his parents were concerned. Where had he been until so late? What had he been doing? But Liping hemmed and hawed, so they didn't press him. Those were hard times in China, and everyone in the family had to look out for each other, but sometimes one couldn't keep an eye on everything. Liping was the second son, after all, and his parents had to worry more about his little brothers and sisters. Much of the time, Liping came and went on his own.

As for the three old men, the local people were sympathetic toward them on account of their advanced years, and because they had made their way there from the heartland of the nation. Their healing skills were welcomed by the people, although the old men revealed comparatively little in order to safeguard their identities as Taoist wizards. Over a period of time, the people came to honor and respect the three ancients, who asked no reward for their services. They used to let Wang Liping do chores for them, and he also got to watch them treat people's illnesses. In between times, they would talk to their young protégé about things that would help orient him on the Way.

Needing a quiet place to train their new disciple, the three teachers found an old smithy, long abandoned, quite out of the way of ordinary traffic. The masters cleaned the place up, planted some trees out front, and started a vegetable garden in back. The people of the mountain villages, being simple, rustic folk, pure and straightforward in their ways, were touched by the good deeds of the venerable old curers, and used to send them gifts of kindling, rice, and other necessities.

With the passage of time, Wang Liping gradually got used to the old masters, who began to guide him in subtle ways to prepare him for the long course of training he was to undergo.

One cold autumn night, as the four sat around a lone lamp the Grand Master Zhang Hodao began to tell stories about ancient Taoists and principles of Taoism. He went into greatest detail about Changchun, the Real Man of Eternal Spring, who lived in the time of Genghis Khan and was the founder of the Dragon Gate sect.

Changchun entered the Taoist path at the age of nineteen and became a disciple of the great Master Wang Chongyang when he was twenty. After his teacher passed away, Changchun traveled to Mount Zhongnan, an ancient center of spiritual studies.

Arriving in the dead of winter, Changchun was snowed in for five days and nights, holed up in a little shrine. In danger of starving or freezing to death, Changchun entered into a deep trance.

In the midst of his profound abstraction, Changchun suddenly heard a voice. Looking up, he saw an old man standing in front of him, bearing a gift of food. Placing the offering before Changchun, the old man turned and walked away.

Following the ancient to the door of the shrine, Changchun looked out to see nothing but a vast expanse of virgin snow. There was not a single footprint. When the snows had receded and travel was again possible, Changchun continued his journey westward, until he came to a huge valley known as Fa River Valley. The riverbed was very wide, and the water alternately rose so high and fell so low that it was impossible to build a bridge or establish a ferry. As a result, travelers had to wade across the river. Seeing the dangers to which people were thus exposed, Changchun resolved to stay there and serve travelers by carrying them across the river on his shoulders.

Fixing up an ancient shrine by the waterside, for six years Changchun lived there by the river, spending the nights in meditation and the days carrying travelers over the water.

During this period of time, Changchun experienced what Taoists call the Great Death no less than seven times, and went through what they call Minor Death countless times. Dying and returning to life, he succeeded in transcending the ordinary world of people, events, and things.

The grand master concluded his talk with these words: "Our spiritual ancestor Changchun had a saying: 'When not a single thought is produced, that is freedom; where there is nothing on the mind, that is immortal enlightenment.' This is how intensely the spiritual immortals and celestial wizards cultivated and trained themselves!"

Then the old man turned to Wang Liping and asked, "Were you listening?" Startled out of his reverie, the boy replied that he had indeed been listening. The old man asked him what he had understood from the stories.

Liping replied with clear assurance, "Only with a sincere heart and a firm will is it possible to learn the Way and develop real potential."

The three old men smiled. The eldest master asked the boy, "Do you want to study the Way?"

"Yes," replied Liping in a most serious and determined tone of voice, "but I don't know how. I don't have a teacher to guide me." He still hadn't realized just who the three old men were.

The grand master said, "If you want to study the Way, don't worry about not having a teacher. Who do you think we are? I am the sixteenth-generation Transmitter of Changchun's teaching, and these two with me are the seventeenth-generation Transmitters. Now that we're old, we want to hand on what we've learned. If you want to learn the Way, just be ready to work hard. Otherwise, how can you rise above the ordinary human condition? The first requirement for learning the Way is hard work; then you need to learn to be a member of society, which means doing good and refraining from evil, building up character. When you have developed virtue and built up character, eventually you enter naturally into the Way."

By now the three old wizards had satisfied themselves that Wang Liping did in fact have the potential, and that the timing was right. As in all things, however, they had to begin from the beginning, bringing the disciple along gradually in order to develop penetrating realization.

The Scripture of Eternal Purity and Calm says,

> *The Way includes clarity and opacity, movement and stillness. The sky is clear, the earth is opaque; the sky is in motion, the earth is still. The masculine is clear, the feminine is opaque; the masculine is active, the feminine is still. Descending from the root to flow into the branches, these produce myriad beings. Clarity is the source of opacity, movement is the foundation of stillness. If people can be clear and calm, the whole universe will come to them.*
>
> *The human spirit likes clarity, but the mind disturbs it. The human mind likes calm, but desires pull it. If you can always put your desires aside, your mind will naturally become calm; clarify your mind, and your spirit will naturally become calm.*

The difficulty in putting this teaching into practice lies in "setting aside desire, clarifying the mind, and entering into stillness." This is particularly hard in the present day, when so many material and human resources are devoted to serving an endless procession of desires and ambitions, without ever really satisfying them, and without ever getting an objective understanding of the effects of this whole process on human society and its relationship to Nature.

The first exercise the old masters taught Wang Liping, therefore, was a practice called "repentance." What this means in the context of Taoism is cleaning the mind, clearing away mundane influences already infecting the consciousness, getting rid of the rubbish.

The way this is done is by temporary isolation and self-examination. The process is subdivided into three parts. First the disciple stays in a dark room for two months with nothing to do. This is supposed to gradually reduce the crudity and wildness in one's nature. The second stage of practice involves sitting still in a dark room for set periods of time, which are progressively lengthened. In the third stage, the disciple is shifted to an ordinary quiet room and required to sit still for at least four hours at a time.

One morning after breakfast, instead of going to school Wang Liping headed straight for the abode of the three old Taoist masters. By this time,

Taoism interested the youth more than school did. He found the old men still engrossed in their morning meditations. In spite of their advanced age, the old wizards had youthful faces and dark hair. Their eyes shone with an uncanny light. Liping sat down to join in their exercise, but the grand master stopped him with a question: "Are you really positive you want to study Taoism with us? Are you sure you won't change you mind?"

Liping insisted that he was most assuredly determined to proceed. So the grand master continued. "Once you have set your heart on learning the Way," he said, "you must start from the beginning. Remember that you must not fear hardships. Today we will teach you the first lesson, which involves no explanation of principles, only actual practice. You must do as I say, for if you fail this lesson you needn't come around looking for us anymore." The old man was firm. With only this brief introduction, he had the youth follow him to the shed they had cleaned out for this exercise.

Pointing into the dark room, the grand master told Liping, "Go inside and stay quiet. Don't start whining to get out, because we're not going to let you out no matter what." With that, the old wizard pushed the boy inside and locked the door.

Wang Liping had never thought the old man would actually do this. The shed was completely empty and totally dark. He couldn't see a thing. Figuring the old man was testing his sincerity and would let him out sooner or later, the boy decided to wait it out calmly.

Easier said than done. After a while Liping began pacing around, groping along the walls after crashing into them a few times. Pacing around until he worked up a sweat, he sat down to rest. Then he got up and started pacing around again. As he kept repeating this over and over, his anxiety mounted; the morning seemed like a year.

Suddenly the door opened a crack, and a beam of light blinded the youth inside. He heard an old man calling him to come out, and he emerged, rubbing his eyes. The boy was extremely upset, but he pretended as if nothing had happened.

Wang Jiaoming asked him, "Can you take more, boy?"

Liping thought the teacher was testing him, so even though he'd already had enough, he said, "No problem. This lesson is easy. Did I do all right?" He wanted to get a good mark.

"All right," replied the old master lightly, "but let's have lunch."

Liping had been unbearably nervous all morning and had already had to urinate in the corner of the shed. When he heard the teacher tell him he had done all right, he figured he had passed the test, though not with very good marks.

This lunchtime was not the same as usual. The three old men spoke very little; no one even brought up the question of how Liping had spent the morning. The boy figured they were feigning indifference, so he decided to play along. Gobbling up his food, he waited to see what the next test would be. He did not expect what happened next.

Wang Jiaoming casually said, "Liping, go back to the shed and stay there." Without even casting a glance at the boy, the old man took him back to the shed and locked him in.

Young Liping had not anticipated this ordeal. He felt he had been tested enough.

Since the old man had given no specific directions as to what he should do, Liping decided to pass the time in sport, shadowboxing in the dark, sitting down to rest when he got tired. Before long, however, the boy realized with growing discomfort that he had not prepared himself properly for this test. The call of nature began to nag him until he thought he would burst. Growing more anxious as the minutes ticked by like hours, eventually Liping wound up pounding and kicking on the door, hollering and screaming for the old men to let him out. Finally he disgraced himself.

As for the three Taoist masters, even while they were occupied with treating the ailments of the local people, nevertheless they focused their inner attention on their young apprentice. By their power of second sight, they were fully aware of his struggle. Lao-tzu said, "Those who conquer themselves are strong." The old masters were not being cruel; they were doing what was necessary to create a new human being. The I Ching says, "Faithfulness and trustworthiness are means of developing character."

From that day on, Liping came back every three or four days to practice "repentance" in the shed. Each time, the length of his isolation was increased, from half a day to a day, from a day to a day and a night. After several sessions, he learned to control himself, and his heart and mind became calm and clear. Having achieved this, he began to use his brain to think about questions. His mentors told him that this "structured thought" was an extremely important subject in training the brain.

Lao-tzu said, "Movement overcomes cold, stillness overcomes heat; clear calm is a rectifier of the world." He also said, "Effect emptiness to the extreme, keep stillness steady; as myriad things act in concert, I thereby observe the return." The essential point here is in calm stillness; when stillness reaches its climax, it produces motion, whereby you observe the subtle. "Structured thought" means that after body and mind have reached the climax of stillness, the brain conceives a "thing," be it a scene, a personage, or an event. One must think ahead or in retrospect, causing the thing to develop and evolve until a "result" is obtained. When this result contains a definite meaning, the exercise is said to have taken effect. This operation of a thought process is called "structured thought."

Now Liping sat quietly in the dark room practicing structured thought according to the directions of his mentor. First he reflected on the fact that even though his body was restrained in a small dark room, his thought could not be locked up and prevented from going out and about.

With this in mind, Liping deliberately focused his thought on his father. What was he doing now? Liping pictured his father at work, his desk and everything on it—pencils, calculator, drafting tools, a cup half full of hot water, an ashtray containing several cigarette butts. Now Liping mentally saw his father, cigarette in his left hand, slowly exhaling a plume of smoke as he wrote on a large chart, making circular and square notations.

Right now his father was absorbed in his work, a job that was, however, terribly dull and boring. Still not finished even by lunchtime, his father continued on through the afternoon, dismayed by the realization that this task would take him days on end to complete. Such drudgery!

Liping decided to change the subject. Now he began to think of his schoolmates, now in class. It is second period, and the math teacher is lecturing. He is talking about the basics of accounting, bookkeeping, double entry, receivables and payables, balancing accounts, and so on. Also incredibly boring. Everyone is there in class except Liping himself. No one is listening very intently, especially Liping's friends, who are looking at his empty seat and thinking how convenient for him not to have come to this torturous class. They are aching to get outside and play!

But none of this was very interesting either, Liping reflected, and here this thought stopped.

Now Liping began to go through books inside his brain. Here is a textbook, he began, and he started to look through it mentally from the first lesson. There is a picture of the Great Wall, very grand and impressive. Gazing at the Great Wall from a distant mountain ridge, Liping mentally saw it like an enormous dragon whose head and tail could not be seen, snaking through the fastnesses of the high mountains. He began describing it to himself. The wall is several meters in height, made of boulders and blocks, built along the spines of the mountains. Truly a breathtaking sight. The Great Wall is a crystallization of the blood, sweat, and skill of countless workers; it is a symbol of the Chinese people.

This was better. Liping concluded his exercise with the thought that he would climb the Great Wall one day, gaze upon the magnificent rivers and mountains of his native land, and take in the pride of being Chinese.

Wang Liping's exercises in structured thought developed his intellectual power and enhanced both his physical and his mental well-being. The little dark room was no longer a confining prison, but an integral part of the whole universe of space and time. In this infinite expanse of space and time, thought can soar at will. Everything Liping "saw"—the people, the events, the things—was very concrete, very realistic, very lifelike. This was a universe full of life, a universe in which he no longer felt alone. And he no longer felt time as a burden, for there were far too many things to do for him to be bored.

Liping was often hungry, however, during his work in the shed, because the old masters didn't bring him out for meals anymore. Instead they would show up suddenly at odd times and toss him something. Sometimes it would be nothing but a rock, as if the ancients were playing a joke on him. Sometimes it would be food, which the youth would wolf down in a few gulps.

It was also cold in the shed. The autumns in north China are cold, especially at night, when the chill gets into your bones. Based on the temperature changes and his bodily sensations, Liping had gradually worked out, through structured thought, first the ability to distinguish day and night, and then the ability to distinguish morning, noon, evening, and midnight.

There is a proverb that says, "It takes a hundred refinings to make solid steel." So it is with human beings; they do not attain great capacity unless they are refined. In Taoist terms, if you want to become a realized human being, while the primal basis is of course important, temporal refinement is even more important, because there is no other way to attain realization.

In the course of two months' isolation in the darkness, Wang Liping had his first understanding of the Way. The three ancients saw that his heart was sincere and his will was unshakable. Based on these qualities, they decided to take him on formally as a disciple.

They chose an auspicious date for the ceremony. That night the sky was clear, the full moon hanging in the eastern quarter, shining on the human world below. A gentle breeze was blowing, and a few flecks of cloud drifted by through the sky. The toil of the day ended, the people were now sleeping. The mountains in the distance were barely visible in the moonlight; they looked like a herd of sheep huddled together unmoving. The grains and pulses stood silently in the fields; occasionally the faint rustle of their leaves came whispering in the breeze, but their colors could no longer be distinguished.

The whole earth was plunged into a profound quiet; only the three elders and their young apprentice remained awake, carrying out the ceremony marking the formal initiation of Wang Liping as the eighteenth-generation Transmitter of the Dragon Gate branch of Taoism. He was given the Taoist name Yongsheng, which means Eternal Life, and the religious name Linglingzi, which means the Spiritually Effective One.

When the ritual was completed, the grand master gave the boy a brief summary of Taoist principles:

"The primal Way is formless and imageless, beginningless and endless, unnameable and indescribable. The word for the Way, 道 which we use as a convenience, is pregnant with hidden meaning.

"First two dots are written. The left one symbolizes light, the right one symbolizes darkness, as in the symbol of the absolute wherein yin and yang embrace each other. These two dots represent the sun and moon in the sky, water and fire on earth, and the two eyes in human beings, which seem to reverse their light and gaze inwardly in the course of refinement exercises.

"Under these two dots is written a single stroke, meaning 'one,' which represents the totality of all things. Below this, the graph for 'self' is written, referring to oneself, meaning that everything in the universe is in one's own body, and the Way is not apart from oneself. When the above pieces are assembled, they form the word 'head,' which signifies that practice of the Way is the best and most essential thing one can do in the world. Finally the sign for 'walk' is written, meaning to travel or operate, signifying the natural working of the teaching throughout one's whole body, the Way being carried out in one's own body, the Way being carried out in the whole world. These are the meanings contained in the structure of the character for the Way."

The grand master paused for a moment, then went on: "Chinese Taoism was founded by Lao-tzu. The essences of its doctrines are all in this word 'Tao,' the Way. The methods of attaining the Way are based on stillness.

"The wonders of stillness are inexhaustible. It is possible thereby to participate in evolution and to embrace all things; heaven, earth, and humanity are all included within it.

"People of the world only know how to talk about stillness; they cannot enter into stillness truly, because they have not found out the source of stillness. The source of stillness is in emptiness. All things and the changes they go through are but temporary conditions, which finally return to nothingness, then revert to emptiness. As long as the human mind is not still and quiet, there will be thoughts of desire remaining, which create tremendous obstacles to the cultivation of refinement.

Once selfish desires arise, the primal spirit is disturbed, the primal energy is blocked, and training has no effect. Get rid of selfish desire, enter physically and mentally into quiet stillness, and the primal energy will be buoyant, while the primal spirit will be lively.

The way to get into quiet stillness is to gradually eliminate random thoughts of personal desires, sweeping away the obstacles to the growth of primal spirit and energy, making the pathway even. This principle of extinguishing one to enliven the other is the great achievement of stillness. When it comes to resting in the highest good, nothing surpasses stillness. Even though myriad things move it from without, one's mind does not stir, even though one does not know why. Then when primal vitality, energy, and spirit are full, stillness climaxes and shifts into movement. Once outward movement is unfailingly sensed within, then one naturally knows how it happens. The enhancement and extension of human life are also accomplished in this way.

Once you have entered the door to the Way, you should understand this principle and apply it diligently. Then the work will naturally make great progress.

Having spoken thus, the grand master stood up and bade everyone good night. It was already one o'clock in the morning.

The next day, everyone rose early in the morning, and the three old men taught Liping some traditional shadowboxing exercises. After breakfast, the Wayfarer of the Infinite and the Wayfarer of Pure Emptiness went off somewhere, leaving the young apprentice alone with the Wayfarer of Pure Serenity. This old man had once been an instructor at a military academy and was adept at both inner and outer exercises. Vigorous and brusque, he was extremely strict and demanding toward students. He called Liping to him and spoke in the following terms:

Today you're starting a new lesson. You've passed through repentance, so now you will go through the second barrier, which requires learning to sit cross-legged in a dark room.

The praxis of the Dragon Gate sect makes a particular point of seeing to it that the foundation is solid, and requires us to make it sturdy. This exercise of cross-legged sitting is essential training for beginners and must be practiced all your life. Every step of the training involves this exercise, so if you learn it properly you can derive endless benefit from it.

There are three styles of cross-legged sitting. One is natural sitting, which is also called informal sitting. Then there is single cross-legged sitting, in which you place one foot on the opposite thigh. Finally there is double cross-legged sitting, in which you place both feet on opposite thighs. Natural sitting is earth; single cross-legged sitting is humanity; double cross-legged sitting is heaven. When the diverse hand positions are added, the postures of cross-legged sitting are innumerably various. Today, though, I'll just talk about natural sitting.

Once seated, keep your upper body straight, with both eyes looking directly ahead, gradually collecting the light of the spirit. With the tongue against the upper palate and the lips shut, let the teeth be lightly closed. Place your hands on your knees, palms down. Still the spirit and meditate quietly, gradually eliminating all random thoughts.

"There are few disturbances inside a dark room," the mentor concluded, "so it is convenient for doing this exercise. Why not go there for now?" The old master's manner was dry and sharp. When he had finished, he stared directly at young Liping. Getting the message, the boy realized he had no choice but to follow his mentor's directions.

This time Liping first got a bunch of dry hay and spread it on the floor of the shack before locking himself in to practice cross-legged sitting. Luckily, the teacher had not presented him with a whole lot of other requirements, letting him suit himself. Being young and still in the process of developing physically, Liping was flexible enough to be able to do all three styles of sitting. He could not, however, maintain them for very long.

Having already cultivated hidden practice in this dark room for two months, although Liping still could not enter into total stillness, nevertheless he had learned to adapt to the environment. On this particular day, he slacked off quite a few times in the course of sitting, but on the whole he persevered, undergoing a variety of experiences as he sat. After a few days of practice, his work in sitting had progressed considerably.

One day the Wayfarer of Pure Serenity called Wang Liping to him and asked him what he had gained from his practice. After giving a detailed account of the process and his experiences, the youth finally said, "I can't clear random thoughts from my brain, and I can't attain stillness. Please teach me some method of handling this."

This was precisely what the old wizard had in mind. "To clear away random thoughts," he began in reply, "first use formal judgment to deal with them. As soon as a random thought arises, immediately pass judgment on it: either declare it right, or declare it wrong, or declare that this is as far as it goes. Having made this determination, stop right away and do not allow rumination to go on and on. Then random thoughts will vanish by themselves, and in this way you can enter into stillness."

Returning to the dark room, Wang Liping sat cross-legged, adjusting his body and tuning his breathing, and began to quiet his mind. Now when he was assailed by random thoughts, he used this method to get rid of them. After repeating the process several times, he found that it actually did work. Liping felt happy inside. After another few days of practice, these random thoughts became fewer and fewer day by day, gradually tending to thin out as the exercise of entering stillness gradually developed. Even though he was only thirteen years old, with little experience of the world and relatively few desires—so his mind was much more pure and innocent than that of an ordinary adult—nevertheless he still had to get rid of random thoughts that occurred to him.

After seven times seven days sitting in the dark shed, Wang Liping had accumulated quite a bit of experience in quiet sitting and had learned an effective exercise. At this point, he had learned the better part of the exercise of repentance, and his wildness had mostly been reined in. Now in his everyday speech and behavior he was rather like a child of the Way. Within a few months, it was as if he had changed into another person.

On weekdays, Wang Liping continued to attend school, so that he would not foul up his ordinary education. After school, he'd go visit the Taoist masters to practice his exercises.

At first, Liping's parents were worried about the change in their son, but when they found out the reason, they realized that the three old men were of impeccable character: they cured the boy's ailments, taught him spiritual exercises, and initiated him into the true Way. When they learned all this, Liping's parents were more than relieved: they were thoroughly delighted.

To return to the story, after Wang Liping had sat for seven times seven days in the dark shed, the three masters called him to them. "Today," began the Wayfarer of Pure Serenity, "we are going to give you a new lesson. Sit here in this room for four hours. After you're finished, you can go home."

After forty-nine days of sitting in the dark, Liping thought, he would certainly have no problem sitting for four hours. Figuring it was just a test, he got up on the platform and sat in the lotus position facing his teachers. After adjusting his posture properly, he closed his eyes and began to sit quietly.

For the first hour, Wang Liping sat immobile as a statue made of stone. Another hour passed, and he still held firm. After that, however, he had to summon up his strength, wondering when the time would be up, telling himself he had to persevere because his teachers were watching.

The minutes crawled by. Liping's legs began to go numb, just like the first time he had practiced sitting cross-legged. His aching thighs felt swollen, but his hips were still bearable, and as long as he kept his waist straight, there was no problem. After a while, however, even his hip bones began to ache, his waist and lower back began to burn, and his whole body broke out in perspiration. Sweating beads as he struggled to maintain his upright position, finally the youth blacked out and collapsed.

"Sit up right!" barked Wang Jiaoming, the Wayfarer of Pure Serenity, like an army drill instructor.

Coming to, the young apprentice sat up again, but his legs were so numb he couldn't cross them.

"Resume the double cross-legged position," demanded the mentor again.

But Liping's legs would not even follow his own commands; he was at a loss. The two mentors took some rope and bound him hand and foot, tying him up into the proper position so that he could go on sitting cross-legged.

Although still a boy, young Wang Liping had a strong will. His eyes filled with tears, but he refused to let them out. Gritting his teeth, he went on sitting. Later in life his eyes would again fill with tears as he spoke with gratitude of the unsparing efforts, relentless severity, and spiritual kindness of his Taoist teachers.

After six months of strict training, the young Wang Liping completed his practice of the phase of repentance. He could now sit quietly all day and all night, his body steady and his mind still, inwardly and outwardly immune to disturbance.

3

Concentrating the Vital Spirit

According to Master Wang Liping, the entire course of his training could be divided into nine stages. At this point in the story, he was going into the second stage, which involves collecting the mind and developing essential nature. This work is still concerned with the refinement of the inner essence of mind, but it is at a higher and more difficult level than repentance; its requirements are stricter, and the external conditions of practice are yet more severe. The aim is to get the practitioner to concentrate the vital spirit, using unified concentration of the whole spirit to examine minute changes within the body, producing extraordinary capacities within the ordinary.

For this exercise his mentors moved Wang Liping to a pit in the earth. The pit was narrow, dark, and dank, without good air circulation. Ordinarily one would not think it a suitable place for doing exercises, but the three wizards had a deep reason for finding this spot for their apprentice to sit and do his inner work. It was not just a matter of using a negative environment to develop extraordinary character, as one would usually imagine; the principle of contrary use of the surroundings has a more positive rationale.

The pit, going deep underground, was dark and wet. Could the principle be herein? Earth and depth both correspond to the earth element in the five elements, so the energy of earth is doubled. Shade and darkness are the extreme of yin; and when yin reaches its extreme, yang arises. Moisture corresponds to the water element in the five elements, and it is the source of life. In both the primal and temporal ordering of the eight trigrams of the I Ching, or Book of Changes, earth and water are both below. The *Traditions on the Changes* says, "Consummate is the creative basis of earth; all beings live on its Concentrating the Vital Spirit sustenance, as it goes along in accord with what it receives from heaven. Earth is thick and supports beings; its virtues are boundless, its embrace is far-reaching, and its glory is great, so all things flourish."

The Tao Te Ching says, "The Way obeys Nature," and it recommends quiet emptiness and keeping centered, which are both virtues associated with earth. In the I Ching trigram symbol for water, yin surrounds outside, and yang is in the center, representing "yang submerged in yin, outwardly empty while inwardly fulfilled." The *Traditions on the Changes* says, "Going through dangerous straits without losing faith, that mind gets through successfully, by means of firmness and balance." This seems to be the rationale for the three wizards using a pit in the earth to train Wang Liping. The young apprentice himself, of course, had no idea of his teachers' purpose in putting him there.

Jumping down into the pit, Liping lit sticks of incense at each of the four corners, according to instructions. The little cavern quickly filled with smoke, and the youth sat down and began to practice his inner exercise.

At first Liping was able to sit calmly and quietly, but before long the smoke got so dense, combined with the wet and cold vapors hanging heavy in the air, that breathing became difficult. Finally his primitive nature lost its patience again, and he shouted, "It's suffocating me!" He was hoping the teachers would let him out of the pit, but Wang Jiaoming had already told him to follow instructions strictly, without any fuss. At this point he knew that if he didn't obey, he'd be severely punished. All he could do was follow the course prescribed by his mentor.

Confined in the dark, dank pit, and suffocating, it was hard to sit cross-legged. Figuring that his mentor had already locked up and wouldn't come back, Liping decided to change positions and relax his body a little. So he leaned against the side of the pit and stretched out his arms and legs.

Just as he was getting comfortable, in a flash an incomprehensible change took place in the appearance of the pit, right before Liping's eyes. Suddenly it seemed to be as big as a banquet hall, and full of light. The grand master and the two mentors were sitting before him, with the air and appearance of people from the immortal realms. The old master's face was red. Speaking solemnly, he said, "What nerve! A mediocre little boy like you dares to fool around in front of the likes of us? How can you go on hoodwinking us? Once you have become a disciple, your commitment stands before you. Whether or not a teacher is present, you should take it to heart. The methods of attaining the Way are transmitted verbally by teachers, but you are required to cultivate them seriously in your own body. The way you are now, unless you eliminate the poisons and delinquent tendencies in your heart as soon as possible, collect your spirit and develop your nature, how can you attain the Way?"

Having finished his speech, the old master closed his eyes. One of the mentors raised a disciplinary ruler, but didn't bring it down. The other mentor pulled out a rope, but stopped there. Wang Liping hurriedly knelt down and cried out an apology and a promise not to be so presumptuous again.

Now when he raised his head again, Liping saw nothing but the interior of the pit, cramped, dark, dank, and suffocating as before. But he felt a pain in the palms of his hands, and he saw that his legs had been bound up tightly. Then he realized that the old master and the two mentors had already administered punishment in some way.

Mortified with shame, Liping now understood how highly developed the accomplishments of the master and the mentors were; he also realized that his mind had not been thoroughly cleaned, and that he was very far from the Way. No longer would he have any illusions and boast of trivial intelligence. He would turn wholeheartedly to the Way, and first he would work on this practice of "collecting the mind and developing the nature," "keeping to the center, silent and empty."

When Wang Liping had learned to sit cross-legged for four hours in the pit filled with incense smoke, the old master and the mentors finally began to transmit to him the teaching of the Dragon Gate sect of Complete Reality Taoism known as "The Art of Inner Exercise of Mental Capacities Attained Through the Classical Spiritual Jewels." As he learned from his teachers, Liping worked on applying the new skills in practice, so his efforts gradually led him into the True Way.

This art of inner exercise of mental capacities according to the classical Spiritual Jewels is one of the ancient Taoist methods of internal work. Its doctrine is "saving one from birth and death is first, comfort and long life come afterward." Its special features are inclusion of both movement and stillness, and cultivation of both essential nature and life energy. The art has many techniques, which are simple and easy to practice, naturally forming a detailed and comprehensive system for training the capacities of the whole human being.

This teaching has been treasured by specialists in method for a long time and has been passed on only by word of mouth and kept only in memory, transmitted individually from teacher to disciple, kept secret and not publicly divulged.

The Art of Inner Exercise of Mental Capacities Attained Through the Classical Spiritual Jewels is divided into "three exercises" and "nine methods." The "three exercises" are the "Three Immortalist Exercises," or quiet sitting exercises, exercises involving external movements known as equilibrium exercises, and sleeping exercises practiced at leisure. The "nine methods" deal with developing mental capacities, stopping illness, curing illness, transmitting awareness, stabilizing mind, settling your birth and death, cutting off the earthly soul, and receiving images.

Among these nine methods, the first four are methods of helping people create happiness; the latter five are methods of overcoming people and methods of controlling people. The fourth method, "transmitting awareness," also includes methods of overcoming people.

One day the old master and the two mentors called Wang Liping to them and started explaining the first method of the Spiritual Jewel attainments, developing mental capacities. Zhang Hodao, Wayfarer of the Infinite, said, "This method of developing mental capacity is a method of exercise in stillness, mainly cultivated while sitting cross-legged. Now that you have learned the basic essentials of sitting cross-legged, you can practice this method.

"This method of developing mental capacity is itself divided into nine steps. The first step is retrospective gazing, returning to infancy. The second step is clear distinction of the real and the unreal. The third step is developing clarity of spirit. The fourth step is knowing the way one is to go. The fifth step is stopping eating to seek life. The sixth step is changing into new clothing. The seventh step is seeing through the mechanism of Nature. The eighth step is revolving time. The ninth step is gazing practice ascending to the moon. Today you will start your practice with the first step, retrospective gazing back into infancy."

Although he gave no sign of it, Wang Liping was delighted. "No wonder they had me learn to sit quietly so long. There are so many things to study!"

Now the Wayfarer of Pure Emptiness, Gu Jiaoyi, continued where the old master had left off. "After you enter into quiet stillness sitting cross-legged, once random thoughts are eliminated, when stillness reaches its extreme, it produces movement. Then various sorts of hallucinations will begin to appear in your brain. When you close your eyes, you will see very lifelike images—birds flying in the sky, animals running and bounding on the ground, flowers, plants, and trees growing in the meadows, people involved in work and other activities. When these images have appeared, they are not actually hallucinations. The brain is beginning to represent real scenes you have seen in the past, so it is memory.

"When ordinary people remember past things, they do not see them so clearly and graphically. Only after accomplishment is achieved in the practice of entering stillness is it possible to 'see' clearly within the brain.

"Slowly, you should then see things that happened a long time ago, things you could never bring up simply by the power of memory or recollection. Now you will be able to see them clearly. You can keep going back all the way through your childhood, because your thinking has gone into reverse. This is called 'retrospective gazing back to infancy.' When thinking has gone back we say it is 'retrospection,' but in reality it is 'gazing,' a clear viewing of images.

"When these scenes appear, don't be afraid. You must let them change as they may. It is most definitely necessary, however, to watch them closely and examine them in detail. You must absolutely avoid letting them go too easily, without clear perception.

"All right now," the mentor concluded, "go sit in your hole in the ground, quiet down your mind, and see what scenes appear."

Wang Liping went back to the hole in the ground again and shut himself in. Lighting three sticks of incense, he sat on a bunch of straw and went into a condition of stillness. After these few days of practice, Wang Liping understood the advantage of doing these exercises in the pit. The incense smoke no longer suffocated him, but instead it created an ethereal atmosphere.

After sitting quietly for a while, Wang Liping felt his whole body become nothing. Inside his brain was a complete blank. Then, all of a sudden, images began to appear. These images were not the same as those that had appeared before when he was practicing deliberate thinking in the dark room. Those earlier images had been deliberately mentally formulated; these images appeared spontaneously. They were very real, distinct, and clear.

Following his mentor's instructions, Wang Liping felt no fear, but watched the images closely, observing how they appeared and how they changed, registering all this in memory. He had no idea how time and space could transform this way: space changed into a mirage, and time reversed its flow. As he sat there quietly, Wang Liping actually went through the experience of "retrospective gazing, returning to infancy."

Liping had no idea how much time passed, but eventually the images faded and disappeared. Then he concluded his exercise and got out of the pit. Outside he saw that it was already late at night; then he realized this sitting had lasted four hours. During his retrospective gazing back into infancy, however, he had seen many places and events spanning several years' time.

When Wang Liping told his teachers about his experiences in inward gazing during this session of quiet sitting, they saw that he was really intelligent, sincere, and quick to learn. Delighted, they urged him to keep on practicing his exercises, to achieve solid stability.

For his part, after this experience Wang Liping became even more attentive to his study of Taoism. One day when he went into the pit to sit, not long after entering into stillness, both eyes gazing inward, unexpectedly he found that he was able to see everything in his own body, from the outside to the inside. His youthful heart was pure, and he felt no fear, only a sense of wonder. Without getting upset or excited, he continued to gaze, observing every detail. When Wang Liping finished this exercise session, he reported his inner vision to the three masters. Exchanging meaningful glances, the old wizards smiled without saying anything. Realizing that they must have something to tell him about this experience, however, Liping asked the mentors for a pointer.

The Wayfarer of Pure Emptiness laughed and said, "You have again progressed further in quiet sitting. Now you have already entered into the second step of the method of developing mental capacities, which is called 'clear distinction of the real and the unreal.' When you gaze inwardly at your own body after entering stillness, even though your eyes are closed and you are in utter darkness, you can see the internal conditions of your own body with perfect clarity. When this happens, you should never be startled or frightened, and you should not engage in any activity. You must observe and make distinctions with accurate precision. See exactly how many bones there are in your head, what shape they are, and how they are joined together. What are the shapes of your internal organs? What colors are they? Are there any spots? When you can see these things plainly and register them clearly, then this becomes useful. This exercise is basic when it comes to diagnosing and curing disease. People may look well from the outside, but when you can see the internal condition of their bodies you know whether or not they are sick, and where the ailment is if they are. So this exercise method is called 'clear distinction of the real and the unreal.' Now that you have entered this domain, you should continue to practice, observing the structure of your body, remembering every detail."

After a moment of silent reflection, the Wayfarer of the Infinite took up the thread. "After these two steps are completed," he began, "the foundation of your inner work is secure, and you need more understanding of the principles of inner work cultivated by ancient health practitioners.

"Inner work cultivates both essence and life. Essence exercises cultivate the spirit, soul, will, awareness, tranquility, and stability. Life exercises cultivate the energy, blood, vitality, sinews, bones, and skin. The methods of cultivation include both stillness and motion. They are orderly and measured, yet adaptable to accord with natural conditions.

"The health practices of the Dragon Gate sect are based on ancient longevity teachings. They are modeled on the principles of yin and yang and are adjusted to calendrical logic. Yin and yang are constants of the sky and the earth; calendrical logic is the organization of hygiene.

"The inner work of the Spiritual Jewel teaching includes aspects associated with heaven, earth, and humankind, used as a means of mating external yin and yang, the five elements, and the eight trigrams with internal yin and yang, the five elements, and the eight trigrams, in order to cultivate them. This work is the basis for establishing essence and life and cultivating essence and life.

Heaven, earth, and humankind are a universe; the individual human being is also a universe, a microcosm. Changes in the macrocosm, the universe at large, all affect the microcosm, the little universe of the individual, and changes in the microcosm all correspond to changes in the macrocosm.

"Refining practices cultivated on the model of the moon circling the earth result in the microcycle, penetrating the three passes, breaking through the gate of heaven, opening the celestial eye, and descending through the three fields. When the aperture of the celestial eye opens, then inner vision is possible.

"The aperture of the celestial eye consists of three points on one line, from outside to inside, combining to form the 'higher elixir.' The 'aperture' is between the eyebrows, the 'eye,' which is popularly referred to as 'nirvana,' is inside that, and the 'heaven,' also called the 'celestial mirror,' is behind that. The aperture is naturally always open, but the eye has to be cultivated; the celestial is primordial. The aperture is open, but does not perceive objects. The eye perceives things even when closed, seeing back into the celestial. Now that your celestial eye aperture is open, you are capable of inner vision and thus can successfully cultivate refinement in conjunction with the cycles of the sun and moon. This is followed by 'external radiation of internal energy,' which can draw small animals to you. This practice links with the work of the third step of the development of mental capacities, which is clarity of spirit."

As the Wayfarer of the Infinite spoke, Wang Liping listened with rapt attention, in complete inner silence, anxious not to miss a single word. There were still some things, however, that he still couldn't remember, some things he couldn't understand. The Wayfarer of Pure Emptiness went over these points with him in detail, until Liping understood them clearly and had committed them to memory.

The Wayfarer of Pure Emptiness said, "The reason I have told you about 'clarity of spirit' beforehand is as a precaution. Whatever may appear, don't let it scare you—you need to have clarity and sobriety of spirit. In the previous two steps, the scenes that appeared to you were all in your brain or were perceptions of inner vision. In this third step, inner energy radiates outward, so sensitive little animals will come to you following the energy, gathering around you. At this time, you must not by any means stir. Don't be afraid, and don't mind them— just let them be. Although the animals will come right up to you, they won't hurt you. When you have finished your exercise, they will leave on their own. These little animals will mostly be rats, weasels, and certain birds. They are quite intelligent and also have an uncanny sensitivity. Some of them can even gaze into the sky and worship the moon, absorbing the vitality of the sun and the essence of the moon, cultivating some of the lesser methods of exercise by following nature. Just act as if nothing were happening. If you don't provoke them, they won't bother you."

Hearing his mentor speak of such things, Wang Liping mused, "What a wonder this world is! Who would have thought that those little animals, which seem so cute to humans, also have this uncanny sensitivity. They too know how to research the mysteries of Nature and have thought of immortality. This is most interesting!"

After that Liping cultivated the "clear distinction of the real and the unreal" for a while. Once he had seen the structure of his body clearly, he then practiced the exercise of external radiation, and small animals actually did come gather around him, crouching nearby, as if they were listening to him tell interesting stories or sing charming songs.

Following his mentor's advice, Liping paid the little creatures no mind. With thorough clarity of spirit, he firmly continued with his exercise. When he was done, each of the little animals went back to its lair, none of them disturbing another in any way. Every time he saw this happen, Liping felt like laughing, but in his heart he was taking another step toward understanding the mysteries of Nature.

Once the first three steps had been completed, his mentors introduced Liping to the fourth step, "knowing the way one is to go."

What is the meaning of "knowing the way one is to go"? It is set on the foundation of collecting mind and nurturing essence, so that there are no random thoughts at all, and one has the ability to gaze inward and radiate outward; at this point it is necessary to advance further to consciously train thinking on a higher level.

The thinking done in this stage is not the deliberate constructive thinking done in the dark room, nor is it the imagery seen in the course of the inner gazing of the first two steps of the method of developing mental capacities. In this exercise, rather, a specific issue is taken up, its outcome is determined, and a method of resolution is presented.

This exercise of "knowing the way one is to go" is not random thinking; it is essential to start out by setting up the topic or the focal issue. Before you have gone through training in entering stillness, your brain is full of random thoughts, so even if you want to settle your mind down to think about a specific problem, it is very difficult to accomplish. But after you have gone through training in entering stillness, random thoughts are removed, and your brain power is ten, a hundred, even a thousand times better than what it was before. The topic that is brought up for this exercise is not pursued retrospectively, but rather prospectively. When the problems that come up in the course of life resist solution by ordinary means, and yet require resolution, they are now brought up in this present exercise, and then a way to solve them is sought. This training of brain power, or thinking, is called knowing the way one is to go.

The "way to go" refers to the immediate problem before you that calls for resolution; that is, of course, as a first step. When it comes to determining the way to go with more long-term and more far-reaching issues, further training is required. The first step of "knowing the way one is to go," nevertheless, is the basic accomplishment, which is extremely important for future development.

The core principle of the method of developing mental capacities is to use it for curing illnesses and helping people, so "knowing the way one is to go" is mainly used for healing. When a daytime examination does not yield a clear picture of an illness or a way of curing it, then this exercise is done at midnight, bringing up the particular problem to make a close examination of symptoms and find a way to treat it.

As Wang Liping put his teachers' instructions into practice step by step, his brain power developed greatly. He was not merely beyond his peers in this respect, but even more advanced than adults. Not only was schoolwork a breeze for him; he had no trouble considering and resolving real problems of life in the world.

But Liping was not only intelligent; he was smart. Whenever he was with other people, he just went along with the flow cheerfully, keeping his true attainments concealed, so that people thought of him as an ordinary youth.

As for the three old Taoist wizards, they devoted a lot of attention to this process. A hundred years of human development, it is said, still just stabilizes the roots. Although Liping was making progress in learning the inner exercises, he had not yet even begun to learn external exercises.

⁓⁓⁓⁓⁓

Inner and external exercises, at their most advanced, both make an issue of subtlety and refinement. The subtle is the recondite, the infinitesimal, the signal of an event, the key to something. The refined is the minute, the profound, the quintessential. The *Traditions on the Changes* says, "The Changes are means by which sages find out the profound and investigate the subtle." It also says, "Cultivated people act on seeing the subtle, not waiting all day." And also, "Cultivated people know the subtle and the obvious, the soft and the hard." Lao-tzu said, "Skilled warriors of old were subtle, mysteriously effective, so deep they were inscrutable." Guan-tzu said, "Thought does not only cognize the coarse; it sees into the subtle, so it is the vital essence of development."

The point of subtlety and refinement is the cultivation of essence and life. Make the slightest error and you miss out completely. If you do not see into the subtle and refined, you cannot reach the sublime realms. With the idea of fostering subtlety and refinement in their young charge, the three old masters next put Wang Liping through more special training.

First Liping was shut inside a large wooden box. This box was con- structed specially for this training exercise. It was as tall as Liping himself, with a bit of leeway around the front, back, and sides. The upper part, however, was studded with spikes several inches long. To avoid being stuck by the spikes, Liping had to stand in the center without moving. As if this were not enough, the old masters added yet another obstacle.

When Liping got into the box, he examined it very carefully. Using the ability he had developed in quiet sitting over the past few months, he stood immobile inside the box, thinking this was not so hard as sitting cross-legged in fact, it was more comfortable than sitting. Little did he suspect that the mentors were then going to hoist the whole box up into a tree and let it hang there, swaying in the wind.

There was no room for the youth to divide his attention as he concen- trated totally on maintaining his balance inside the box, to avoid getting stuck by the spikes. Carefully studying the subtle relationships among the movements of the wind, the tree, the box, and his own body, Liping gradually discovered a sort of regularity. Then he no longer had to make any physical effort, all he needed to do was concentrate with complete attention.

After two months of this practice, Wang Liping had developed the ability to notice even the slightest movement of the grasses in the breeze. Doing this exercise in the mountains at night, he could physically sense even a rat scurrying by several meters away.

Once Liping had passed this barrier, the three Taoist wizards reduced the size of the box a little, so that Liping could only just fit inside, with no leeway whatsoever for movement. To avoid getting spiked, he was going to have to keep his body absolutely still. Since he already had months of basic training in quiet sitting and quiet standing, however, this exercise was just a matter of enhancing the degree of perfection, so Liping was able to master this exercise completely after a while.

The teachers also used to set "booby traps" for their apprentice, to test his concentration and foster an intelligent capacity of swift reaction. Once Liping crept up stealthily to where the old masters were staying, hoping to see what they were doing. All of a sudden there was a thunderous shout that sent him tumbling backward several yards, raising several lumps on his head. The Wayfarer of Pure Serenity laughed out from inside the shack—"You rascal! Why were you sitting outside our door?" Now Liping realized the old Taoists had been aware of his doings all along. From now on, he knew he had better watch out and not get careless.

Another time, when Wang Liping went to the outhouse, as he squatted over the cesspit he heard someone cry out below. Apparently someone had fallen into the sewage. Just as Liping was going to call out he heard the sound of the three old masters laughing. "I've been tricked by the old Taoists again," he realized, restraining his upset. "I'll get even! Just wait and see!"

As it turned out, this was one of the schemes of the Wayfarer of Pure Emptiness. His intention was to tune Liping, see to it that he maintained a high level of alertness at all times in the course of daily life, not being careless about details and subtleties. After this lesson, Liping certainly increased his watchfulness.

One day Wang Liping happened to see a thumbtack on the wall and hatched a plot of his own. Taking the tack, he put it on the bed of the Wayfarer of Pure Emptiness. Then, occupying himself with other matters, as though nothing were afoot, he quietly waited for the old wizard to get stuck, in revenge for past pranks. Little did he imagine that he himself would be the one to get stuck, that evening when he sat on his bed to practice inner exercises. Sharp as the pain was, however, he didn't want to let on.

The Wayfarer of Pure Emptiness saw Liping was in pain, but just vaguely remarked, "Young fellow, you're still soft!"

Getting his meaning, Wang Liping laughed bitterly and said, "You're too ferocious!" Nevertheless, these little tests between teachers and disciple added no little amusement to the life of spiritual cultivation.

The next barrier was to practice internal exercise inside a huge urn. When inverted the urn was just large enough for Wang Liping to squat inside with lowered head. There were two bricks inside for him to squat on. The urn was placed over a cesspit, leaving just a seam of opening at the edge of the urn. The weather was very hot at the time, so when the sun was overhead, the urn was really boiling inside; anyone inside it would be running with sweat. The stench of the cesspit, furthermore, and the flies and vermin, all made Liping feel like vomiting. His mentor used this method to get Liping to be able to practice concentration single-mindedly under any conditions. In such an out-of-the-way place, this cesspit may have been the best tool for the purpose. The three old wizards really knew how to make use of the terrain and the items of the locality, taking from them the materials to set up places to practice Taoist exercises. Just as Wang Liping was finding it impossible to enter stillness and practice his exercise because of the disturbing conditions in and around the urn, he suddenly heard a rapping on the urn. Then he heard the coarse, powerful voice of the Wayfarer of Pure Serenity scolding him, "Stop thinking of other things! Focus on your exercise!" After a time, the Wayfarer again came and deliberately spoiled the atmosphere by scraping on the urn with a piece of brick; he wanted to see if the screeching would upset Liping. Feeling this test might not be severe enough, furthermore, he scooped up some slop from the cesspit and dribbled it over the top of the urn, intensifying the stench and causing maggots to crawl up into the urn.

Wang Liping couldn't stand it anymore and cried out for mercy. He would have been better off not seeking pity, though, because asking for mercy only got him into deeper trouble. Seeing that Liping couldn't quiet down, the old mentor added oil to the fire, pouring filth through the crack in the urn, fouling the youth with ordure. Liping knew that the Wayfarer of Pure Emptiness was the most severe of the masters in the process of training, never once showing him any quarter. All the youth could do was endure silently.

Ever since the first day in the dark room when he had embarrassed himself by incontinence, Liping had been making sure to prepare himself before each exercise. This time, though, when he needed to relieve himself, it was too much for him to bear. He wanted to tip the urn over and get out of there. But his mentor, seeing movement inside the urn, grabbed a stick and poked inside, jabbing Liping and wounding him in several places.

Liping couldn't get out, yet he couldn't hold it in. He had no choice but to relieve himself right there inside the urn. Knowing what had happened, his mentor scolded him for fouling his exercise place, demanding that he clean it up. Liping knew that the rules of conduct do not allow disobedience; since he had already sacrificed himself to the Way, he couldn't do other than follow his teacher's commands. He had no choice but to wipe up the mess with his own clothing.

After a few days of this exercise, Wang Liping gradually adapted to these surroundings, and his mentor no longer came to disturb him during his exercises. A truly extraordinary youth, he got through this barrier too, using stillness to master disturbance, master odor, and master filth, collecting his mind and nurturing essence, refining the nature of his mind to even greater purity.

Subsequently, seeing that the nearby cemetery could be used for exercises, the three old wizards added another item to the process of collecting the mind and developing essential nature. This they called "pacifying the spirit and guarding the house."

Since this practice is hard to do, the three elders first called Liping to them and spoke to him seriously. "You have been practicing the Way for some time now," they said to the youth, "and you have made great progress. Now we want to add another exercise to strengthen your courage and stabilize your higher soul. Do you dare to undertake it?"

Wang Liping knew only that he had to learn whatever exercise he was given. Without knowing what he was getting into, without any further thought, he replied in the affirmative.

The Wayfarer of the Infinite laughed and said, "Very good! This technique is carried out alone in a graveyard at night. Do you have the nerve?"

"That's not so hard!" the youth replied.

Feeling that the youth's spiritual state was favorable, the Wayfarer explained, "The ancients said that the relationship of the vital spirit to the physical body is as that of a sovereign to a country. If the spirit is restless within, the physical body deteriorates externally, just as a country falls into chaos below when the rulership above it is benighted.

"So educated people know that the physical body depends upon the spirit; while the spirit needs the body to remain present. Therefore they cultivate essential nature to preserve the spirit, and pacify the mind to keep the body intact. When body and spirit are intimate with each other, outside and inside are both taken care of.

"Those who live well are clear and open, calm and serene, with minimal selfishness and few desires. They do not keep the burdens of external things on their minds, so their purity of spirit is outstanding. Open-minded and unruffled, peaceful and unworried, maintaining this state by unity, nurturing it with harmony, they take care of daily affairs reasonably, equanimously attaining universal accord.

"Now you have already experienced the effects of collecting the mind and nurturing its essential nature, but you have not realized stabilization of the higher soul and strengthening of the earthly soul. That is why we are giving you another exercise, to stabilize your spirit."

Liping nodded, getting the general meaning of what the old master said, supposing that all he had to do was practice whatever the masters taught him.

Later that night, when all was still, the graveyard was silent as death itself. There was no moonlight, and dark clouds blacked out the stars in the sky. There was no one in that desolate place but the three old wizards and their youthful apprentice, practicing inner exercises.

The three elders had already picked their spots and sat down. The Wayfarer of Pure Serenity told Wang Liping to choose a place for himself and sit there. He was to sit for four hours, concluding the session at one o'clock in the morning.

As Liping sat down to concentrate, he thought to himself that this exercise wouldn't be hard, seeing as how his three teachers were right there. Little did he know that the three old wizards had already disappeared silently into the night: two had gone back to their abode, and one had stayed behind to watch over Liping from a distance.

The one who remained to supervise was the Wayfarer of Pure Serenity, who was a great practical joker. After Liping had entered into stillness, the Wayfarer began to produce all sorts of banshee cries and wolf howls to disturb the youth's exercise. By now Liping had considerable accomplishment, however, and was completely unfazed by the bloodcurdling, spine-chilling shrieks and howls. He heard but didn't listen, stolidly cultivating his inner work.

At the end of the midnight hour, Liping concluded his exercise. When he opened his eyes and looked, he saw that the three old masters were gone. Without another thought, he turned and set off on his way. Suddenly the youth saw a black shadow flitting back and forth in front of him, not very far away yet not too near, trying to block his way out of the graveyard.

Liping wondered whether he was really seeing a ghost. Even if it was a ghost, he thought, he wasn't afraid. He just kept on walking, but now the black shadow flitted from side to side, trying to lead him around in circles. Steeling his nerves, circulating primal energy through his body, Wang Liping stretched his right hand out like a sword blade and thrust it with a tremendous shout directly into the black shadow.

Suddenly the black shadow disappeared, and Liping heard a laugh, crystal clear, right by his ear. Distinguishing the voice of his mentor the Wayfarer of Pure Serenity, Liping hurriedly said, "You're still testing me!" The mentor then appeared, bragged a little about baffling the boy, then took him by the hand and led him back.

As it turned out, this exercise in the graveyard had numerous advantages. After practicing for a while, Liping felt yin and yang harmonize throughout his whole body; filled with pure energy, he also mastered the basis for the practice of stabilizing the spirit and guarding the house. Wang Liping learned that with courage, self-control, and calm assurance, it is possible to bring everything into silence, into absolute stillness. One is thoroughly solitary: both body and spirit are there, the self is their master, and the self enters into stillness, silence, tranquility, calm. "Once the mind is spontaneously quiet, the spirit is untroubled; when the spirit is untroubled, it is forever clear and calm." Once the mind is quiet and the spirit is at peace, the only realization is emptiness; this emptiness is the Way. This is also an individual universe, an individual realm of experience.

After repeating these practices over and over again, Wang Liping developed further stability and self-possession. He went in and out of the graveyard like going in and out a door; the countless dead buried there didn't bother him a bit. Spirit and soul untroubled, he had reached a considerable degree of attainment.

The three old wizards formed a powerful team, now devoting their total attention to the work of developing the next Transmitter. The Wayfarer of Pure Serenity was indeed very stern and harsh, but there was no question that he had a good heart. Now past seventy years of age, once again he was at his old work as a drill instructor. By day he would search all over for the best places to have Wang Liping do his exercises, making special spots into instruments to help the training. By night, he would oversee and supervise Liping doing his exercises. Having instructed and guided the youth, he also egged him on and helped him out, devoting a truly extraordinary effort to developing the new Transmitter of Dragon Gate Taoism. He treated Liping as a son; indeed, their relationship was even closer than that of father and son.

And how are ordinary relationships between fathers and sons? Some people are loving and close. Some are loving but unable to provide guidance, leaving children to do it for themselves. There are those who provide everything, including guidance, but with questionable contents and methods. Although they have fine food and clothing, their hearts are not good. Cases of problematic behavior in children of good families are not rare. The work of education is important for the evolution of the human race.

In going through this systematic course of training, Wang Liping passed through one barrier after another. Adding studies of external exercises, he had by now cultivated a solid foundation in both inner and outer exercise. From the point of view of ordinary people, he was already extraordinary, but the old wizards knew that their youthful apprentice was as yet operating in the lower triple world, still quite far from the middle triple world.

4

Cultivating the Triple World

Han Zhongli was one of the Eight Immortals of popular Taoist legend. His disciple Lu Dongbin, another of the Eight Immortals, is among the greatest and most beloved Taoist wizards of all time. There is a book called *Annals of Transmission of the Way from Zhong to Lu*, which consists of dialogues between these two giants on the practice of inner spiritual alchemy. Collected, edited, and disseminated by the Taoist Master Huayang, this text includes the following discussion.

Lu asked, "*What is the principle of the Great Way that is hard to know and hard to practice?*"

Zhongli said, "*Since minor auxiliary methods easily produce visible effects, and they have been popularized by worldly people who never wake up all their lives, this has become such a trend that it has come to the point of spoiling the Great Way.*"

Lu asked, "*I already know about minor auxiliary methods. Can I hear about the Great Way?*"

Zhongli said, "*The Way basically has no question; the question basically has no answer. But when true energy divides, total simplicity is already gone. The Way produces one, one produces two, two produce three. One stands for substance, two stands for function, three stands for creation and evolution.*

"*The substance and function are not beyond yin and yang; creation and evolution are caused by their interaction. The higher, middle, and lower are the three fundamentals; heaven, earth, and humanity collec-*

tively realize one Way. The Way produces the two energies, the two energies produce the three fundamentals, the three fundamentals produce the five elements, the five elements produce all beings.

"Of all beings, the most intelligent and most noble are human beings. Only human beings search out the principles of all things and fulfill their own nature; finding out principle and fulfilling nature, we arrive at destiny. Fulfilling our destiny, preserving our lives, we conform to the Way, to become as stable as heaven and earth, and to last forever in the same way."

Lu said, *"Heaven and earth last forever, but the human life span is only a hundred years, and indeed few even live to be seventy. How can the Way only exist in heaven and earth while being remote from humankind?"*

Zhongli said, *"The Way is not remote from people, but people distance themselves from the Way by trying to nurture life without knowing how. The reason they don't know how is that they don't know the right timing to make effort. The reason they don't know the right timing is that they have not understood the mechanism of heaven and earth."*

The "mechanism of heaven and earth" refers to the laws by which the universe operates. Humanity is born between heaven and earth. A human being is a microcosm that is influenced and regulated by the macrocosm. Unless you know natural laws, proper timing, and appropriate method, there is no succeeding in learning the Way. Polish away the temperamental nature of acquired habit, and fundamental essential nature appears of itself. Casting aside the ordinary mind, keep the true mind. Where does the true mind resort? To Nature.

The work of collecting the mind to nurture its essential nature was completed in one year. Wang Liping emerged from the dark room, the earth pit, the giant urn, and the graveyard, heading toward Nature itself.

Everything in the triple world of heaven, earth, and humanity is a partner in cultivation in the process of realizing the Way—sun, moon, stars, and plants; mountains and rivers; flowers, plants, and trees; birds and beasts; wind, rain, thunder, and lightning; heat and cold; spring, summer, fall, and winter; east, west, south, and north. Everything contains creation and evolution; everything conceals subtleties. Now, under the tutelage of the three old wizards, Wang Liping began intensive cultivation of the triple world.

The sun rises and sets, the moon waxes and wanes, the poles revolve, and the stars shift; spring gives birth, autumn kills, summer grows, and winter stores; seas dry up, and rocks emerge; dynasties change, and eras pass. The triple world of heaven, earth, and humanity, the middle of the three realms, fluctuates, one thing waning while another grows, alternately emptying and filling, with countless changes and transformations always going on. And yet all of it forms one single, complete system, wherein oppositions tend toward balance from imbalance and nurture imbalance within balance, producing regular and harmonious movement. Humanity, being in the midst of this, lives and acts in conformity to the commands of Nature, subject to many pressures from both Nature and society.

The forces not only differ in direction; they are also unequally distributed in time, and are of countless different characteristics. Some people's senses can perceive them, while others' cannot; some are beneficial to the human body, some are harmful. Modern science has made minute analyses of those forces that can be perceived, but it does not recognize the existence of countless imperceptible forces. Yet the effects of these forces on the human body and human life are even greater than are those of perceptible forces.

This shortcoming does not exist in the ancient cultures of China and other peoples. First of all, these cultures accepted the existence of such forces; what is more, they investigated these forces, using different methods, testing them and learning to operate them. The excellence of traditional Chinese culture is in its totalistic view, in which heaven, earth, and humankind are united into one; this view avoids partiality and bias. When it comes to the issue of what degree of perception they attained, and how they expressed it in words, that is another question.

Taoist culture is one of the main pillars of traditional Chinese culture. Its methodology and degree of attainment in perception of the universe and the human body is truly amazing to modern man. It may even be that Westerners appreciate its value more than the Chinese themselves do, seeing it as a lustrous jewel of human civilization.

Heaven, earth, and humanity are one continuity, one totality, one system, with humanity living in the middle. The Great Way works throughout the universe, unresisting harmony balancing itself.

Taoists have cleaved to this Way for thousands of years, using it to perceive the universe and to cultivate and refine the human being, leaving behind them an inexhaustible treasury of countless writings. The three old Dragon Gate Taoist wizards from Mount Lao were using the teachings transmitted by their spiritual ancestors to train their young disciple Wang Liping. Liping's mentor now taught him an equilibrium exercise from the Spiritual Jewel techniques of inner exercises to master mental capacities.

This equilibrium exercise, one of the Spiritual Jewel Power exercise methods, is in the category of external exercises; it developed from elaboration of even older breathing techniques. The practitioner combines harmonic physical movements with strictly regulated breathing patterns, then goes on to use intent, energy, and the whole system of sensitive spots in the body to exchange energy masses with plants, animals, human beings, and other natural entities. It is called an equilibrium exercise because it enables the practitioner to attain a state of balance or equilibrium in the mutual opposition and antagonism of energy masses in the interaction between humanity and plants, between humanity and animals, among human beings, and between humanity and other natural entities.

This practice, in name, principle, and method, actualizes a kind of deep philosophical thinking. Considering the relationships between humans and other beings within the context of the total system of the universe, handling these relationships seriously in a comprehensive manner, the premise is to avoid disrupting the equilibrium of the total system while maximizing the expression and employment of useful energy in oneself to establish a new equilibrium between the self and the external world, with the purpose of nourishing life, strengthening the body, and increasing longevity.

The Wayfarer of Pure Serenity began this lesson by facing a huge pine tree. "See this tree?" he said to Liping, "Today we're going to work with this tree. It is an enormous tree. It has been through years of fierce heat and bitter cold, blown by the wind and beaten by the rain. Its life force is truly powerful, containing something useful to our cultivation.

"In the human body are routes of energy circulation, routes of blood circulation, and routes of waste elimination. The tree also has routes of energy circulation, routes of water circulation, ways of absorbing nutrients, and ways of eliminating waste products. Equilibrium exercise mainly consists of methods of radiating and absorbing auras of ethereal force.

Working with a tree involves exchanging energy with the tree to attain an equilibrium of yin and yang and the five elements in the human body.

"Trees have different color bases, associated variously with the five elements. The color base of this pine tree is green. Among the five elements, this corresponds to wood. In the human body, it corresponds to the liver. If people have liver disease, it comes from water weakness. When water is weak, wood does not grow. The kidneys manage water, and the color associated with water is black. The tree associated with black is the cedar. So to cure liver disease you first work with cedar to replenish kidney water, then you work with pine after that.

"Liver disease can also come from excessive fire energy, which causes a leakage of wood energy, so control of fire energy is needed to cure the liver effectively. Liver disease can also come from an excess of metal energy, which causes tension in wood energy. So it is also necessary to control metal energy to cure the liver. In any case, it is necessary to find a corresponding tree to work with. Only then can you harmonize the yin and yang and five elements in the human body, getting rid of sickness and strengthening the body."

Wang Liping had already heard about this principle of the five elements fostering and overcoming each other from the Wayfarer of the Infinite, so now he took in the explanation of the Wayfarer of Pure Serenity with perfect clarity. He even knew what the Wayfarer meant by an "aura of ethereal force."

The Wayfarer of Pure Serenity continued, "There are altogether nine kinds of equilibrium exercise. Starting today, we will study them one by one." Then the Wayfarer walked over to the huge pine tree and stood about half a meter from it. "Watch what I do," he said to Liping.

Standing with his feet at shoulder width, knees slightly bent, the mentor held his upper body in an erect position. Raising his arms, he extended them in front of him, straight but not stiff, his sides open, his palms toward the tree. Gazing straight ahead with his eyes nearly closed, the old wizard slowly bent and straightened his legs, moving up and down while maintaining his torso upright, both hands slowly sweeping up and down along the trunk of the tree. As he demonstrated the movements, the Wayfarer explained, "Pay attention to the attunement of the breathing. When you move upward you breathe in, and when you move downward you breathe out. As the physical movements are performed slowly, the breathing must be slow, subtle, deep, long, and even. At the same time, certain conscious thought needs to be added to this combination. The attention is placed in the palms of the hands, and you imagine the tree to be an enormous pillar of energy of a particular color. In this case, the pine tree I am using is a pillar of green energy. Imagine your palms emitting a mass of energy of the same color, exchanging it with the tree's energy mass." Now Wang Liping began the exercise, imitating the teacher. The old wizard stood by watching carefully, alerting him where he needed to pay attention, stopping Liping when he had gotten to the point where he could execute the movements correctly and had clearly experienced certain feelings.

In the mountains of that region, there are many varieties of trees, making it a good place to practice this exercise. Every morning at dawn and every evening at dusk, Wang Liping would perform the exercise for a period specified by his mentor, choosing a different species of tree, one after another. He also learned a number of different postures.

The Wayfarer of Pure Serenity was very serious about teaching, and his requirements were strict. For this exercise, he decided to add an extra challenge. Rigging a pulley up in the tree, he attached a rock to a rope and ran the rope through the pulley so that the rock could be raised and lowered by pulling on the rope. As Wang Liping performed the exercise, the old wizard held onto the rope in such a way as to keep the rock right over the youth's head, thereby forcing him to control the speed of his movements accordingly, while keeping his upper body consistently erect. The old mentor worked the rope so that it took fully half an hour to go up and down once, so the movement was extremely slow, even more difficult than standing still; and since the breathing has to be matched to this pace, that added yet another degree of difficulty to the exercise. Over a period of four hours, Liping made the excruciatingly slow movement up and down just a few times. His knees burned with pain, his thighs turned to jelly, and his sacroiliac became numb. There was that rock over his head, however, and the sternest of his teachers there watching, so no matter how hard or painful it was, he had to continue steadfastly.

When the exercise period was over, Liping's clothes were soaked with perspiration. He didn't have the strength even to walk. The old wizard, his mentor, was pained by the sight, but how could he foster exceptional attainment in his disciple without such training? The aged Wayfarer half carried his youthful apprentice away, but in fact he himself had also had quite a workout.

After he got used to doing this exercise under the stone, Wang Liping had already achieved more than usual skill in tuning his body and breath and exchanging energy with trees in this exercise. Even without his mentor there, he was able to do it quite well.

Liping's mentor wanted him to establish a solid foundation once he started working on equilibrium exercises, so he pursued a new tack with this subject. The three old wizards had discovered an extremely good place on the mountain. It was not a large spot, but it had five huge trees of different species, one in each of the four cardinal directions and one in the center. In the east was a pine tree, in the south was a paulownia, in the west was an aspen, in the north was a cedar, and in the center was a willow. Felicitously, they formed a natural array of the five elements and their associated directions, so it was a natural place for using the external five elements to refine the five elements within the human body.

When the three old wizards discovered this spot, they spontaneously looked at each other in amazement. The grand master, the Wayfarer of the Infinite, clapped his hands and said, "This is a boon from heaven!" Subsequently they rigged up a rope net among these trees, about half the height of a man; then they had Wang Liping walk under the net, his legs crouching but his upper body erect, the crown of his head just touching the net, so he could neither stand tall nor squat too low.

After practicing like this for two months, Liping could walk in this "horse step" all around the area within the five trees. He could even carry a bowl of water on his head, prancing about at a rapid pace without spilling a drop, keeping the surface of the water level as a mirror.

With the five trees arrayed around the spot, as one walked among them, the five elements in the human body corresponded to the external five elements in the trees. Liping's mentor had him walk along a certain prescribed route, based on the interrelations of the five elements to tune the internal five elements within the human body, using the external five elements to exert a pull on the internal five elements, so as to arrive at equilibrium of the internal five elements, in order to get rid of diseases and prolong life. By varying the route, and adding different hand positions and matching breathing patterns, it was also possible to bring out latent capacities hidden in the human body and cultivate extraordinary powers. From these very ordinary trees in the natural world, Wang Liping was ultimately able to elicit and to absorb unusual capacities.

Trees are the largest of plants; just as trees can be classified according to affinity with the five elements, so it is with other plants, which also contain vital energy and can be used for Taoist exercises. Depending on their own physical condition and need for power, practitioners use a specific form of equilibrium exercise to take in that vital energy, exchanging energy bodies.

Animals, like plants, can also be differentiated in terms of the five elements, and humans can use a relationship with them to cultivate themselves. Wang Liping's mentor gave him specific instructions on exercising with each species.

One day the Wayfarer of Pure Emptiness called Liping to him. Pointing to a basket on the ground, he said, "There's something in the basket. Take a good look!"

Peering through the slats, Liping saw a long snake coiled up in the basket, creeping up the side. Unconsciously he started. People of the north aren't used to snakes and are likely to be frightened if they see one. Wang Liping asked his mentor what the snake was for. The old wizard replied that it was for doing exercises. Liping didn't understand what he meant.

The teacher explained that the subtlest equilibrium exercise is paired cultivation, which requires a partner of some sort. There is nothing in the triple world that cannot be an object or a partner in paired cultivation. The snake is a kind of animal that usually lives in places that are shady, cool, and moist, so its nature is extreme yin. Paired cultivation with a snake makes it possible to develop extraordinary capacities in the human body.

When the old wizard had finished this explanation, Liping saw the wizard's lips convulse, emitting an eerie sound much like the hissing of a snake. The snake in the basket immediately lay down quietly, completely immobile. Directing his disciple to have no fear in working with the snake, the old wizard taught Liping a method of paired exercise. After several days of practice, Liping noticed extraordinary sensations.

One moonlit night the Wayfarer of Pure Emptiness led Wang Liping to the mossy opening of a small mountain cave. Ordering his apprentice to stand a ways back from the cave, the old wizard began to make a sound with his mouth. Before long, snakes of all sizes came out of their hiding places, slithering toward the mouth of the cave from all directions. Liping saw the snakes stop near the cave, glistening with a cold light under the moon, coiling on the mossy ground, their tongues darting out every now and then.

No longer afraid, Wang Liping first steadied his spirit. His mentor told him to exercise in the manner he had been taught, so Liping took up the appropriate posture and began to work. Closing his eyes, he relied on only inner sensations to exercise in tandem with the snakes.

The snakes, a dozen or more of them, began to circle Liping, all moving in the same direction, following the movement of his hands and the movement of his energy. Slow at first, they speeded up, then gradually slowed down again; and then they began to dance and frolic about, shimmering in the moonlight.

Liping then switched the technique he was employing. Immediately the snakes stopped cavorting and lay motionless on the ground, finally becoming so still they virtually seemed dead.

When four hours had passed and it was time for Liping to conclude his exercise, the snakes revived and left, each going the way it had come. Seeing that Liping had mastered the techniques of this exercise, his mentor, who had been there watching over him all along, felt a surge of happiness in his heart.

Later the Wayfarer of Pure Emptiness also taught Liping methods for working with other animals, such as badgers, weasels, rats, and so on. Liping practiced each one of them in the fields at night until he had mastered them all. All the exercises with small animals are practiced at night because the animals are pure yin entities and are mostly nocturnal. Yet these little bundles of vital awareness have a lot of spiritual energy; sometimes they can be seen worshiping the moon on quiet, windless nights, and some of them have attainments in developmental exercises.

According to the Taoist theory and practice of three realms, every living thing with form and substance has an aura of ethereal force. But this is still viewing the issue from the level of the lower three realms—people, events, and things. If we rise higher to the level of the middle three realms—heaven, earth, and humanity—the mode of existence of events and phenomena rises to a higher level, and we encounter this issue immediately. It is at this level that the gravity with which Buddhists and Taoists view the taking of life has its profound logic.

One clear moonlit night the Wayfarer of the Infinite called off the midnight exercises. Instead he led the other wizards and their young apprentice down the mountain to a hill at a bend in the river. Gazing fixedly for a while, at length the Wayfarer turned to his disciples and said, "Do you see the energy in this hill?" The other two Wayfarers replied that they saw a blue energy, very powerful.

Now the old master said to Wang Liping, "This spot is very good. Yin and yang energies merge and combine here. When pure energy is rising on a mountain, that is the best condition for refinement work. Let's do our exercise here." Then the grand master gave Liping a detailed account of the method for practicing with mountains. When he had finished, all four of them began the exercise.

Wang Liping had been taught methods of developing mental capacities and had already attained the minor cycle; the aperture of his celestial eye was opened, and he had also successfully practiced various methods of equilibrium exercise. Now as he practiced this teaching tonight, after just two hours he had already seen the blue energy rising over the mountain, gazing with his celestial eye. As he used this energy to develop himself, the power in his body grew in a rapid spurt. After four hours had passed and the four of them had concluded the exercise, Liping told the old wizards that he had really seen the energy and had made tremendous gains from working with it.

One day the Wayfarer of Pure Serenity took Wang Liping to a small reservoir, where he had already prepared a large plank. The Wayfarer had Liping sit cross-legged on the plank, then eased it out into the water, where it gradually came to a stop in the middle of the reservoir. Liping sat on the plank in a state of silence, doing inner work; following his mentor's instructions, he raised his work to a whole new level.

After four hours had passed, and the Wayfarer was sure that Liping had reached the right state, he disturbed the surface of the water with his hand, sending a wave of ripples toward the center of the reservoir. When the ripples approached the plank, Wang Liping's reflection in the water was shattered; he himself just felt a shudder in the heart, and his body stirred. When the ripples had passed, the surface of the water again became smooth as ever, and Liping's body and mind returned to their former state of quietude. The Wayfarer tested him in this way several times, and Liping successfully sensed the ripples each time. Seeing that his attainment was quite deep, the Wayfarer had Liping conclude the exercise and paddle in to shore. The young apprentice told his mentor all about the sensations he'd had on the water, finding it quite beyond his understanding.

When they had returned to the wizards' abode, Wang Liping was finally given an explanation of the principle of this exercise. As the youth practiced paired cultivation work with all sorts of things and beings, his inner and outer accomplishments grew together. Now the yang celestial soul and the yin earthly soul in his body had both been strengthened and sensitized. From the point of view of ordinary people, shadows and reflections are unreal, things that have form but not substance, of no value to the human being. From the Taoist point of view, however, these "unreal shadows and reflections with form but no substance" also have ethereal force, which can be felt by the human body on contact. People who have not been refined by inner work are insensitive to these impressions, but those of high attainment can sense even such subtleties quite clearly. This is why Liping's body and mind stirred when his reflection was disturbed in the water. When one gets to the "middle three realms," shadows and reflections are no longer insubstantial forms; now they not only have form, they also have substance. This is the principle underlying the practice of curing illness by working on people's shadows, as Wang Liping later learned from his mentor.

At this point, Liping reviewed the "eight trigram mental balls" taught him by his mentor, practicing over and over again. Once he had built up from one to nine energy balls of different colors, they whirled around his body, above and below, left and right. Wang Liping determined the positions of the eight trigrams, set a fixed direction and order, and then ran from one position to the next, so lightly and swiftly that he virtually flew, his upper body remaining erect and balanced throughout, blending different hand positions and different breathing patterns into an infinitely varied flux, while those nine colored energy balls revolved around him, above and below, left and right, according to regular patterns.

Once he was capable of doing this, Wang Liping was able to mentally extract his own internal organs, whirl them around in the air, massage them, and put them back into his gut. This exercise, which strengthens the internal organs, is simply inconceivable to an ordinary person without the requisite mental training.

As Liping cultivated the three realms intensely, his accomplishments became finer day by day. The Wayfarer of Pure Serenity also transmitted to him methods of exercise while sleeping and natural circulation of energy, part of the Spiritual Jewels techniques for developing mental capacities.

Sleeping exercise is one of three kinds of Taoist work, to be done at leisure. The practitioner is physically in a sleeping position, but mentally in an active state, so that it is possible to work even while sleeping. "The body is still, but the mind is in movement," attention inducing energy to flow, stabilizing the spirit and strengthening the body. Sleeping exercise is divided into eleven forms; when a certain degree of efficiency is attained in each form, then they are combined into a total system, which produces an equilibrium of yin and yang throughout the whole body.

The method of natural energy circulation is one of the auxiliary techniques of the Spiritual Jewels system. It is also called the method of natural absorption of energy. There are no limitations of time or place in doing this practice, but it is best to do it where there are lots of flowers and trees and fresh air.

The basic method of work is to walk naturally, with matching attention and breathing. For example, one walks three steps with each inhalation, and three steps with each exhalation. After this pattern of breathing becomes natural, then one increases to six steps with each inhalation and six steps with each exhalation. The ratio is further increased, to twelve, then twenty-four steps with each inhalation and each exhalation, in such a way that both walking and breathing remain natural and relaxed, without any sense of strain.

Once this practice has been mastered, another method of training is introduced. Now one walks three steps while breathing in, three steps holding the breath, and three steps breathing out. This pattern of inhaling, stopping, exhaling, and stopping is repeated over and over, while walking according to the prescribed pattern. When that has been mastered, then the period of energy circulation is again increased, so that one walks six steps inhaling, six steps holding the breath, six steps exhaling, and another six steps holding the breath. Then this is again increased until one can go twelve steps, then up to twenty four steps, with each interval.

Just as the circulation of energy through breathing is matched with walking, the thought must also be matched. When breathing in, one imagines breath-energy being absorbed through the skin from all directions. When breathing out, one imagines breath-energy radiating out from the whole body in all directions. When holding the breath after inhaling, one imagines the body has become a single whole. When holding the breath after exhaling, one imagines one is in the clouds.

As Wang Liping followed the instructions given him by his mentor, he was able to use both walking and sleeping for doing exercises, plunging his whole body and mind into continual inner work.

Delighted to see their young apprentice making such progress in his training, the old wizards took him deeper into the mysteries of Taoism. Liping had already learned basic principles such as the Infinite, yin and yang, the three fundamentals, the four forms, the five elements, the six energies, the seven treasures, the eight trigrams, the nine chambers, and so on. He also knew the ideas of old Taoist classics like Lao-tzu and Chuang-tzu, and had even memorized some of the most important passages. The old wizards, the grand master, and the two mentors now began to teach him about many important texts in the Taoist canon, such as the The I Ching or Book of Changes, The *Yellow Emperor's Classic of Internal Medicine,* the *Book of Hidden Correspondences,* the *Book of the Yellow Court,* and the *Book of Pure Serenity.* They also talked about the ancient Taoist adepts, their practices, activities, and teachings.

In school, meanwhile, Wang Liping was studying ordinary subjects such as language, mathematics, nature, geography, history, and biology. What he was learning from the three old wizards, in contrast, was immensely broader, richer, and deeper.

One night the Wayfarer of the Infinite taught Liping some practical principles of Taoist exercise transmitted in their lineage: "Our ancestral teacher Wang Chongyang said there are five classes of immortals. Ghost immortality is not worthwhile. It is not necessary to talk about human immortals. Earth immortals remain in the world forever; spiritual immortals go from being into nonbeing. Those who can disappear and appear unfathomably, have embodiment outside the body, and can double their bodies, are called spiritual immortals. Celestial immortals are ranked even higher than spiritual immortals.

"Students of the Way should not follow the mediocre and the lesser. They should study the principles of the supreme one vehicle, the supreme, ultimate, sublime Way, clearly understanding the yin and yang of heaven and earth, profoundly comprehending the creative evolution of the five elements. The principle of yin and yang is incomparably great; heaven and earth, sun and moon, and the five elements, all evolve from it. Once the Absolute has divided, clear energy rises, becoming images in heaven; opaque energy descends, becoming forms on earth. The essences of wood and fire produce major yang. The essences of metal and water produce major yin. Heaven and earth and the sun and moon develop from the influence of this bipolar energy.

"This bipolar energy is perpetually operating throughout heaven and earth, circulating everywhere endlessly, producing all species of creation. So a human life is born of a father's sperm and a mother's ovum, the yang energy of the sun and the yin energy of the earth, and a solar yang celestial soul and a lunar yin earthly soul, a fiery yang spirit and a watery yin vitality. So the creation of a human body is the same one energy as that of the universe.

"So heaven and earth are the great father and mother of human beings. Those who realize this transcend the universe and all its fluctuations, while those who miss this are trapped in an ocean of suffering in the midst of myriad forms. Those who are not constrained by the five elements or bound up by yin and yang are called celestial immortals of the highest rank.

"These statements express the supreme design. As people on earth see the courses of the sun and moon, they follow continuous cycles, each having its specific cycle. Speaking in terms of the sun, as the sun rises warmth increases and energy heats up; this is symbolized by fire. When the sun goes down, warmth decreases, and energy recedes; this is symbolized by water. When the sun's course is farthest from the earth, warmth disperses and energy scatters; this is symbolized by wood. When the sun's course is nearest the earth, warmth gathers and energy collects; this is symbolized by metal. When the sun's course is parallel to the earth, warmth stops and energy rests; this is symbolized by earth. Thus from spring to summer to autumn to winter, and back again to spring, the five elements are inherent in the course of the sun, forming the cycle of the year.

"Speaking in terms of the moon, when the moon descends, warmth increases and energy heats up; this is symbolized by fire. When the moon ascends, warmth decreases and energy withdraws; this is symbolized by water. When the moon is on this side of the earth, warmth dissolves and energy dissipates; this is symbolized by wood. When the moon is on the other side of the earth, warmth gathers and energy collects; this is symbolized by metal. When the moon's course is even, warmth ceases and energy rests; this is symbolized by earth. Thus the moon waxes and wanes, wanes and waxes; the five elements are inherent in the course of the moon, also forming a cycle, the cycle of the month.

"The method of training the Spiritual Jewel powers involves using the correspondences between the internal five elements within the human body and the external five elements in the sun and moon, and the external five elements in the earth, collectively cultivating the three realms of heaven, earth, and humanity, returning from nine to eight, from eight to seven, from seven to six, from six to five, from five to four, from four to three, from three to two, from two to one, finally returning to the Absolute. When the Absolute becomes a single sphere, then the work of the Spiritual Jewel powers is done."

Now that Wang Liping had practiced cultivation of the three realms for some months, the old wizards introduced him to the supreme one vehicle. Following their instructions, secret methods transmitted from the founders of their lineage, Liping experienced the changes of the five elements in extremely subtle conditions within his own body, taking primal energies from the sun and moon to augment the primal energy in his body, gradually comprehending the pattern of nine, eight, seven, six, five, four, three, two, one. At this point, however, the work he was doing was transitional, and still required refinement.

One evening, as the full moon was rising, Wang Liping chose a spot amidst a luxurious, fragrant growth of plants and trees and sat there to exercise. Having tuned his body, breath, and attention, and gone into a state of stillness and concentration, he mentally gazed at the golden moon slowly rising in the eastern sky. He saw the moon drift closer and closer to him, gradually becoming larger and larger and brighter and brighter, like an uncanny ball of energy, radiating myriad beams of ethereal light, engulfing his whole body. Liping felt that his own body had also completely transmuted into energy and no longer existed corporeally—nothing in the world was there anymore. There was only a feeling, that of a body like a mass of energy, rising to merge and disappear into that vast energy mass of the moonlight. Time and space no longer existed.

As the east began to pale, the clouds over the horizon became visible, turning from black to grey to white. Then a thin layer of pale golden glow appeared below. In a moment, the sky was deep blue. The stars vanished, the moon had set in the west, a new dawn had arrived. Scarlet light spewed from the east, announcing the rising of the sun.

As the shining golden orb of the sun rose over the earth, Wang Liping still sat unmoving. He had already sensed the sunrise. Opening his eyes, he looked directly at the sun for a moment, then closed his eyes and gathered in spiritual light, which he sent down into his body, so that a golden sun was now revolving within him. As Liping bathed in the sunlight, the miniature sun in his body was bright and lively as a newborn baby.

By now, Wang Liping was able to sit unmoving for days and nights on end. While sitting, he minutely examined the patterns and laws of movement and the shifting of the celestial bodies, finding out the corresponding changes in the subtle conditions within his own body, gradually coming to a realization. As he found, the workings and transformations of the human body correspond to the workings and transformations of heaven and earth. When there is external movement, there is always internal reaction; when there is reaction, there is sensing; with sensing there is knowledge. There is knowledge, that is, but no further reversion. This sort of accomplishment is already quite profound from an ordinary perspective, but Liping was still far from meeting the requirements of the old wizards teaching him. He had to know and yet also revert back, return from nine to one, going back to hold to oneness in quiet stillness, thus to reach the Great Way. This method of reversion is something that needs practice to accomplish.

While Liping was in the process of cultivating the three realms, his mentor also taught him some of the ordinary concepts of Taoist practice and hygiene.

Hygienists consider heaven and earth to be the greatest things, and humankind to be the most intelligent of beings. The human body is a microcosm, a miniature universe, having within it a sun and moon, yin and yang, and the operation of the five elements—metal, wood, water, fire, and earth—fostering each other and overcoming each other, taking advantage of each other and dominating each other, thus achieving balance.

The numbers associated with the five elements were already established three thousand years ago in the "Universal Model" chapter of the *Classic Documents*: "One refers to water, two refers to fire, three refers to wood, four refers to metal, five refers to earth." It also illustrates the natures of the five elements: "Water refers to moisture and descent, fire refers to heat and ascent, wood refers to curvature and straightness, metal refers to adaptation and change, earth refers to sowing and reaping." In *The Yellow Emperor's Classic of Internal Medicine* there is more detailed discussion of the five elements. The "level energies" of the five elements are described in these terms: "Wood refers to expansion and harmony, fire refers to rising and illumination, earth refers to completeness and transformation, metal refers to alignment and leveling, water refers to quiet and obedience." "Insufficiency" in the five elements is described in these terms: "Wood refers to combination, fire refers to subdued light, earth refers to close supervision, metal refers to adaptive change, water refers to evaporation of flow." "Excess" in the five elements is a illustrated in this way: "Wood refers to explosive growth, fire refers to intense daylight, earth refers to richness, metal refers to hardness, water refers to overflowing." The way to lengthen life is to become thoroughly familiar with the natures and relationships of the five elements, as well as the correspondence of the five elements in the body with the five elements of the universe, fostering and nurturing true energy. The most significant relationship with the operation of the human body is that of heaven and earth. Crudely defined, heaven and earth consist of the earth, the moon, and the sun. The rotation of the earth takes a day and a night; in terms of its correspondence with the operation of the human body, this is the morning–evening cycle. The revolution of the moon around the earth, in terms of its correspondence to the operation of the human body, is the minor cycle. The revolution of the earth around the sun, in terms of its correspondence to the operation of the human body, is the major cycle. These cycles are different periodicities in the operation of life. Even uncultivated people know enough to work and rest in accord with the cycles of operation of heaven and earth; this is called conformity. Cultivated people consciously accord with the cyclic operations of nature by attuning the yin and yang energies in the body; this is conformity as practiced in the highest vehicle of Taoism.

Those who are highly cultivated use the pure energies of the external five elements to nurture pure energy inside the body, opposing the operation of nature to rise above it, combining water and fire, producing and culling medicine, crystallizing the alchemical elixir and incubating it, thus becoming immortals.

The *Hundred Character Tablet* by Ancestor Lu (Dongbin) says,

> *Nurturing energy, forget words and guard it.*
> *Conquer the mind, do nondoing.*
> *In activity and quietude, know the source progenitor.*
> *There is no thing; whom else do you seek?*
> *Real constancy should respond to people;*
> *in responding to people,*
> *it is essential not to get confused.*
> *When you don't get confused,*
> *your nature is naturally stable;*
> *when your nature is stable,*
> *energy naturally returns.*
> *When energy returns,*
> *elixir spontaneously crystallizes*
> *in the pot mating fire and water.*
> *Yin and yang arise,*
> *alternating over and over again,*
> *everywhere producing thunder.*
> *White clouds assemble on the peak,*
> *sweet dew bathes the polar mountain.*
> *Having drunk the wine of long life,*
> *you wander free;*
> *who can know you?*
> *Sitting listening to the stringless tune,*
> *you clearly understand the workings of creation.*
> *The whole of these twenty verses*
> *is a ladder straight to Heaven.*

When the sun rises at dawn, the air of the eastern direction rises in temperature, exposed to the sunlight; its volume expands, and it slowly rises. This is considered the productive energy of minor yang. At noon, the hot sun is overhead; the temperature of the air increases, its volume expands, and it rises rapidly. This is when things grow most strongly; this is considered the growing energy of major yang. At dusk, the sun sets, the heat in the air disperses, its volume contracts, and it slowly descends; now things begin to withdraw. This is called the gathering energy of minor yin.

At midnight, the sun is gone and the night is deep; the air cools, contracts, and sinks. This is called the storing energy of major yin.

The energies inside the human body correspond to this process. Liver energy is the productive energy of minor yang. Heart energy is the growing energy of major yang. Lung energy is the gathering energy of minor yin. Kidney energy is the storing energy of major yin. At midnight, energy arises in the kidneys; at dawn, it reaches the liver. At noon, energy reaches the heart; accumulated energy in the heart produces fluid, which reaches the lungs at dusk and gets to the kidneys by midnight. Kidney energy is like water, heart energy is like fire, liver energy is like wood, and lung energy is like metal. Water is wet and flows downward; fire flames upward. When fire and water do not balance each other, we do not live long. When the work of human refinement is mastered, water is above and fire is below; water and fire balance each other, so life is extended.

When Wang Liping worked on the minor cycle, or the cycle of the moon, by inner concentration and plenitude the energy broke through the three passes in his coccyx, midspine, and the back of his head. When it reached the "gate of heaven" at the top of his head, however, he needed a mentor to attend him.

Around the aperture on top of the head there are always four flashing points of brightness; the ancients called these the "four great spirits of the gate." Their adamant guardianship makes it hard for the pure energy inside the body to burst through here. It is necessary for a teacher to move these "four great spirits of the gate" before the "gate of heaven" can be opened.

What impressed Liping as most novel in his new experience came after completion of the minor cycle, when he could feel something warm and moist inside his body slowly rising up his back to his head, then descending slowly from his face downward. The whole process took exactly one lunar month, corresponding to the cycle of the moon, this occurring completely naturally and spontaneously. Even if he was shut up in a dark room for several days and nights, he could still determine the trajectory of the moon accurately and know what day of what month it was.

The earth revolves around the sun once in a year. The Chinese divide this into twenty-four seasonal energies. For the purposes of Taoist exercises, the four points considered most important are the spring and autumn equinoxes and the summer and winter solstices. Heaven and earth are represented by a human being: the heart is heaven, the kidneys are earth, the liver is the position of yang, the lungs are the position of yin; "energy" is yang, "fluid" is yin. On the winter solstice, the sun, coursing in the south, begins to turn north; people in the Northern Hemisphere of earth perceive this as yin culminating and yang arising, with the kidney energy in the body beginning to grow. On the spring equinox, kidney energy rises to the liver. On the summer solstice, the sun, coursing in the north, begins to shift south; people in the Northern Hemisphere perceive this as yang culminating and yin arising, with the yang energy in the body rising to the position of the heart, where accumulated energy produces fluid, and the fluid begins to descend. On the the autumn equinox, the heart fluid reaches the lungs, thence to reenter the kidneys on the winter solstice.

On the key days of transition of seasonal energies, the solstices and the equinoxes, Wang Liping closely examined the subtle changes in his body, under the careful guidance and protection of his mentors.

Lao-tzu says, "The valley spirit undying is called the mystic female; the opening of the mystic female is called the root of heaven and earth. Though subtle, it does exist; its use is not strained." This opening of the mystic pass fits cosmic space. A Taoist scripture says that there are 84,000 miles between the heights of heaven and the depths of earth, so the center of heaven and earth is 42,000 miles up. If the human body is a miniature heaven and earth, and the heart and navel are 8.4 inches apart, then the center is 4.2 inches from each. This opening is right in the center, where all channels connect, an empty opening with a tiny pearl hanging in space. This is the true center of the universe in the body, the aperture where the original generative energy is stored. Therefore the master teacher Chunyang said, "The mystic female, the mystic female, the true mystic female; it is not in the heart and not in the kidneys. Find out the beginning of life where energy is received; do not think it strange the celestial mechanism has been divulged." From this the importance of that aperture can be seen.

In cultivating refinement to this point, Wang Liping also experienced minor death several times.

5

The Elixir of Life

As Wang Liping cultivated the three realms, three years passed by in a flash. Seeing their apprentice grow and develop, the Dragon Gate wizards led him on to even loftier domains. Liping was given an alchemical pill for the first time, one of the most unforgettable experiences of his life.

～～～～

Ancient methods of hygiene and refinement were divided into inner cultivation and outer development. Outer development refers to ingestion of special substances, which eventually evolved into alchemy.

These dietary practices began during the Warring States era, flourished during the Qin and Han dynasties, and became especially popular in Wei and Jin times. The famous Taoist work *The Simpleton* by Ge Hong devotes an entire article to it.

"External alchemical elixir" is made by refining and combining substances such as lead and mercury. Ge Hong considered external alchemical elixir very important, and his encyclopedic work lists dozens of alchemical formulas. He wrote, "If you want to see spiritual immortality, just get the quintessential. What is most essential is to treasure vitality, circulate energy, and ingest elixir. That is enough; not much is required. There are, however, relatively shallow and deep versions of these three things. If you do not meet an enlightened teacher and do not go through intense effort, you cannot know everything in a hurry."

Treasuring vitality refers to the bedroom art. Ingesting elixir, circulating energy, and treasuring vitality are three essential factors in attaining immortality. Ge Hong also gives detailed cautions for alchemy: "Alchemical elixir should be compounded on a special mountain, in an uninhabited location, with no more than three people in the group. First fast for a hundred days and bathe in perfumed water; keep pure, do not approach anything polluted, and do not associate with vulgar people. Also do not let people who do not believe in the Way know about it, because if the spiritual medicine is slandered and repudiated, the elixir will not develop." The special mountains have righteous spirits guarding them, so they are good for making alchemical elixir. When Taoists go into the mountains to refine elixir, they first choose an auspicious day and go in armed with a talisman.

The practice of taking alchemical elixirs must have had some extraordinary effects to have continued for so many thousands of years. There are many popular legends of the miraculous effects of "gold elixir," which have been further embellished in literary works, where they are described with exaggerated marvels. Over the ages there have been many people who died from taking alchemical elixir. Cinnabar is definitely useful to the human body, but it has to be refined and processed correctly, and it has to be ingested in the right way.

Taoists have learned profound lessons on refining and ingesting alchemical elixir, based on deep experience, so they are extremely cautious in the refining process. Those who come from the Dragon Gate sect of Complete Reality Taoism in particular lay special emphasis on the cultivation of internal alchemy, but they still take external alchemical elixirs to assist the cultivation of inner work. Both the preparation and the ingestion of external alchemical elixirs equally depend on the guidance of an enlightened teacher with a great deal of experience.

~~~~~~

Under the protection of the three old wizards, Wang Liping swallowed a grain of "gold elixir" that they had brought from Mount Lao. He took it on an empty stomach, and the "gold pill" gradually melted inside him, permeating his whole body through his circulatory system. The three teachers had him sit cross-legged and commence inner work, using the power of inner exercise to push the liquefied elixir inside his body out to the surface of his skin.

The night was very quiet. The abode of the wizards, so far out of the way, was totally silent. Under the dusky light of a lamp, Wang Liping quietly worked, surrounded by his three teachers. The expression on the old wizards' face was most solemn. All three of them and their student were engaged in a sacred task, a grand experiment.

Again the mentors tied up Liping's legs with rope to ensure that he remained in a cross-legged position. This was the first time this had happened since he had been cultivating the three realms. He knew the seriousness and gravity of the situation. Based on his present degree of accomplishment, in ordinary situations, under normal conditions, the rope would not have been necessary anymore. Settling his spirit, Liping circulated his inner energy and worked on the method indicated by his teachers, holding firm as hour by hour ticked by.

A day passed. As the toxicity in the gold elixir gradually began to act, Wang Liping felt as if his insides were burning. He became dizzy, and his vision blurred. Finally he lost control and collapsed unconscious. Because his legs were tied up, however, he didn't lose his cross-legged position. The Wayfarer of Pure Serenity doused him with cold water to revive him, and helped him up. All three wizards also employed certain techniques to assist their apprentice invisibly. Wang Liping continued to hold on, performing the exercise.

The night passed. On the second day, the three wizards saw that Liping's skin had gradually changed colors, from sallow to ruddy to dark. In their judgment, based on their experience, the period of danger had passed. They breathed a sigh of relief.

Through the action of the gold elixir, the toxins in Liping's body had been pushed to the surface of the skin; this was what caused the changes in skin color. Liping's life was no longer in danger, but he could not conclude the exercise just yet. If he stopped now, the toxins would crystallize in his skin, causing the hair to fall out all over his body and spoiling the work already done.

Although Wang Liping's attainment was already quite profound, after this depletion of inner energy he had reached the limits of his endurance. The burning pain in his gut was gone, but now the skin all over his body was experiencing a variety of inexplicable sensations that were difficult to bear, burning and aching, swelling and itching. He wanted to scratch himself all over, but his mentor told him to keep still and not move at all.

Another difficult night passed.

On the afternoon of the third day, Liping's body became quite comfortable and relaxed, and the color of his skin went through an extraordinary change. The darkness, ruddiness, and sallowness changed to a healthy rosy white, and each pore became a crystalline point of brilliance, such that his skin glistened under a strong light. The gold elixir had completed its circulation throughout the body and all of it had been ejected. The "energy routes" of Wang Liping's body, from outside to inside, had all opened up freely.

After making a careful examination of the youth's condition, the grand master pronounced the results excellent. All of them were so happy they cried and danced about, congratulating each other.

Now the old wizards took Wang Liping into the mountains. As they passed through grassy glades into the woods, the evening scenery was extraordinarily beautiful. They decided to do some deep breathing facing the evening sun in the fresh mountain air. The old masters were very much at ease in mind. Liping was at ease too, but now he had an unusual feeling. He no longer needed to use his nose and mouth to breathe as usual; all that was necessary was a slight movement of the abdomen, whereupon the energy of heaven and earth poured into his whole body from all directions through his pores, clear and cool, fluid and easy, thoroughly penetrating. Once the energy was circulating in his body, it seemed as if he had merged with the universe.

Making a careful examination of Wang Liping's eyes and skin, the old wizards realized that his body had undergone a fundamental change, inwardly and outwardly. Now they considered conditions ripe to transmit the fourth step of the work to their apprentice, abstention from grain.

Wang Liping was unusual from birth in having been naturally vegetarian without even having been taught about it. His diet was plain, consisting of grains and vegetables. Now that Liping had learned some of the techniques of the Spiritual Jewel capacities, he was able to absorb power directly from Nature. His teachers had planted cereals and vegetables around their camp, and their garden yielded enough to sustain them. Sometimes when he was engaged in exercises, moreover, Liping didn't even think of eating for days on end. When his mentor began teaching Liping how to abstain from grain, he got into it gradually, so it wasn't terribly hard. He hadn't realized, however, how much there was to be explained about this practice.

Taoists say there are three harmful morbidities in the human body. One morbidity is attached to material wealth; another is attached to fine flavors;

the third is attached to sexual pleasure. Taoists also say there are three parasites in the body: one lives in the brain, one in the chest, and one in the belly. These are also harmful to the human body. The three parasites live on the energy of grain, so if you want to get rid of them it is necessary to stop taking in energy from grain. If you want to destroy the three morbidities, it is also necessary to abstain from grain.

The practice of abstention from grain evolved from the ancient Qin dynasty practice of ingesting energy. In his *Elegies of Chu*, the famous Taoist poet Qu Yuan wrote, "Eating the six energies and drinking the fog, I gargle with the first sunlight and swallow morning mist. Preserving the clarity of spiritual luminosity, vital energy is absorbed and coarse pollution ejected." Qu Yuan was already practicing energy ingestion when he left court to live a life of freedom.

By the end of Han, and on into the Wei and Jin dynasties, the arts of spiritual immortality flourished, so the practices of ingesting energy and abstaining from grain became very popular. There are many references to abstention from grain in the dynastic histories. The chapter "Traditions of Methodology" in *Documents of the Latter Han Dynasty* says, "Mengjie could ingest date stones and go without eating for five or ten years. He could also freeze his breath and remain immobile as death for as long as a hundred days, or even half a year."

In the inner chapters of *The Simpleton*, it says, "I have seen a number of people who abstained from grain, many of them for as long as two or three years. Their bodies were light, their complexions were good, and they could endure wind and cold, heat and humidity. None of them were fat." Also, "There is someone who relies on Life itself, who only ingests energy and has abstained from grain for three years already. He can climb a mountain with a heavy load and never get tired all day. From time to time he practices archery, but he hardly speaks. When he does speak, he won't raise his voice. Questioned about this, he says that when abstaining from grain one should utterly avoid losing one's vitality and wasting one's breath." Nowadays there are still sometimes news reports of people who can do without grain.

The method of grain abstention transmitted by the Dragon Gate wizards to Wang Liping is divided into three successive stages of training.

The first step is not eating grains, just consuming enough fruit and vegetables to maintain life. This practice greatly reduces the burden of the digestive tract and purifies the internal organs; it must be continued for at least two months, preferably longer. While working on this step, Liping went to school and pursued ordinary activities as usual. He used to go off to a densely wooded area rich in flowering plants to do his regular inner exercises at dawn, noon, dusk, and midnight, in order to strengthen the true energy in his internal organs. He carried out this step in ninety-eight days, just over three months. Afterward he felt physically comfortable and mentally clear.

The second step is fasting, or abstention from all food, just drinking a cup of cool water in the morning and evening. When practicing this exercise, there is no filth in the body; there is hardly even any urine. With the mind already clean, the body is purified. One only exchanges true energy with Nature, feeling as if the body has been put in a totally different realm. Wang Liping persevered in this exercise for more than fifty days.

After completing the first two steps, Wang Liping's body had a rosy glow and a crystalline sheen, as if he had just come from a bath; his spirit was clear, his mood refreshed, thoroughly clarified from inside out. The old wizards were overjoyed to see him like a reborn infant, having refined his flesh and blood into a body pure as ice and jade, cleared of years of accumulated worldly pollution. They had spent four years of total devotion to raising this resplendent flower, completely absorbed in carving and polishing a raw jade into a gem.

Liping was now ready for the third step, "suspended animation." The day they started this step, the wizards told Liping, "Just sit here without rising, and without even drinking water. Just do the inner work properly."

At this time, it was autumn of the year 1966, when turmoil arose throughout China. The Dragon Gate wizards and their apprentice paid no mind to the unrest, but they made more urgent use of what time they had to practice their exercises. Every day at dawn, noontime, and in the evening, a mentor poured some pure water on the floor to humidify the air in the room somewhat. Wang Liping was supposed to moisten his whole body with this little bit of water vapor, while using true energy to sustain his life. Both mentors took turns watching over him.

One day passed, then another. A third day passed, then a fourth and a fifth. Liping sat like a stone statue, completely immobile, his mind as still as death. The sun, moon, stars, and planets; the mountains, rivers, lakes, and seas; the flowers, plants, and trees; his parents and siblings, his teachers and classmates, the grand master and the mentors; the four seasons; day and night; north and south; up and down; right and left; heat and warmth, cold and cool, birth, old age, sickness, and death; joy and sorrow, sourness, sweetness, bitterness, and piquancy—everything he had ever seen, heard, felt, or imagined in his life in this world disappeared from Liping's brain and body. In a state of profound abstraction, he gradually lost all sense of himself. There was no more time and space; all was empty, utterly void.

Ten days passed. Wang Liping remained stable. Seeing his complexion rosy and moist, and noting that the other changes in his body were right, the grand master and the mentors were much relieved. The two mentors still took turns pouring the water on the floor every day and watching over the youth.

Fifteen days passed. Twenty days passed.

Wang Liping seemed completely normal; he sat there quietly like an immortal, mentally and physically calm and composed. The three wizards observed him carefully.

The twenty-fifth day passed. That night, there was a fierce rainstorm, with lightning and thunder. The wizards hurriedly shut the windows; aware of the emergence of an abnormal condition, they changed into Taoist garb, took up ritual swords, burned incense, and performed a rite. The senior master conveyed a spiritual message to Liping: "Since ancient times the Transmitters of our Dragon Gate sect of Complete Reality Taoism have sought the Way with their minds and accepted the Way with their bodies. Fasting and suspended animation is the border pass between life and death. As a Transmitter of the Dragon Gate sect, you should do as our ancestral teachers did, and put life and death out of your mind, and do not distort your own future."

In a trance, Wang Liping saw a vision of a realized man instructing him. Remembering everything, he continued to sit silently, spirit and soul clinging to their abode.

The twenty-sixth day passed. The twenty-seventh day passed.

The twenty-eighth day passed. It stormed again that night, with frightening ferocity. In the mountain shack there was only a dim lamp. The atmosphere was tense; the three wizards surrounded Liping, ritual swords in hand, totally oblivious to the roar.

Suddenly the lamp flickered. Wang Liping slowly toppled and collapsed; his legs unlocked and stretched out, and both hands lay limply at his sides. He looked completely calm, not stirring at all.

The wizards checked Liping's pulse and respiration; both had stopped. They knew he was dead. Immediately they sat in a battlefront formation, held their precious swords upright, and performed an esoteric rite. The grand master first caused the wind and rain to stop in the area, and saw to it that the spirits did not interfere; he also forbade pure yin entities from approaching. The two younger masters both exercised their extraordinary arts to create a protective seal around Wang Liping's body. The three wizards worked unremittingly, keeping careful watch day and night.

Earlier on, the grand master had placed a memorial tablet for Wang Liping by the memorial tablets of the ancestral teachers, burning incense before it on an altar in a traditional gesture of respect for the dead.

As for Liping himself, after fasting and entering suspended animation, he felt all was void; subsequently even the feeling itself disappeared. His body had suddenly begun to float, and he was no longer aware of anything familiar in his daily life. Although he had just been through an excruciatingly painful experience, it had already faded from his memory. Now he just felt lightness and plenitude, extremely comfortable.

In an instant, there was absolute blackness all around, empty and silent, vacant and cold. Feeling he was about to plunge into an abyss, Liping began to struggle desperately, as if to climb out, but he could find no handhold or foothold; he was powerless as a floating strand of thread.

Then, all of a sudden, a dazzling brilliance appeared. Seeing it was an open road, radiant with light, Liping began to follow it. Breezing airily along, all he could see were green mountains on both sides of the road, with rushing valley streams and masses of aromatic grasses and fragrant flowers. The scene was thoroughly tranquil, clear, and fresh, without a trace of worldliness.

Wang Liping had no idea where he was going. Suddenly he saw a number of people on the road, coming toward him. All of them were dressed in old-fashioned clothing and were very proper in manner. They greeted Liping smilingly. The one who seemed to be the eldest, an old man with flowing silver sideburns, came up smiling and took Wang Liping by the hand, leading him to a cluster of houses in the shade of a mountainside wood. All the houses were simple and clean. The elder led Liping into a room and indicated that he should sit down. The others in the group filed in courteously, taking their seats in an orderly manner.

Now the elder had people bring tea and wild fruit for Wang Liping. Liping didn't refuse, thinking to himself that this was just what he wanted. He held up the cup and drank, but he got no feeling of warmth or coolness, only a sense of fragrance bathing his lungs and chest. Then he picked up a piece of fruit and ate it. He heard no sound, but only sensed the freshness and fineness of the flavor enriching his spleen and moistening his liver.

Everyone was delighted to see Wang Liping so frisky, but the elder seemed to have something on his mind. "Your life has a long way to go yet," he finally said to Liping. "Why are you here now?"

Wang Liping didn't understand what the old man meant. He just kept gobbling up fruit, totally absorbed. Seeing that Liping didn't answer, the old man didn't ask again. Instead he began to introduce everyone, beginning with himself.

The moment he heard the old man explain that he was Liping's own ancestral forefather, Wang Liping put the fruit down and immediately bowed to him in respect. The others, it turned out, were some of his ancestors. He also paid respects to them one by one.

Wang Liping realized that he was still young. Here he was roaming around visiting the homes of his ancestors and relatives, and even the homes of their friends, as if he already knew them. How could he have ever seen his ancestors before? Now that he was seeing them, he was happy without consciously realizing why. Liping had been cultivating refinement for several years, his nature was free, and he had now reached this splendid resort. But how could he have ever seen it in the past? In this realm not only was the scenery beautiful and elegant; the human relations were also very fine, and the organization of the settlements was orderly, with nice buildings and houses. People were all sitting at leisure, conversing or playing chess.

Liping had no idea how much time passed. All he sensed was having interacted with numerous people and having learned many things from them. In terms of terrestrial time, his experience was equivalent to several decades in our world.

The only things that Wang Liping couldn't understand during this time were that no one worked, no one fought or held grudges; and even though he spent quite a long time there, he never noticed any births or deaths, nor did he see any sickness or aging. This was all quite strange to him.

Now one day as Liping was watching a couple of elders playing chess under an enormous pine tree on the mountainside, the eldest ancestor suddenly showed up, took him by the hand, and said, "You have to go back. You can't stay here too long." Then a bunch of people came and escorted Liping back to the luminous road and bade him farewell.

In the darkness, Liping heard an insistent rustling by his ear, and his physical sensations gradually returned. Slowly opening his eyes, in the dimness of the lamplight in the room he saw the three Dragon Gate wizards sitting stock still, the pale shine of their ritual swords glimmering. Realizing he was still inside the room, Liping hurriedly sat up. The whole experience seemed like one long dream.

Seeing him revive, the wizards stopped their inner work and rose to bow to the sky. Then they embraced Liping, weeping with joy and relief.

Only when he had heard his three teachers relate what had transpired did Liping know that he had been in suspended animation for twenty-eight days, and then had been dead for three days and three nights, during which time the three wizards had all kept up a relentless, exhausting vigil over him.

As he listened to their story, Wang Liping wept until tears streamed from his eyes.

Part II

REFINING THE SPIRIT

Attain the climax of emptiness,
preserve the utmost quiet;
as myriad things act in concert,
I thereby observe the return.

—Lao-tzu

6

Life After Death

Having fought a life-and-death battle for days on end, and having finally won complete victory, the wizards and their apprentice sank into a complex mixture of feelings—hardship and toil, happiness and rejoicing, fatigue and relaxation. The Wayfarer of the Infinite was the first to dry his eyes. He personally ladled out a cup of hot water and gave it to Wang Liping to drink. Immediately Liping felt refreshed and relaxed. The old masters also drank hot water to help their bodies recover from their ordeal.

Now the Wayfarer of the Infinite took Wang Liping to a makeshift altar and had him kneel before it in respect to the ancestral teachers. When he rose, the Wayfarer said to him, "See what's written on this particular memorial tablet," indicating one of the markers on the altar.

Taking a close look, Liping found the tablet was inscribed with these words:

IN MEMORIAM
WANG YONGSHENG
"LINGLINGZI"
EIGHTEENTH GENERATION TRANSMITTER
DRAGON GATE BRANCH
COMPLETE REALITY PATH

Seeing this, Wang Liping couldn't help being startled—now he realized he had died. When he thought back to what he had just experienced, it all seemed as if it were still right there before his eyes. When he told his teachers what had happened, they all nodded in affirmation. All of them had been through the same thing.

Later, in his adulthood, Master Wang Liping described his experience to us in these terms: "This was the most unforgettable experience of my life. It was so real that there is no way to forget it. People living in the world all know there is birth and there is death, but people have no way to remember what it felt like to be born, and only the dead have personally experienced what it feels like at the moment of death, and what it is like after death. When people die, though, they don't come back to life, so they can't tell you about the experience of death. "Birth and death are critical stages in human life, but still little research has been done in this area by modern science. Taoist culture has done quite a bit of research and accumulated a lot of literature on the subject; but there is no way to apply this literature usefully without a change in mode of thought, and so no way to pursue deep investigation of this critical issue.

"I myself am a man who has died several times, and this first experience made me come to an understanding of a number of questions. In terms of the questions of time and space as usually considered, for example, my knowledge became quite unlike that of ordinary people. This established a stable basis for my later Taoist studies."

Master Wang Liping also said of his unforgettable experience: "The moment of death was certainly extremely painful; even when I tried to break free, I had no strength whatsoever. Had I had any strength, of course, I wouldn't have been dying.

"This sensation, however, very soon disappeared, followed by a rapid flow of time in reverse and a corresponding transformation of space. Everything I ever experienced, whether I had remembered it or not, now appeared before me. Finally someone came and led me to a completely unfamiliar place, with very beautiful scenery, where I met deceased relatives. In three days of terrestrial time, I spent several decades there. After reviving, I clearly remembered the things I learned there. I had never seen the old folks there before, but when I described them to my parents, they confirmed their identities. My father and mother were also amazed, because that showed I had actually seen those people and wasn't making it up."

After returning to life, Wang Liping's mind was clear, yet he was in a sort of a trance. Looking around, he found his room small and dark—where is there room for people to live? How boring! Then he thought about the vast masses of humanity all in this enormous yet tiny space, working all day for a living, struggling for their future, exhausting their vital energy. What are they to do? Boring!

Seeing this seventeen-year-old youth in a daze, quite different from before, the three wizards knew the reason. He had already understood certain things and realized certain truths. The Wayfarer of the Infinite said to him, "Now you are a different person; the former you has died. The person who died turned sincerely to the Way and tried the Way with his own being, without hesitation or fear. He was, however, still a denizen of the lower three realms; the work he left unfinished is up to you to bring to completion, so you should proceed bravely into the middle three realms."

Wang Liping understood the old master's admonition, but his emotional state was still unsettled for the time being. Perhaps too much of the true energy in his body had been expended in the last half year; though he had been reborn and "changed his bones," his constitution was still weak, and he was somewhat prone to depression.

It was a late autumn night; the cold wind blew Liping's shirt open and tousled his hair. Paying no mind, the youth wandered aimlessly. It was extremely dark and cloudy; Liping had no idea where he was going, nor did he care. He walked into a frigid valley stream, wetting his clothes to the waist. Unminding, he just walked on. Liping had no sense of fear; life and death were no different to him.

Rain began to fall, thoroughly soaking and chilling the youth. What a thrill! Finally he wound up lying down in the grass and falling into a deep sleep.

In the course of human life, in the struggle to reach the goals they have set for themselves, people may exhaust the energy of half a lifetime, only to feel, when they have reached their goal, a sense of anticlimax. Everyone has this kind of experience, and in this Wang Liping was no exception. He had traveled even further than most people on the road of life; he had gone beyond time; he had gone through death, had seen many things that cannot be seen in the human world, and then had returned. Nothing could fool him anymore, so he had even more right than most people to feel a sense of anticlimax, a sense of the limitations of human life.

Wang Liping was now a living dead man. He was alive, yet he had died; he was dead yet still living. Only seventeen years old, he had just gone through a heart-wrenching life-and-death struggle; he had died and then returned to life. Now that he had shared the joy of his victory with his teachers, things settled down; back in ordinary life, he had only one thought, a dislike for this humdrum existence, a feeling of disinterest and ennui.

Wang Liping was beginning the fifth stage of his Taoist training, that of the "living dead."

Having gone through it themselves, the master wizards knew that the stage of the "living dead" is psychologically very painful, and one needs some time to gain strength. So they generally kept close by and slowly helped their apprentice shape up.

For the next two months, Liping was like a different person. He hardly talked, and his behavior was not as usual; a bystander might have thought him somewhat mad. Winter had arrived, the trees were bare, and the wind was cold; Liping wandered around in a ragged old jacket, not even buttoning up. The whole country was in turmoil, and everyday life had already lost its normal order; people watched out for themselves, and no one thought anything of it when they saw Wang Liping in such a state. People had all they could do to look out for themselves; they asked after others as little as possible.

Wang Liping had no idea where he was going; sometimes he'd sit by the road, or under the eaves of a house, and simply cry, weeping piteously. Sometimes he'd go back home and not speak a word. When asked a question, he'd speak in such a disjointed manner that no one could make heads or tails of what he was saying.

On one occasion during this period, when Liping's mother sent him out to buy some oil, he went out and got on the bus without buying a ticket. Seeing the youth's ragged appearance and eccentric air, the ticket taker kept an eye on him. Finally, after going round and round on the bus route, Liping came back and got off at a little grocery store not far from his home. In front of the store there was a long, long line of people waiting to purchase their ration of oil. Liping walked right to the head of the line, as if he didn't even see the other people waiting, and said he wanted to buy some oil. People who had been in line for half the day got upset and began to tussle with him; a civil patrol guard standing nearby tried to take him away, but Liping refused to go. When the guard brandished a gun at him, this emboldened the youth even further. Striking his chest with his oil jar,

Liping cried, "Go ahead and shoot! Shoot me right here! Rebel or right, dead or alive—it's all the same to me!"

Seeing him in this state, the people didn't contend with him anymore, but just let him buy his oil and get out of there, to avoid provoking an incident.

As for Wang Liping, he again went off somewhere in a melancholy mood for half the day. When he got home, and his mother asked where the oil was, he couldn't say. It was as though he'd never been sent on the errand at all.

Liping's mother found it very trying to see her son in such a state. She went to find the "old doctors" to ask them what caused it and to have them cure him. Zhang Hodao, the grand master, laughed and said, "The boy is fine. He's not ill. 'Who can become a spiritual immortal without going mad?' Your son is destined for greatness, so put your mind at ease." Trusting in what the old man said, Mother Wang let Liping do as he wished.

The strange thing was that even though Wang Liping spent the days wandering around aimlessly, still he went to visit the old wizards regularly every day. And every day the wizards had him pay respects to the memorial tablet of Wang Yongsheng—himself, that is—seeking help. Liping didn't understand why he had to bow to himself and seek his own aid; after all, he was dead and yet still alive.

Seeing he didn't understand, the Wayfarer of Pure Emptiness told Liping, "You are a living dead man. Though alive, you are dead. Yet though dead, you are alive. Now you are not the same as other people. Now all you need in this world is a bowl of food to eat. The rest is all extra. Understand?"

This made no sense to Liping, so the Wayfarer had to guide him patiently. "There are three realms in this world," he began. "After death, some people go to the lower realm; some go to the higher realm. The higher realm is a thousand times better than the lower realm. If you want to go to the upper realm, you'll have to work hard at further training and refinement. Later you'll understand all this on your own."

Although he couldn't get over a feeling of upset, Wang Liping continued to follow his teachers' instructions, paying respects to his own memorial tablet every single day.

One day, after Liping had finished the usual rite before his memorial tablet, the grand master sat him down and talked to him about the training of their spiritual ancestor Chongyang, hoping thereby to inspire an awakening in the youth.

The old wizard related, "Master Chongyang was forty-eight years old when he was initiated by Master Chunyang. The next year, he met another realized immortal, who transmitted several esoteric works to him. Now he began to cultivate refinement seriously. After a year, he dug a grave, raised a mound, and hung up a tablet on which he had written his own name: 'In Memoriam: Mr. Wang.' Then he took up residence in the grave, which was over ten feet deep, living in it for more than two years. He personally composed a number of verses entitled 'Living Dead Man' to commemorate this event." The the old master recited a few of the poems.

> *A living dead man, Wang Che's strange;*
> *Rivers and clouds are a special happy harmony.*
> *His Taoist name is Chongyang,*
> *His joking name is Buried in the Ground.*

> *The entry of the road to life is not forgotten,*
> *But on interment it's necessary to hang up a tablet.*
> *This is not to delude people for profit,*
> *But to make them aware assemblage is followed by dismissal.*

> *Living dead man, living dead man!*
> *Finding death in life is a good cause.*
> *In the grave is peace and quiet,*
> *true emptiness and calm,*
> *Quite apart from the dust*
> *of the ordinary world.*
> *There is a free man roaming;*
> *Simple, natural, he alone knows why.*
> *Minding the spirit, nurturing energy,*
> *keeping true essence complete,*
> *His material body temporarily*
> *mixes with the world.*

> *Humanity can spread the Way,*
> *the Way is close to humanity;*

The Way of humankind has always
been the highest cause.
If you make the dark clouds all recede,
You free the mind-moon to shine
on this complex world.

Who knows this man in a grave?
He goes along with how things are,
Neither artificial nor contrived.
White clouds take him
along with wind and moon;
Shedding material toils,
he leaves the dust of the world.

The old wizard went on, "Master Chongyang's verses are very deep in meaning, very clear in expression. Now that you are a living dead man yourself, you should understand what he meant."

With these instructions, Wang Liping suddenly woke up; immediately he bowed in thanks to the wizards for teaching him the Way. Renewing his commitment, Liping began a whole new life, continuing his upward ascent.

Practicing the Way

The sixth step of Wang Liping's training was called "practicing the Way." Although he had already been studying the Way for four years, had firmly established the basic foundation, and had accomplished something in both inner and outer work, nevertheless Liping had still only accomplished the attainments of an ordinary mortal. Anyone can learn to master these practices, provided they use the proper method and do the work consistently.

Wang Liping's learning of the Way was, however, superior to that of ordinary people in two respects. For one thing, he was learning the Way while still very young. Wang Liping was naturally bright and pure of heart, an essential condition for Taoist learning. The curriculum of the Dragon Gate branch of Complete Reality Taoism emphasizes twin cultivation of essence and life, first cultivating essence and then life, employing both inner and outer exercises, but especially valuing cultivation of inner work. "Repentance" and "gathering the mind to nurture essential nature" are both practices for cultivation of essence, requiring considerable time and energy to establish a good foundation. Even these two steps are hard for most people to master, but Wang Liping had accomplished both very thoroughly.

The second condition favoring Liping's Taoist learning was the fact that he was personally instructed by enlightened masters. All three of his teachers were highly experienced and very accomplished. The opportunity to transmit the knowledge and arts of three wizards to one individual is very rare in the history of Taoism. Lacking these conditions, most people would not be able to accomplish the preliminaries to fasting in just a few years.

These attainments, however, are no more than preparatory stages for even higher work. Having gone through death, Wang Liping was now a new person, and the wizards were ready to give him a new curriculum.

On the second day of this new phase of study, seeing Liping outwardly crazed but now inwardly sober, the grand master told him, "When you have gone through the border pass of life and death, you have shed ordinary limitations, but you are still quite far from the Way.

"The Way is divided into three vehicles. You should start practice from the lower vehicle, progress from the lower to the middle, and from the middle to the higher, advancing step by step. Only thus can you achieve great success.

"Many people practicing the Way do it in the morning but then change their minds at night; they do it while sitting but then forget it when they stand up, enjoying it momentarily but tiring of it in the long run, starting out diligently but winding up slacking off lazily. Their learning is not clear, their work is not earnest, their hearts are not calm, and their spirits are not true. Although they study for years, after all they do not attain; and yet they say the Great Way has turned away from humanity. In reality, it is not that the Great Way turns away from anyone; but people themselves turn their own backs on the Way."

Wang Liping listened quietly as the grand master continued.

"Master Chongyang dug himself a grave, put life and death out of his mind, and practiced quiet cultivation inside the grave for two years, thus completing the great work. You should go a step higher, again beginning with building the foundation. This is true practice of the Way."

The grand master went on to talk to Liping about Chongyang's work *Fifteen Statements on the Establishment of a Teaching*, discussing several critical passages in considerable detail. This famous document includes the following essays:

On Sitting

Sitting does not mean physically sitting still with the eyes closed. This is artificial sitting. True sitting requires that the mind be unstirring as a mountain all the time, whatever you are doing, in all action and repose.

Shut off the four gates—eyes, ears, mouth, and nose—and do not let external scenes get inside. As long as there is the slightest thought of motion or stillness, this is not what I call quiet sitting.

Those who can sit quietly in the real sense may be physically present in the material world, but their names are already in the ranks of the immortals. It is not necessary for them to call on others, for the century of work of the saints and sages in the body is fulfilled, and they shed the shell to climb to reality; a pill of elixir is made, and the spirit roams throughout the universe.

On Overcoming the Mind

If the mind is always calm and still, dark and silent, not seeing anything, indefinable, not inside or outside, without a trace of thought, this is the settled mind, which is not to be overcome. If the mind gets excited at objects, falling all over itself looking for heads and tails, this is the disturbed mind, and should be quickly cut away. Do not indulge it and let it go on, for it will harm spiritual qualities and cause a loss of essential life. Whatever you are doing, always strive to overcome perceptions, cognitions, and feelings, and you will have no afflictions.

On Refining the Nature

Putting your nature in order is like tuning a stringed instrument. If the string is too tight it will snap, and if it is too loose it will not respond. When you find a balance between tautness and slackness, the instrument can be used.

It is also like making a sword. If there is too much hard metal it will snap, and if there is too much soft metal it will bend. When hard and soft metals are in balance, then the sword can be cast.

If you embody these two principles in refining your nature, it will naturally become sublimated.

The grand master also handed on a living tradition from Master Danyang's talks on the Way at the assembly of Chongyang on Dragon Gate Mountain. Master Danyang said, "You must not neglect your everyday tasks. These everyday tasks are twofold; external and internal. External everyday tasks include not watching for others' faults, not boasting of your own virtues, not envying the wise and able, not plunging into the fire of ignorance, not getting mired in vulgar thoughts, not aspiring to overcome others, not judging others, not talking about likes and dislikes. Internal everyday tasks include not thinking up doubts and suspicions, never being unaware of what goes on inside you. Whether you travel around or stay put and sit, in either case you clarify the mind and eliminate desire, free of hang-ups and obstructions, unaffected and unattached, truly pure and clear, roaming freely."

The grand master also taught Wang Liping the standards set by Master Changchun, the founder of the Dragon Gate sect:

"Living in a hermitage means clarity and openness, coolness and aloofness, freedom and serenity. Seeing essence is the substance; nurturing life is the function. Flexibility is normalcy, modesty is character, compassion is basic, and expedient technique is initiatory.

"When in a group, always be humble. When the outside environment is quiet, don't give rise to mundane feelings. Whatever worldly toils you have, work according to the measure of your strength; do not go too far. Eat and dress without going to excess. Plan your upkeep, and do not overstock. The necessities of life are not to be sought greedily. If there is a permanent endowment, use what is extra to help out penurious travelers.

"Never cling to artificialities; always be clear and true. Getting rid of pollution, do your chores selflessly, without irritation. Let each individual live in a separate room, clarifying the mind and working on the Way, organizing yourselves so that each occupies a specific role; or you may alternate with each other, meanwhile tuning and refining true essence.

"Do not perform your tasks obsessively, and do not attack each other judgmentally. Strive to conquer your mind, get rid of egotism, be oblivious to reputation and appearances, detach from the body and the intellect, be calm and desireless. When you see Taoists, Buddhists, or Confucians, treat them equally. Don't be lazy."

There are many rules and regulations for those who would enter the Way, but essentially they are all about how to regulate oneself, how to treat others, and how to deal with all sorts of situations. They are permeated with the philosophy of Taoism, which is to deal with things in accordance with natural laws, to help the country and the people, to honor ancestors and respect teachers, to do good deeds, to eliminate evil, to cultivate essence and nurture life, and to transcend the ordinary and enter into the sacred.

Listening quietly to the master's talk, Wang Liping registered everything in his mind. He also minutely discerned the pragmatic effects of cultivating essence in his body during his daily activities, whether he was walking around, sitting still, or lying down.

One day, the old master gave Liping another lecture on the Way, this time talking about Ancestor Lu's *Song on Tapping the Lines*. Reciting the text from memory as he expounded it, the ancient wizard talked Liping into a state where it almost seemed as if the gold pill had already crystallized within him and he had taken off into space.

The *Song on Tapping the Lines* concludes with these statements:

> Reputation is not valuable; the Way is what's most noble:
> Distinguished ancestors of rulers and advisers,
> gold at their waists, saddles of jade, riding ostentatious
> horses, are all as floating dust, in the twinkling of an eye.
> Floating dust, flint-struck sparks—
> how crazy it is to keep your mind on them
> as if they were going to last,
> suffering miserably, burning hot, beyond recall,
> grabbing for profit, competing for reputation,
> like a boiling cauldron!
> To be like a boiling cauldron, sunk in it forever,
> is due to losing the Way and missing the Real.
> If anyone levels the brambles in the mind,
> then I'll explain the celestial mechanism to you.
> Life science must be transmitted,
> essence requires awakening;
> entering sagehood, transcending the ordinary,
> is up to you to do.
> Few people travel the road to the pure heavens;
> they struggle to get into mundane ways.
> I announce to the wise and good,
> give up clinging attention!
> The mechanisms of essence and life
> should be protected and guarded:
> if you lack one, that is not fine
> if you cling to the raft on the waves,
> you will lose the road.
> To cultivate only essence and not cultivate life
> is the foremost disease of practice.

If you only cultivate original essence
and do not cultivate the elixir,
a shadow spirit forever,
you cannot attain sagehood.
If you attain the source of life
but miss the original essence,
that is like trying to look at your face
without having a mirror;
an ignoramus with a life as long as heaven and earth,
you have no handle on use of the family treasure.
Twin cultivation of essence and life is most profound of all;
enormous waves on the ocean floor
carry the ship of truth.
When you catch the fierce dragon alive,
you'll know experts do not teach in vain.

As the old master sat talking half the day, reciting and explaining text, Liping remained completely still, not moving a muscle, not even taking so much as a drink of water. The two mentors also sat there, upright and unmoving, seeming to be listening and yet apparently in meditation.

Wang Liping listened intently to every word, gaining a clear understanding of these Taoist principles. The question in his mind, however, was how to put them into practice. When the old master had finished, Liping asked him how to proceed.

The wizard replied, "Don't rush. Listen to Ancestor Lu's *Three-Character Secrets*":

This Way is not an ordinary path;
it's the root of nature and destiny,
the opening of life and death.
To speak of it is constraining,
to practice it sublime.
People all dislike it, everybody laughs.
The great key is a matter of inversion.
Don't detest impurity,
don't make comparisons.
When you get it,

you immediately see the effect;
tranquility of heaven and earth
is one of the indications.
Transmitted by mouth and mind,
when you absorb it yourself,
then you know the Way.
Freshness of the herbal sprouts
is a sign of the primordial.
Finding the spot between the brows,
practice the way of reversal.
Material things perpetuate themselves;
when yin and yang are abundant,
there is the absolute marvel.
When you want to practice the Way,
let people howl;
your mood must be stable,
your spirit must not be exhausted.
If you do not practice,
you will age in vain;
if you recognize the real,
even if old you'll be young again.
If you're not a connoisseur,
don't speak of the essential;
this teaching accords with the Great Way.
Vitality, energy, and spirit,
elixirs of immortality,
are complete within quietude,
effective in enlightenment;
riding on a phoenix,
you hear the summons of Heaven.

Simply reciting this time, the old master did not give any further explanation; Liping already understood the meaning. In particular, he heard the words "vitality, energy, and spirit" with exceptional clarity.

The old master closed his eyes, nurturing his inner spirit. One of the mentors, the Wayfarer of Pure Serenity, went on to explain initiatory technique to Wang Liping.

This initiatory technique is still called constructing the foundation. This foundation practice is also divided into three levels, in which one works on vitality, energy, and spirit.

First it is necessary to cultivate the lower elixir field. In the case of the body of an ordinary person, which is already leaking, it is first necessary to cultivate a restoration of the original basis, repairing leakage. When vitality is full and does not run off, then one proceeds to refine vitality back into energy, refine energy back into spirit, and refine spirit back into spaciousness.

Most people think, however, that when the elixir field is full of energy, this itself is crystallization of the elixir. In reality, they do not even know where the elixir is produced, or what the gold liquid and jade liquid are. They are still in the lower three realms of persons, events, and things. Wang Liping was now already starting to cultivate the middle three realms of heaven, earth, and humanity; the initial task was still building the foundation, and refining vitality, energy, and spirit, only now the cultivation was carried out at a higher level.

The grand master and the mentors now transmitted a secret Dragon Gate teaching to Wang Liping. Known as the *Threefold Immortalist Exercises*, this teaching originated in the *Ultimate Teaching of the Spiritual Jewels*, which was composed by Zhongli Quan, known as Master Zhengyang. In his preface, Zhengyang wrote,

"Aspiring to emulate the sages of yore, my heart embraced the Great Way. As fate would have it, war unexpectedly broke out, making the times perilous and the world chaotic. At first it was to flee for my life that I took to rivers and lakes, crags and valleys. When I stepped back and recognized my true nature, however, I set my mind exclusively on clarity, purity, and ethereal refinement.

"I diligently read alchemical texts and repeatedly called on Taoists, but they only spoke of hygiene, which is relatively minor, and did not talk about the Great Way of true immortals.

"I originally found a thirty-volume *Spiritual Jewels* scripture inside a stone wall on Mount Zhongnan. The first part, 'Golden Proclamations,' was composed by the Original Creator. The second part, 'Jade Records,' was written by the Original Emperor. The third part, 'Principles of the True Source,' was transmitted by the Ancient Master.

"I spent a great deal of time and effort, thinking extensively and reflecting deeply, until I realized that there is yang in yin and there is yin in yang, based on the regularity of rise and descent of heaven and earth, and the principle of interaction of the sun and moon. Liquid is produced in energy; energy is produced in water. That is also the principle of the interaction of the heart and the genitals.

"Like the abstract images of objects, the Way is not far from people. Join the climax and beginning of the yang cycle, and only then will you prove that alchemy has rules; subtract and add morning and evening, and the firing process will naturally be unerring. Red lead and black lead after all do not produce the great medicine; only the gold liquid and jade liquid are ultimately the restorative elixir.

"When you enter from nonbeing into being, you always harbor the mood of a military campaign. When you rise to the heights from lowliness, you gradually enter the domain of ethereal subtlety. Extracting lead and adding mercury, cause the negative to vanish; changing your bones and refining your body, cause the positive to grow. The clarity or cloudiness of the water source is discerned at the time of settlement; the reality or falsehood of inner experiences is perceived when sitting forgetting.

"The profound doctrine of the mystic mechanism is hard to formulate completely, so I have compiled subtle principles of the *Spiritual Jewels* so they can be used to enter into sagehood and transcend the ordinary. In all, it consists of teachings of three vehicles; it is entitled *Ultimate Teaching of the Spiritual Jewels*.

"These are words of sages on the Great Way; I dare not let my individual subjectivity enter into it. This I hand on to Dongbin; when you have attained the Way, do not hide it, but leave it to posterity."

When Lu Dongbin journeyed to Mount Zhongnan, he met Zhongli Quan for the second time, and the two discussed Taoist arts for nurturing life. Their conversations were recorded, edited, and disseminated by Shi Jianwu. This collection, which was included in the Taoist canon, deals with ninety issues about eighteen aspects of Taoist science, systematically expounding the essentials of inner work.

In his final question, Lu asks Zhongli, "Now that I have heard you expound the great principle of ethereal abstraction and the hidden mechanisms of the universe, I know the sublime principles, but what about the practice? Without application, there is no effect. Please tell me how to practice. How do I start, and how do I work?"

In reply, Zhongli promised to transmit the *Ultimate Teaching of the Spiritual Jewels*. So this is where that teaching comes from.

The *Ultimate Teaching of the Spiritual Jewels* is divided into methods grouped by three vehicles, referred to as celestial, earthly, and human.

The lower vehicle is for human immortals and consists of four methods of happiness and longevity: pairing yin and yang, gathering and dispersing water and fire, mating dragon and tiger, and refining elixir.

The middle vehicle is for earthly immortals and consists of three methods of living longer without dying: the Flying Gold Crystal Talisman, the Jade Liquid Restorative Elixir, and the Gold Liquid Restorative Elixir.

The greater vehicle is for celestial immortals, consisting of three methods of transcending the ordinary and entering into sagehood: resorting to the source, inward gazing, and transcendent release.

The *Ultimate Teaching of the Spiritual Jewels* delves deeply into principles of practice, but on the whole it explains comparatively little about concrete methods. After Wang Chongyang had gotten this teaching, he compiled a set of exercise methods based on its principles, so that they could be put directly to use in practice. This is the *Three Immortalist Exercises*. Wang Chongyang handed this on to Qiu Chuji, (Changchun), so the *Three Immortalist Exercises* came to be transmitted secretly within the Dragon Gate sect.

The theoretical basis of *Three Immortalist Exercises* is the idea of the union of Nature and humankind, aligning the yin and yang and five elements of the human body with the yin and yang and five elements of the celestial bodies, cultivating a sort of cubic mode of practice on the basis of technical calculations, proceeding from plane to line to point, reaching the achievement of the higher vehicle step by step. These three sets of immortalism exercises are exercises in quiet sitting, which are combined with equilibrium exercises in external movement and with sleeping exercises, all together forming the system of twin cultivation of essence and life used in the Dragon Gate sect, a mode of Taoist exercise combining movement and stillness.

In the three immortalist exercises, the "methods of inducing immortality" are basic exercises for returning to the source and repairing leakage. There are twelve of these methods altogether:

1.   collecting the mind and sitting quietly

2.   tuning the body
3.   no looking, no listening
4.   gathering in the vision, listening inwardly
5.   tuning the ordinary breathing
6.   three-step exercise in stabilizing the spirit
7.   tuning the real breathing
8.   cultivating nonleaking
9.   looking inwardly and listening inwardly
10. freezing the spirit and perceiving silently
11. listening to the breathing and following the breathing
12. nurturing the mind and bathing

The whole methodology of practice revolves around working with stillness, tuning the body, tuning the breathing, refining the physique and refining the spirit.

Tuning the body means mastering the sitting postures, and closing the nine major openings of illumination so that "the eyes do not look, so the higher soul remains in the liver; the ears do not hear, so the vitality remains in the genitals; the tongue does not speak, so the spirit remains in the heart; the nose does not smell, so the lower soul remains in the lungs; the limbs do not stir, so the intent remains in the spleen."

Tuning the breathing means bringing the real breathing with ordinary breathing, so that when ordinary breathing is stilled, the real breathing goes into operation. The most important methods and secrets are these: "Inhale energy all the way past the lower abdomen, exhale energy not behind the heart. Inhaling energy with the body collected, take in the universe. Exhaling energy, let it go outside, radiating in all directions, forming a sphere."

Refining the physique comes after not seeing, not hearing, and activating the real breathing. It involves inward gazing and inward listening, listening to one's own mind, listening to the mind of the Way, listening to the celestial mind, listening to one's own heartbeat, listening to how real breathing follows the operation of the celestial bodies and the universe. When the five elements in one's own body have returned to their proper places, then one determines the route of the mutual production of the five elements to silently operate the five elements within the body, from kidneys to liver, from liver to heart, from heart to spleen, from spleen to lungs, and again from lungs to kidneys, repeating this cycle over and over again.

In refining the spirit, one makes thought enter into the universe within one's own body, into the pores and energy apertures of the whole body, ultimately to attain a state beyond consciousness. "In refining the spirit, it is necessary to refine the nonpsychological spirit; the spirit that is not the psyche is the nonpsychological spirit."

Finally one nurtures the mind, bathing, thus entering into great stabilization. There is a work called *On Forgetting* that says,

> *By forgetting things, you can nurture your mind. By forgetting feelings, you can nurture your essence. By forgetting stillness, you can nurture your spirit.*
>
> *By forgetting sensuality, you can nurture your vitality. By forgetting desires, you can nurture your body.*
>
> *By forgetting your body, you can nurture energy. By forgetting your self, you can nurture emptiness. By forgetting things, you can nurture the Way.*

There is also a work called *Secrets of Minimization* that says,

> *By minimizing speech, you can nurture your energy.*
> *By minimizing affairs, you can nurture your reputation.*
> *By minimizing hearing, you can nurture your intelligence.*
> *By minimizing thinking, you can nurture your mind.*
> *By minimizing desire, you can nurture your essence.*
> *By minimizing activity, you can nurture your spirit.*
> *By minimizing favor, you can nurture your vitality.*

There is also a work called *Secrets of Energy*:

> *By speaking little, you can nurture inner energy.*
> *By lessening sensual desire, you can nurture vital energy.*
> *By dining on plain food, you can nurture plain energy. By controlling fluids, you can nurture gut energy.*
> *By avoiding anger, you can nurture liver energy.*
> *By moderating appetite, you can nurture stomach energy.*
> *By equilibrating the womb breath, you can nurture lung energy.*

By minimizing rumination, you can nurture heart energy.
By not leaking vitality, you can nurture genital energy.
By carefulness in behavior, you can nurture spirit energy.

Before Wang Liping had fasted and died, the wizards had already transmitted to him numerous methods of exercise from the Spiritual Jewel arts of inner work for development of mental capacities. Now that he was at a higher level, they transmitted the *Three Immortalist Exercises* to him.

The Wayfarer of Pure Serenity explained, "The *Three Immortalist Exercises* originated in the *Ultimate Teaching of the Spiritual Jewels*. It is a kind of method of cultivation by which the human body is aligned with the celestial bodies, and the temporal is aligned with the primordial. The whole method is divided into three vehicles, ten gates, and forty-five stages; it requires nine years 'facing a wall' and one year 'bathing,' so it is completed in ten years.

"The four lesser vehicle methods of happiness and longevity are exercises for human immortalism, comprising seventeen stages altogether. The three middle vehicle methods of living longer without dying are exercises for earth immortalism, comprising sixteen stages altogether. The three greater vehicle methods of transcending the ordinary and entering into sagehood are exercises for celestial immortalism, comprising twelve stages altogether.

"You have actually worked through the lesser vehicle exercises already. At present, you are a member of the lower three realms, and yet you are not a member of the lower three realms. You should start cultivating the exercises of the middle vehicle, beginning with work on vitality, energy, and spirit."

The Wayfarer of Pure Serenity now taught Wang Liping a more advanced foundation exercise. Vitality, energy, and spirit were referred to by Taoist masters as the Three Flowers. By night, these three flowers grow in the liver; by day, they abide in three places—vitality is in the ears, energy is in the mouth, and spirit is in the eyes. That is why listening too long harms vitality, talking too long harms energy, and looking too long harms the spirit.

The vitality spoken of here is formless yet substantial vitality. When cultivating refinement, the ears are sealed, the eyes closed, and the mouth shut; vitality, energy, and spirit are concentrated at the crown of the head.

This is called the three flowers gathered at the peak.

The five elements in the human body also have to be directed toward a particular place by means of refinement exercises. When the eyes do not look, the higher soul is in the liver. When the ears do not listen, vitality is in the genitals. When the tongue does not taste, the spirit is in the heart. When the nose does not smell, the lower soul is in the lungs. When the limbs do not move, the will is in the spleen. Causing the energies of these five internal organs to focus and gather in the "mystic pass" inside the forehead is called "the five energies returning to the source."

This higher foundation work is a means of cultivating the human body to replenish the three bases. Refining vitality into energy is the first pass of inner refinement; when the union of the basic vitality, basic energy, and basic spirit is attained, they congeal into a more refined energy in which vitality and energy are combined. This is also called "the great medicine."

Refining energy into spirit is the middle pass of inner refinement, combining the great medicine with the basic spirit to produce a spirit in which the three bases have coagulated. This spirit abides in the chamber of nirvana in the top of the head. The nirvana chamber is also called the upper elixir field; the open aperture there is where the spirit is stored.

~~~~~~

After going through a certain period of training, Wang Liping's inner gaze could see a spot of brightness in the nirvana chamber at the crown of his head. The wizards also saw this bright spot and knew that the aperture at the top of his head had opened, meaning that the foundation work was done. Now they began to guide him in the cultivation of the nine chambers in the head.

It was before the break of dawn, and the sun was still below the horizon. The stars glittered in the sky, an occasional meteor streaked through space and then disappeared in the blink of an eye. The distant mountains only showed a black silhouette. Every now and then the crowing of a rooster or the barking of a dog was heard very faintly, coming from far away. The human world was still immersed in sleep and dreams. On the summit of this mountain the three wizards and their disciple were already sitting, staring fixedly at the eastern horizon, gazing at a bright celestial body moving slowly among the stars.

The grand master told Wang Liping that this celestial body was Mercury, which is usually not easy to find, except sometimes before dawn or around dusk, when it may be found above the eastern or western horizon, closer to us than the stars. As this planet moves through the heavens, it silently affects Earth and everything on it.

"Lightly close your eyes," instructed one of the mentors. "Forget yourself, and examine the extremely subtle changes the planet brings to you. See what response there is in your body. See what changes take place in the nirvana chamber in your head."

Following these instructions, Wang Liping entered into stillness. As if in a trance, he saw the planet coming toward him, moving closer and closer. Vaguely, dimly, an extremely subtle tremor went through his kidney system. A point of brightness appeared ethereally in his nirvana chamber. This bright dot also seemed to be in motion, appearing and disappearing.

Wang Liping told the old wizards that he had in fact "sensed" the presence of Mercury. They too saw that a chamber in his head was in motion. They told him that Mercury influences the human nervous system.

At dusk, the remaining glow of the sun lightly brushed the sky over the western horizon, before the curtain of night fell. On the western horizon a big, bright celestial body gradually emerged. His mentor told Liping that this was Venus. People in olden times used to call this the evening star when they saw it at dusk, and the morning star when they saw it at dawn. Venus has an influence on human glands, and the human head also has an aperture corresponding to it.

There was also a fiery red celestial body visible in the sky, moving among the stars; this was Mars. Mars has an influence on the vitality and physical strength of human beings, and there is also a corresponding point on the top of the head.

The planet Jupiter, furthermore, has a direct influence on the human liver. Human liver function varies in strength according to the changes in the relationship between Jupiter and Earth.

There is also a very slow-moving body, so slow that its movement can hardly be discerned without continuous observation. It is, however, quite bright; as bright as the stars Altair and Vega. This is Saturn. The planet Saturn has an influence on the human digestive system.

His mentor had Wang Liping practice inner refinement as he gazed at the stars. In the process, the wizard talked about astronomy to direct his apprentice's thoughts to the starry sky, relating the cultivation of the human body with the movements of the celestial bodies.

Taoists in the mountains also practice cultivation in this way. In the daytime they gaze at scenery; by night they gaze at the stars. Over a long period of time, they have accumulated a rich knowledge of the movements of the celestial bodies and have found a correlation between the movements of these bodies and the activities of the human body.

In *The Yellow Emperor's Classic of Internal Medicine*, in the "Basic Questions," there is a "Discussion on Life Energy Communing with Nature," which says, "Communion with Nature is the basis of life, rooted in yin and yang. Everything in the universe, the energies of the nine land masses, the nine apertures, the five inner organs, and the twelve major joints, all commune with the energy of Nature."

Later another discovery was made, through the efforts of generations of Taoists cultivating their own bodies. The human body, they found, has even more parts corresponding to celestial bodies (including Earth). This was a very significant discovery for research on the human body. Later use of the human body to study the secrets of the celestial bodies and the Earth also had similarly great importance.

The Taoist canonical work called *Classic of the Celestial Mechanism* says, "The nine openings correspond to the nine planets in the sky, the nine land masses on earth, and the nine apertures in human beings." The exercise the wizards were now teaching Wang Liping works not with the nine major luminous apertures in the human body, but with the nine occult apertures atop the head.

The presence of these apertures is illustrated in the recently published *Diagrams for Cultivating Realization*: there is a large sphere on the practitioner's head, within which are arrayed nine smaller spheres. When cultivation reaches a certain level, an aperture opens up in the head, known as the nirvana chamber. There is another chamber within the nirvana chamber, with nine openings on the circumference of a large point of light; by inner vision it is possible to see nine small points of light revolving around the large point of light. The large point of light corresponds to the sun; the nine small points of light correspond to the nine planets. This small section of the head thus forms a miniature version of our solar system. This is one of the most valuable aspects of the corresponding relationship between the human body and celestial bodies revealed by Taoist methods of cultivation. This scientific discovery made by Taoists has still not received full recognition even today, as if no one has done the appropriate research, thus leaving an enormous gap between Taoism and science. Taoist external alchemy, for example, has now been recognized by science as the beginnings of chemistry and has been accepted as such by chemists and other scientists. But this acceptance has been confined to this one point; modern science has little to offer on such questions as whether there is any value in further research into alchemy, or whether alchemical elixir is useful to the human body.

In astronomical observation as well, science has pursued its own path, paying no attention to other methods of studying the celestial bodies, such as the Taoist method. Through cultivation of the human body, Taoists discovered early on that there are nine planets; science, in contrast, only ascertained this fact after the invention of new measuring devices.

After Uranus was discovered by means of the telescope, people started to study its orbit. After a period of observation, it was discovered that the orbit of Uranus around the sun departs from the expected course; the actual orbit and the theoretically calculated orbit do not match. It was moving more slowly after 1822 than it had been before 1822; this made people hypothesize that there might be another planet beyond Uranus exerting a gravitational pull on it. After making more detailed observations of the orbit of Uranus, based on the orbital laws governing other planets, they finally found the planet Neptune on September 22, 1846.

The greatest stellar and planetary influences on the human body are naturally those of the sun, moon, and Earth. It can be said that Earth has left its reflection on the human body, but only the cultivated can truly understand what this means.

India is another country with an ancient culture; over the ages there have also been many people there who cultivated refinement. They have their own theories and methods of cultivation, the most famous being Yoga. It is interesting to note that Indian Yoga and Chinese Taoist hygiene both apply the theory of union of Nature and humanity to cultivation of the human body. There are also quite a few points in common in their practical methods and concrete processes. Because India and China are located in different latitudes of Earth, there is a difference in the "equator" or "line of the center" of the human body brought out by cultivation in the two climes.

Taoists regard Earth as a universe, and they regard the human body as a universe. Just as Earth has longitudinal meridians and latitudinal parallels, the human body also has longitudinal meridians and latitudinal parallels. The question of "acupuncture points" on the Earth's meridians and parallels has already been raised; this is in itself a major breakthrough in the domain of theory. The Chinese theory and application of longitudinal meridians in the human body are known to the whole world, but the theory and practice of the latitudes of the human body has long been held secret by Taoists, completely unknown to the world.

When we first visited Master Wang Liping, he told us about the existence of the latitudes of the human body. This phenomenon is sure to provoke the interest and attention of people all over the world, and inquiries into the mysteries of the human body should make a major advance.

Earth has a central line, which is the equator; the human body also has a central line. Taoists divide the human body into three elixir-producing segments, which are the upper, middle, and lower elixir fields everyone talks about. People who do meditation exercises generally know the lower elixir field is in the lower abdomen, below the navel, but they cannot accurately determine the precise location. Taoist practitioners over the ages have also given many different explanations of this point. The conclusion at which Master Wang Liping has arrived through his own personal experience in training is that the exact location of the lower elixir field in the human body varies according to the geographical location of the individual. In Chinese people, it is between 1.2 and 1.5 inches below the navel; in people who live nearer to the equator, the lower elixir field is closer to the navel; while in people who live farther away from the equator, the lower elixir field is farther from the navel.

Extending this similitude, the human body, top to bottom, corresponds to the earth from south to north. People usually refer to north as above and south as below. Why is the relationship of correspondence between Earth and the human body the reverse of this? Master Wang Liping explains that when people are in the womb, the normal position is in fact head down, body above, precisely corresponding to Earth having south below and north above.

Why do Taoists emphasize the need to sit cross-legged when cultivating refinement, and why is the full lotus posture considered best? Practitioners have to imitate the situation of the fetus in the mother's womb, with all the lower passages and apertures sealed shut, the luminous openings not leaking, thus facilitating the development of the "fetal breathing" or "womb breathing," as well as the clearing of this tenth great opening located in the umbilical region. Another important function is that the cultivation of the cross-legged posture can enable the practitioner to sense the existence of the longitudes and latitudes of the human body. Taoists say, "Nine years facing a wall, maturity in ten years; two years of bathing, and you return to the primal," meaning that they use twelve times the length of time spent in the womb to refine the primal energy that is constantly wearing out under temporal conditions, in such a way as to attain the special effect of Taoist hygiene.

Lao-tzu says, "Carrying vitality and consciousness, embracing them as one, can you keep them from parting? Concentrating energy, making it supple, can you be like an infant?" Rejuvenation is one of the aims of Taoist hygiene. Once people have grown old, they cannot return wholly to the stage of infancy, but it is possible to cultivate some of the special characteristics of the state of the infant. One of these special characteristics is the complete set of longitudinal meridians and latitudinal parallels on the body of a newborn infant.

The existence of longitudinal meridians in the human body is a fact now known to all the world, though ordinary people cannot see them, even using scientific instruments and the methods of Western medical science. Only by using the methods of inner work is it possible to see the longitudinal meridians on the body of a living human being clearly with the celestial eye.

The latitudinal parallels of the human body also exist; in conjunction with the longitudinal meridians, they form the total system of energy channels and energy lines in the human body. The existence of the latitudinal parallels is a perennial secret; even among people who practice refinement there are few who know of the presence of these parallels. Once their presence is known, however, then the pattern of the array of acupuncture points becomes clear at a glance; it is then possible to rapidly memorize the hundreds of points that have already been discovered, and to find out the locations and functions of points as yet unmapped.

The historical mission of Taoism has been to seek out the secrets of the human body, the secrets of the celestial bodies, and the secrets of the relationship between humankind and Nature, through this method of cultivating and refining the human body.

Having reached this advanced stage in his practice of the *Three Immortalist Exercises* under the tutelage of the three old wizards, Wang Liping's task was precisely the task of all scientists in the world, albeit by a different methodology, taking a different route.

According to Master Wang Liping, there are many ideas and discoveries in Taoism that can deeply inspire people and could be very beneficial to the evolution of the human race. There are, in fact, too many such things to even mention them all.

As noted before, the layout of Earth and the human body match each other, with the South Pole corresponding to the human head. Taoists knew early on that the South Pole is a place of special value. Humans discovered the continent of Antarctica in the 1830s. At approximately the same time, people began depth studies of brain function, which in the West gradually developed into psychology. In the view of Master Wang Liping, this was not a fortuitous coincidence. Here is something even more remarkable. In the course of his training, Master Wang Liping discovered that there are some energy channels in the body that are not complete. Some have a beginning but no end, or no beginning or end; they subtly fade out after having extended to a certain spot. Dragon Gate Taoists call them "terminal channels." The human body also has some "apertures of death" and "forbidden apertures," whose precise location can be determined only by the power of inner work. The problem with "terminal channels" is that if a death spot or a forbidden spot is disturbed, that can produce serious illness, or in severe cases possibly even death.

Does Earth also have similar "terminal channels" and "apertures of death"? When we mention "apertures of death" in relation to Earth people may naturally think of the notorious Bermuda Triangle. Situated at the juncture of the Atlantic Ocean and the Caribbean Sea, this is a place where airplanes and ships are always mysteriously disappearing, such that people call it the Triangle of Terror. From the point of view of Master Wang Liping's theory of correspondence between the human body and the planet, the Bermuda Triangle corresponds to what in the human body would be a "terminal channel" or "death hole."

The terminal channels and death holes in the human body are not always open or closed, so it is plausible that the Bermuda Triangle also has times when it is open and times when it is closed. So when this "death hole" of Earth in the Bermuda Triangle is open, anyone or any vehicle that crosses it can hardly return. As for when the death holes on Earth open and when they close, there must be a pattern that follows some natural law. To discover this, it is necessary to study the operative mechanisms of Earth itself, not treating it as if it were an inert object but studying the planet as a living microcosm. Here the theory of longitudinal parallels and latitudinal meridians in the human body can provide an edifying theoretical framework for the study of the longitudes and latitudes of Earth. It is also necessary to study Earth in the context of this solar system, to find out the interrelationships of the Earth's orbit with other planets inside and outside this solar system. Here again, the Taoist theories of unity of Nature and humanity and correspondence between Nature and humanity also contain very revealing meanings.

According to the elevation of one's state of refinement, it is possible to find some new, even more obscure terminal channels and apertures of death.

Having reached this point in their writing, the authors of this biography visited Master Wang Liping again. At the time, the master was right in the midst of a class on Taoist hygienic arts, attended by more than fourteen hundred people. Coming right to the point, we described a circle an inch in diameter in the region of the spot at the back of the waist known as the "gate of life" or the "door of fate," and confronted Master Wang with the question of whether there is not at least one aperture of death or death hole there.

Slightly taken aback, Master Wang Liping said, "How did you know that?" "We figured it out from looking at the Earth." While writing this chapter, we had placed a globe before us, occasionally putting down the pen to look at the globe to stimulate original thinking. We went on to explain the process to the master, still full of the excitement of discovery.

According to Master Wang Liping, while in the womb people draw nutrition from the placenta through the navel, so the navel is the point where nourishment is supplied. Thus there must be a corresponding Earth navel where nourishment is supplied to the planet.

Wang Liping told us that when he was young, his senior teacher told him that if one proceeds directly southward from the central plain of China, there is a line by which one can find the spot where Earth is supplied with nutrition. Hearing this, we immediately thought of the vast oil reserves in the Middle East: might this be the Earth's supply point? In the human body, the navel is directly opposite the "door of fate" region at the back of the waist; in terms of the "inner work lines," the line between the navel and the door of fate is called the "line of life preservation." So what does the Middle East correspond to? Turning the globe round, to our amazement we find that, longitudinally and latitudinally, the Middle East basically corresponds to the Bermuda Triangle.

Might these two regions have some sort of mysterious connection? The Bermuda Triangle is a death spot on Earth, so if the human body has a deep relation with Earth, it follows that there must be at least one aperture of death in the region of the door of fate in the human body.

Master Wang Liping drew a picture and explained that the nine apertures of death in the human body are all concentrated in the region of the door of fate and are arrayed in the pattern of nine chambers. From this knowledge it might be deduced that the death spots on Earth must cover an area even wider than that of the already discovered Bermuda Triangle.

～～～～

To resume our story, at this point in his training Wang Liping was in the process of cultivating the earthly immortal exercises, the second of the *Three Immortalist Exercises*, under the guidance of the three old wizards.

The *Three Immortalist Exercises* are a more concrete and systematized version of the *Ultimate Teaching of the Spiritual Jewels*, made by Founding Master Chongyang on the basis of the older work. The *Three Immortalist Exercises* consist of three vehicles, ten stages, and forty-five parts, as follows.

A. The lesser vehicle, exercises for human immortalism, consists of four methods of well-being and extension of the life span.
    I. Pairing yin and yang
        1. The yang embryo and yin breathing
        2. True fetal breathing
        3. Mating water and fire
    II. Gathering and dispersing water and fire
        1. Absolute unity containing true energy
        2. Minor physical refinement

3. Natural innocence, natural maturity

III. Intercourse of dragon and tiger

  1. Culling restorative elixir

  2. Nurturing the embryonic immortal

  3. Settlement of water and fire

  4. Meeting of the true husband and wife

  5. Intercourse of energy without physical change

IV. Cooking and refining medicinal elixir

  1. The firing process

  2. The minor cycle

  3. The cyclic firing process

  4. Gathering the spirit to nurture energy

  5. Gathering energy to nurture the spirit

  6. Refining yang to nurture the spirit

B. The middle vehicle, exercises for Earth immortalism, consists of three methods of living long without dying.

V. The flying gold crystal at the side

  1. Returning vitality to boost the brain

  2. Starting the waterwheel

  3. Intercourse of dragon and tiger

  4. Extracting lead and adding mercury

  5. Rejuvenation

VI. Jade liquid restorative elixir

  1. The jade liquid talisman for refining the body

  2. Bathing the embryonic immortal

  3. Minor restoration of elixir

  4. Major restoration of elixir

  5. Seven-reversion elixir

  6. Nine-transmutation elixir

VII. Gold liquid restorative elixir

  1. The gold liquid talisman for refining the body

  2. Starting the fire to immolate the body

  3. Gold flowers and jade dew

  4. Major settlement

  5. Material alchemy

C. The great vehicle, exercises for celestial immortalism, consists of three methods of transcending the ordinary and entering into the sacred.

VIII. Returning to the source and refining energy

1. Inner transcendence
2. Refining energy to perfect the body
3. Violet gold elixir
4. Refining the yang spirit
5. Gathering the three flowers on the peak

IX. Inner gazing and exchange

1. Concentrating the yang spirit
2. Igniting the celestial fire
3. Exchanging the immortal for the ordinary
4. Paradise in the world and in heaven

X. Transcendent liberation and replication of the physical form

1. Going in and out of body replication
2. The spiritual immortal sheds substance
3. Transcending the ordinary to enter the sacred

In the level of training based on the triple realm of heaven, earth, and humanity, Wang Liping experientially realized the profound relationship between humankind and Nature, searching out the secrets of the human body and the universe. Plunging his whole body and mind into his training, he experienced realms of perception impossible to describe in words, cracking the mysteries of heaven, earth, and humanity.

Our thinking also has to rise a step higher and stand on a more elevated level in order to understand the relationship between human beings and the universe.

People commonly say that Earth is our mother, but if this is only understood to mean that the Earth gives us life and nourishes us, then it is hardly an adequate statement. Earth and the universe have nurtured humanity with their forms and images; a human being is a miniature Earth, and a miniature universe. The mysteries of the human body, the mysteries of Earth, and the mysteries of the universe have to be understood from this angle; and it is from this angle that we must reflect on the relationship among ourselves, Earth, and the universe.

Our technological development should not be aimed at the endless extension of human sensual desires, it should not employ methodology that exploits and exhausts natural resources, and its price should not be the destruction of the equilibrium in the interdependence between humanity and Nature. Humankind is the most intelligent of creatures; the manager of the world is humanity, and yet it is not humanity. That is to say, the managers of the world are people with reason and sensitivity, not the irrational and insensitive. By "reason," here we mean a profound recognition of the nature of the universe. And by "sensitivity" we are referring here to a deep sensitivity to the universe. The place of humanity in the universe dictates that there are things that should be done and things that should not be done; there is that which should be taken and that which should not be taken; that which should be promoted and that which should be prevented. Pursuing that which is beneficial and avoiding that which is harmful, we emphasize communion, integration, harmony, and balance. And these should not be irreconcilable extremes, which would ruin the foundation of human existence and evolution.

The human body is a miniature universe, a macrocosm. Information of the universe is registered in the human body. So is information on the evolution of humankind and human society.

One day the three old wizards told Wang Liping something interesting about information registered in the human body. They talked about the famous book of prognostication, the *Back Figuring Charts*. According to Taoists, the name "Back Figuring" comes from the practice of reading out information registered in the human body.

During the Tang dynasty (619–906) there were two mathematicians by the names of Li Chunfeng and Yuan Tianwang. Li Chunfeng mastered all sorts of subjects in youth and was an expert at calendry. He was appointed royal astronomer in the time of Emperor Taizong (627–650). His prognostications regularly turned out to be true. As for Yuan Tianwang, he was an expert physiognomer, able to read people's character in their features with uncanny accuracy. Li and Yuan collaborated in making prognostication charts foretelling the rise and fall of dynasties and the changing of the ages. These are called *Back Figuring Charts*. Li and Yuan saw things in each other's backs; observing the information provided in their backs, they calculated major events. Li and Yuan corroborated each other's findings, coordinated this information with sixty hexagrams made of eight trigrams, and constructed sixty diagrammatic prophecies according to a temporal order. This is the popular book *Back Figuring Charts*.

The basic structure of *Back Figuring Charts* consists of sixty sections, each comprising a hexagrammatic symbol, a diagram, a prophecy, and a verse. The prophecies and verses are recondite, and the diagrams and symbols are mysterious, giving people a sense of not knowing what is what.

In reality, the *Back Figuring Charts* is a prognostication manual, for predicting future events. There are, furthermore, several varieties of *Back Figuring Charts*; the version composed by Li and Yuan is for figuring out trends and events in society. The book used by the old wizards to locate a successor was the *Back Figuring Charts* passed on from generation to generation by the Transmitters of the Dragon Gate branch of Taoism. In theory, it is possible to make one's own "back figuring charts" in other areas, but the contents would be different, and some would be on a higher level than others.

In the process of training the human body, Taoists are very thorough in their investigation of each part of the human body. The information Taoists see in the various parts of the body does not only indicate sickness and change in the internal organs and the courses of the celestial bodies; it also contains information on the evolution of society.

The *Back Figuring Charts* that the old wizards taught Wang Liping to study records information found in the back. This information refers not only to the past, but also to the future. In the eyes of the ordinary person, however, there is only the physical structure of the back; no deeper information is visible. Only those who are highly developed through inner work can see in people's backs what others cannot perceive.

To locate their successor, the old wizards had used a copy of the *Back Figuring Charts* that had been passed on from generation to generation by the Transmitters of the Dragon Gate branch of Complete Reality Taoism.

The *Back Figuring Charts* composed by Li Chunfeng and Yuan Tianwang is a "state secret," because its predictions have to do with major events in the development and evolution of society. Generation after generation of rulers have considered the *Back Figuring Charts* of Li and Yuan a state secret. Not only were commoners not allowed to see it; even officials below a certain rank were not permitted to read the book. After it had been banned, the book still circulated in the world, but few people could actually understand it.

8

Roaming the Four Directions

Before they even left the mountains, the three old wizards knew from the *Back Figuring Charts* that the country was going to go through a period of chaos. They didn't know, however, just how chaotic it would turn out to be.

All over China the Red Guard swarmed, holding aloft the Little Red Book. All sorts of atrocities occurred in the name of a Clean Sweep, leaving nowhere to hide in all the land. Society changed so much that even the spirits could do nothing!

Even in the high mountains and deep valleys, sacred grounds of spiritual immortals rarely trod by human footsteps, Buddhist and Taoist schools that were not in competition with anyone and had no quarrel with the world, temples and shrines of purification and calmness, were unable to escape systematic destruction and "purgation." The mausoleum of Confucius was desecrated, and the woods around it were chopped down.

Red Guard brigades from over a dozen prefectures and cities banded together in a mass action and occupied Mount Wudang, one of the most sacred of Taoist sites. Several thousand Red Guards carrying red flags broke into the Shaolin temple where Chan Buddhism started. The holy mountain Omei was turned upside down. White Cloud Monastery in Beijing, one of the most important Taoist centers, was ruined.

The precious shrine of the Three Purities on Mount Lao could not be secure. The three old wizards were growing uneasy and restless. They realized a major calamity was imminent and knew they should move quickly to escape it.

The ancient city where Wang Liping lived was also in ferment. The three old Taoists had been living in the mountains to the west, avoiding the noisy city. Concealing themselves and appearing to be ordinary, they had kept their unusual abilities hidden, except when the local peasants had problems or ailments and needed help. The old masters were very effective in curing illnesses by uncanny methods and had won the good will of the people; but with the change in the times, and the unpredictability of human hearts, this sort of activity might actually put them in a vulnerable position and bring on trouble.

From the chaos of the last years of the Qing dynasty through the conflicts of the warlords, the war of resistance against Japan, to the struggle between the Nationalists and the Communists, the three old wizards had been through a lot and seen a lot. Yet even in times of unrest, there had always been quiet places to get away from the clamor of the world; there had always been places in ancient forests deep in the mountains where people could hide and cultivate themselves. Each of the three wizards had extraordinary spiritual powers, and though they may not have been able to change the world at large, they were certainly capable of preserving themselves. But now their old nest was being swept away, and even their humble abode outside the city was no longer safe.

The task of teaching a successor, however, had never been interrupted for eleven hundred years, even up to the present day, and the three old wizards took their responsibility most seriously. The treasures of knowledge and wisdom had to be passed on to posterity, so that the Great Way could be disseminated in the future. The old masters figured it was about time to go on the road, taking their apprentice with them.

At this time, Wang Liping was no less anxious than the Taoist masters. From the very beginning of his apprenticeship, he had been instructed to record everything he went through and experienced in the course of his training. This record would be a valuable resource for later people. Taoist literature is as vast as the ocean; even the Taoist Canon alone comprises more than five thousand scrolls, part of which consist of principles and methods of practices for hygiene and refinement. These principles and methods, however, are often hidden in puzzling symbolic codes, and the rules are inflexible and hard to operate.

There are also 3,600 auxiliary techniques, each of which has a history, all of which were developed through the accumulation of generation after generation of long-term practical experimentation. But if people study only these minor techniques and do not know the way to practice the major teaching, they will be limited to a low level of realization even if they work all their lives.

According to old cultural tradition, those who held secret teachings would guard them jealously, keeping them to themselves, so very few were disseminated. Thus while there are many unique techniques, very few of them have been opened up to the public. This is a flaw in the old culture and it is an important reason why China's high culture has not flourished in the world for a long time.

Although the transmission of the Dragon Gate does not have the obstacle of being limited by blood relationship like a family tradition, nevertheless it is limited to transmission from teachers, whose disciples are not many, so very few outsiders have access to the teachings. Since he began studying Taoism, Wang Liping intended to do something creative and new by making a detailed record of the process of learning the Way and cultivating its exercises, thereby to amend the gaps in the Taoist Canon, in order to fulfill the needs of researchers and practitioners. Now, however, the environment was hostile, so it was very difficult to avoid being seen as old-fashioned, and it was hard to prevent this material from being destroyed.

Wang Liping's diary recording his Taoist practice was the product of four years of intense effort. Comprising dozens of notebooks containing tens of thousands of words, it filled a box two feet long by a foot high and a foot wide. His record of the process and experience of fasting in particular, including parts written by his mentor based on observations, as well as his own personal experiences and visions later recovered from memory, constituted extremely valuable firsthand resource material. This material, obtained with such difficulty, was valuable not only for the individual, but for the whole country, and even for the whole of humankind.

Unfortunately, Wang Liping's father had already been made out to be a "reactionary technocrat," so Liping could not safely keep his notebooks at home. And yet there was no other place to hide them anywhere else either. Now that it had become imperative to run away, the old wizards were already preparing to go on the road; they couldn't take this diary along, so they told Liping to burn his notebooks. The wizards explained that he had to prevent these materials from falling into the wrong hands; later on, when it was safe, they told him, he could reconstruct his notes. They might not be the originals, but he could recover enough from memory to enable people to gain understanding.

Though his heart was burning too, Wang Liping finally reduced his notebooks to ashes. Now there was nothing hanging him up; he prepared to go on the road with the wizards, traveling to who knows where.

Travel is one of the processes necessary to Taoist training; but Liping's was quite different in intent from the ordinary sort of travel familiar to most people. Ordinary travel is no more than a change of surroundings and enjoyment of scenery. Literati and esthetes mostly use travel to augment their experience: to take in the beauties of nature and observe different climates and local characters; to refine their sensibilities and stimulate their sensitivities. Taoist travel, in contrast, has three general objectives: self-cultivation, seeking out realized people, and exploring.

Self-cultivation here means using the living energies of the different mountains and rivers of various regions to develop the true energy inside one's own body, causing one's inner work to reach further into the realms of sublimation day after day.

Seeking out realized people means finding the real human beings in the esoteric domains of the famous mountains in the various regions.

Exploring means searching out natural laws in different environments and life situations in order to find out how to survive.

Taoists do not go traveling until they have reached a certain degree of accomplishment. This shows how very important a place travel occupies in the life of Taoist training.

The Taoist observation of the natural world is extremely minute and detailed; it is permeated with a kind of philosophy, the doctrine of the unity of Nature and humanity. Changes in heaven and earth are intimately connected to changes in the human body. Only people of high attainment, however, are able to sense subtle changes in the outside world within their own bodies.

Now the departure of the old wizards with their young apprentice had become unavoidable; now that the natural course of events had come to this, all the four Taoists could do was adapt. Although Wang Liping was not as accomplished as the old masters, still he was young and had already become a "living dead man," so there would be something positive for his development in going through trying hardships.

As far as we can tell from written records, Chinese culture has existed for thousands of years, and its main thread, quite evidently, is Taoist culture. Over the long era of feudalism, however, the marrow of Taoist culture was officially suppressed time and again. Why? Because Taoists knew too much about heaven, earth, and humankind, so they were hard to dominate.

When the Qin (Ch'in) dynasty unified China (in the third century B.C.E.), first it unified Chinese culture. All histories and documents not written by Qin officials were burned, scholars were buried, and books were destroyed. All that were left were books on medicine, divination, and forestry. Anybody who wanted to study had to be instructed by a government official. This idea of making government officials the educators was a significant invention, and it has been emulated by rulers ever since.

There is a notably peculiar phenomenon in the development of Chinese culture. As everyone knows, whatever object exists in space must have latitude if it has longitude. The human body also has longitudes and latitudes, as mentioned earlier. These ancient books also had longitudes and latitudes; now only the longitudinal books survive, while the latitudinal books are lost. The reason for this is that after the Qin emperor burned the books, the following Han dynasty only honored Confucianism, so the "longitudinal" Confucian classics naturally were preserved, while the "latitudinal" books based on Taoist thought evolved among the populace. These latitudinal books all dealt with the strategic points of heaven, earth, and humanity; and they were subjected to government bans.

Similar phenomena continued to occur throughout history. From the point of view of the ruling classes, it was too dangerous to allow the peasantry to obtain the knowledge of astronomy, geography, calculation, and military science. Such books could hardly be called superstitious; feudal rulers knew what they were about, and they had their own reasons for banning such books. A notable example of this is the banning of the *Back Figuring Charts* mentioned earlier. Originally a prognostication manual, this book was a state secret; it was inaccessible not only to peasants, but even to officials below a certain rank. Eventually it leaked out to the public somehow, and in spite of official prohibitions people continued to keep secret copies. When Zhao Pu, prime minister of the first emperor of the Song dynasty, memorialized the throne about this matter, the emperor replied, "There is no need to multiply prohibitions and bans. Just scramble the internal order of the contents of the book."

Later on, as these scrambled copies circulated in society, the more the book was read the more confusion there was. Thus, even though everyone knows of the importance of the *Back Figuring Charts*, very few people can really understand the contents.

Another example is seen in the case of the highly successful Ming dynasty general Liu Ji. Skilled in astronomy, military science, and calculation, Liu helped the founder of the Ming dynasty wrest China back from the hands of the Mongol Khans. He also designed the enlarged capital city. When he was on his deathbed, Liu ordered his son to turn all of his books on astronomy in to the government. There had actually been an imperial edict forbidding people from keeping such books, banning private study of astronomy. This goes to show how Taoist books were not superstitious trivia.

So these treasures of Taoist culture have repeatedly been suppressed on account of political changes over the ages. A relatively small number of texts have survived, transmitted by various lineages and concealed in secret caves deep in the mountains. This is like a secret passed on in a family, actually a method of preserving culture, done for lack of feasible alternatives. Since the essence of Chinese culture has been preserved and transmitted in this way, in that sense it is laudable; but it is also lamentable that the transmission and development of Chinese culture have also been severely constrained in this way. At the point in our story now, the movement of time had come to the latter 1960s, when an immense tide of cultural destruction engulfed all of China. The hearts of the three old wizards and their young apprentice were filled with a sorrow that had no bounds.

The four Taoists took off one night, very late, in a cold, howling wind, a night when the sky was covered with black clouds. Having paid symbolic respects to the spiritual adepts of heaven and earth, concealing the memorial tablets of their spiritual ancestors and gathering up their other implements, in the depths of the night they stole away in absolute secrecy, taking nothing but the barest necessities.

The eighty-six-year-old grand master, the Wayfarer of the Infinite, strong and swift of foot, took the lead. The Wayfarer of Pure Serenity and the Wayfarer of Pure Emptiness followed up behind with Wang Liping. Together the four disappeared into the darkness, slipping away into the unknown.

The teachers and their disciple sped along without stopping. Using their Taoist walking techniques, the three old wizards went so fast that Wang Liping could barely keep up with them in spite of his youth.

Seeing the teenager gasping for breath, the old men stopped and told him to go on ahead by himself while they rested. They instructed him to wait for them in about two hours under a big tree somewhere down the road. By the time they had finished speaking, the old wizards were already sitting down.

Figuring the grand master and the two mentors were, after all, old men, Wang Liping thought he might as well let them rest while he went on ahead to wait for them down the road. Traveling at a rapid pace by himself in the dark, in two hours Liping had covered well over ten miles when he saw a huge tree on the hillside.

Making straight for the tree, as he was going to sit down and rest a bit, Liping unexpectedly heard a laugh. "You slowpoke! We three have been resting here for quite a while already!" Suddenly Liping felt shamed and embarrassed. There were the three old wizards!

Sitting their young apprentice down, the Wayfarer of Pure Serenity said, "To travel over the land, it is imperative to cultivate this footwork. Otherwise you will waste time and energy as you go. At the rate you're going, anyone would be completely burned out and unable to go on after crossing only a few mountains.

"Although this walking is external work, you first have to have a pure practical basis in inner work, so that you can use attention and thought to lift your body up so that it is light as a feather. Only then can you move swift as lightning when you get going. Add the balance work and natural circulation you have already learned; then with each fifteen, thirty, and sixty miles you walk, you sit for a while, rest your legs, relax your muscles, circulate your energy, and nurture your spirit. In this way you can keep on going without getting tired out." The Wayfarer of Pure Serenity taught Liping some concrete techniques, which Liping took to practicing over and over on the way as they went along, gradually learning the walking art.

The mentor also taught Wang Liping methods of determining direction and location. When working at the level of the lower vehicle, one determines direction by reference to the moon and stars, and one determines location by reference to features of the landscape such as mountains, rivers, boulders, trees, houses, and so on.

When working at the level of the middle vehicle, it is possible to determine direction and location even on a pitch dark night; the method involves operating the minor cycle within the body while resting in order to locate the position of the moon, then opening the celestial eye and examining the scenery in all directions to determine location.

When you reach the level of the higher vehicle, none of this is any longer necessary; you only need to follow your intuitive sense, which is none other than your own original spirit.

These three levels of heaven, earth, and humanity, furthermore, pertain to all phenomena and all beings. The methodology becomes more profound, and yet more simple in structure, the higher you go. That is why it is said that the Way is unaffected simplicity.

In this case, the purpose of the journey was to avoid calamity and chaos, just to find peace and safety. All along the way, whenever an occasion arose, the three old wizards taught Liping a practical exercise. On occasions when they had a chance to rest in a quiet place, the masters would expound classics and recite texts, going deeper and deeper step by step, until Wang Liping was able to understand quite a bit of Taoist theory.

On one occasion when the four were taking a rest, Wang Liping's "Little Red Book" slipped out of his cap, and he didn't pick it up. His mentor said, "You'd better pick that up and put it back. It is now our life-preserving amulet, our passport!"

Liping didn't understand, so the mentor went on, "In the lower three realms, everyone needs a protective talisman, because people cannot control their own fate and are not masters of themselves. We are now traveling in the lower three realms, so we have to rely on this object, this Little Red Book, to conceal us. When you have reached the middle three realms, you have become master of your own fate, and then you no longer need this 'protective talisman.'" As they made their way along, the three wizards and their young apprentice avoided the cities, taking to the mountain villages and open wilds. When they were hungry and thirsty, Wang Liping would first settle the three old wizards down to rest, then go by himself to find some drinking water and something to eat. Sometimes Liping and the old masters would all disguise themselves as refugees fleeing famine, begging from village to village for some simple fare. When the weather got too cold, they'd find anyplace they could to take shelter from the wind and snow. In this way, before they knew it several months had passed.

Coming to the foot of a mountain one day, the four travelers saw that it was getting late and rain was on the way. The grand master suggested they find a place to stay nearby. Scanning the area, at last they spotted a tiny settlement of a dozen or so houses nestled on the mountainside.

It was a quiet, rustic village; most of the houses were made of piled stone with thatched roofs. The county seat and the commune garrison were far away, the mountain paths were hard to travel, and very few Party cadres ever went there. Although the villagers were also members of the commune, they lived in extended families, with the elders still having relatively high status.

There was a small level area in the village, where there lay a millstone under a large tree. This appeared to be the community gathering place. Walking into the village, the three old wizards put their bundles on the millstone and sat down to rest while Wang Liping looked around. Soon a crowd of children began to gather. Few people ever came to this remote mountain village, so the appearance of these four strangers was a major event.

Seeing the evident poverty of the hamlet, the ragged clothes of the villagers, and the hungry looks on the children, the three old Taoists were suddenly moved to pity. As the crowd of children grew, the Wayfarer of the Infinite forgot the weariness of the road and suggested to the Wayfarer of Pure Serenity that they should have Wang Liping put on a performance to entertain these village folk.

The Wayfarer of Pure Serenity agreed, and the next thing anyone knew he was ringing a broken gong. All at once the whole village was astir—rarely was there any such excitement around there. Bracing the old and carrying the young, they crowded around the four strangers, eager to see what kind of performance they would put on.

The Wayfarer of Pure Serenity made the rounds with cupped hands, for all the world like a mountebank, expressing gratitude for their kindness: "We are fleeing famine and have nothing rare with us. We've just learned some minor feats to earn a bite to eat. Today we'll present a performance, in hopes of your generosity."

Seeing the three old men homeless at such an advanced age, the villagers were quite sympathetic. They also had good feelings toward the youth, who seemed like a good boy. These mountain peasants were simple folk, and quite a few offered the four strangers places to stay and food to eat. The Taoist travelers, teachers and apprentice, were very moved by this hospitality.

Without needing to be told, Wang Liping was already in the center of the clearing, bowing deeply and thanking everyone for their good will. Then he struck a pose in a state of supreme alertness, so magnificently dignified, even awesome, that everyone was startled at what they had thought was just a quiet student. Liping then went into a display of rapid-fire kicks, punches, and footwork, going through a whole routine that dazzled all eyes and drew rounds of applause.

Gradually Wang Liping grew still; then he slowly took up another posture, with his hands positioned as if he were holding a ball, which he began to roll all over his body. In a short time there actually appeared to be something in his hands; it looked to be about the size of a hen's egg, shining with light, dazzling the crowd. Everyone stared wide-eyed, wondering if they were just seeing things. But the fireball didn't disappear. Instead, it grew bigger and bigger, becoming more and more beautiful in the process, like a colored ball dancing in Wang Liping's hands.

With his feet, Liping now did some kind of step that was not clearly visible, whereupon the colored ball began to circle his body. Stunned, the villagers shouted applause, and just as they were marveling at this, they saw Wang Liping shake his hands, somehow turning the ball into three balls. Now he had one ball in each hand, and a third hung suspended in front of him at the level of his abdomen. Then the three balls spun around him, appearing like a colorful brocade wrapping his body, making a sound like whispering wind. Everyone stared in rapt wonder.

A moment later, there were nine colored balls flying around, encircling Wang Liping's whole body, revolving vertically and horizontally, flabbergasting the whole crowd. Even the old wizards, seeing Liping's accomplishment, nodded and smiled imperceptibly.

Suddenly Wang Liping came to a halt, and the colored balls disappeared in the blink of an eye. Slowly lowering his hands from his chest and opening up his eyes, Liping concluded the exercise. The whole crowd of villagers went wild. That day their eyes had really been opened!

The reader will already have realized that these were the "eight trigram mental spheres" about which Wang Liping's mentor had taught him. The marvelous thing about these eight trigram mental spheres is not their visual beauty, which may please villagers, but in their special function.

This function is known as "distributing the body." Once a colored ball appears, one's own body has already been put inside it, although this "body" is invisible. When Wang Liping was seen manipulating the colored ball, in reality he was massaging a certain part of his body.

The eight trigram mental spheres also have another marvelous function, which is they can be used as a means of sending true mental impressions over vast distances. Because the "self" is in the ball, the ball is a hologram; everything in the self is therein, and it has life, thought, and spirituality like the self. There is no way for ordinary people to comprehend this.

The "information" of which modern people speak and the "true impressions" spoken of by the ancients are not the same thing; they are not even on the same order of reality and should not be confused. The word "impression" here is key, dividing the animate and inanimate worlds, and the universes of the lower and middle three realms.

Watching this young, gentlemanly scholar perform such feats, the villagers wound up seeing him in a different light.

Now the Wayfarer of Pure Serenity came forward and did a little performance to keep up the excitement. To their surprise, the villagers saw how powerful his martial art technique was. Several of the youths brought a large rock and asked the old man if he could split it. Seeing the enthusiasm of the villagers, the Wayfarer didn't refuse. First, he performed several flourishes, worked up the combined energy of his inner organs, and then brought his hand down forcefully with a great shout. Cracking with a dry sound, the rock split into several pieces. The villagers were stupefied. The youths who had brought the rock examined the old Wayfarer's hand, finding it to be like that of an ordinary person, with nothing strange about it. This seventy-six-year-old man was still able to make jaws drop.

Wang Liping was also deeply impressed on witnessing his mentor's uncanny power. He knew how dangerous the Wayfarer's hands could be, for once the old man had hit him during a sparring session. In spite of the protective gear he was wearing, young Liping was knocked back several yards, and his ribs were broken. The grand master remarked on how lucky it was that Liping had a body protector on, because an ordinary person might have even died from such a powerful blow.

The village youngsters surrounded the Wayfarer of Pure Serenity, but when an old man came forth from the crowd, they automatically made way for him. The old man said, "It's getting late. Why don't we let these people rest and eat? Everyone go home!" Then he turned to the four strangers and politely invited them to spend the night in the production brigade barn.

The barn was simple, with nothing in it but some agricultural equipment, room enough to sleep there. Several children who had continued to tag along brought some hay to spread on the floor. The clan elder took a lamp off the wall, lit it, and placed it on a stone stand inside the room. Then everyone sat down on the hay and began to talk about all sorts of things.

Before long, people began to come, one after another, bringing gifts of food, rice cakes, and vegetable soup. Apologizing for the simplicity of their humble fare, the village elder invited the travelers to eat. The wayfarers didn't refuse; it had been days since they'd had such good food. Young Liping's eyes were already red as he began to eat.

After some time, quite a few people also sent the travelers some dry provisions, or a small coin or two. All four Taoists requested that everyone who came take their goods back. Seeing this state of affairs, the clan elder felt he could only ask everyone to go home and let the wayfarers rest.

All of a sudden a terrific thunderstorm broke out. The Taoist masters and their apprentice put out the lamp and sat in meditation before getting some sleep.

This is an illustration of what life was like in the late 1960s. Here were four Transmitters of Taoist sciences, made homeless by a storm of civil strife, left with no choice but to conceal their identities, assume disguises, and flee to the mountains and countryside, dining on wind and sleeping in the dew, putting on performances in the streets, and begging for food in villages.

With all of China plunged into turmoil, quite a few people seemed to go crazy; culture was destroyed, business was disrupted. It was a tragedy for the people. This was an extremely critical period, following the postwar reconstruction of the 1950s. While quite a few nations were developing in areas of economics, culture, and government, China fell into turmoil; its balance was disrupted, its creativity was lost, and its basic health was severely injured.

Oh, China! When you have advantage of terrain, you lack opportunity;

when you have opportunity, you lack harmony! How could you not fall behind, how could you not be beaten, how could you not be poor!

Oh, China! Yours is great wisdom, great wisdom that awes people of the West! But you also have great folly, great folly that makes people of the West laugh!

A famous Westerner once said that what he feared most was the awakening of this slumbering giant of the East. Now it would appear that this giant had awakened, but was still dizzy on standing up, groggily engaged in self-destructive internal conflict. When it finally came to itself, it had fallen way behind others. Foolish giant! Take care of your wounds, then see about gradually catching up. What a tragedy for the people!

This bitter fruit was one that everybody had to bite.

The rain continued for a long time. The Taoist masters and their disciple slept for a few hours, then rose very early to sit. By the time they had finished their inner exercise, the sky was already light. The four then went outside to practice some external exercises, enjoying the exceptional freshness of the mountain air.

Presently they saw the clan elder coming over. The Wayfarer of the Infinite hurriedly went to greet him, and the two exchanged courtesies. The Wayfarer said, "We've caused you a lot of trouble by coming here, and you've treated us so well we don't know quite how to acknowledge your kindness."

The clan elder said, "Think nothing of it, brother. Once you go out the door, there's trouble and misery aplenty. Here in this rustic mountain village we really don't have anything suitable for guests. I'm afraid we've wound up mistreating you. I've been worried about this rain all night, wondering whether the barn roof leaked on you."

The Wayfarer of the Infinite said that the barn hadn't been leaking, and they'd had a comfortable night. The clan elder was relieved. Seeing the old peasant keep looking worriedly at the sky, still darkly overcast, the Wayfarer realized what was on his mind. "What is the problem?" he tactfully inquired of the village elder, already knowing what it was.

The clan chief sighed. After a silence, he finally explained, "Here in our mountain fields we have very little arable land. All of us depend on nature for our livelihood. Right now the wheat is ripe and ready for harvest, but the weather remains overcast and rainy, so we don't know what to do."

The Wayfarer of the Infinite said, "Don't let this worry you, respected younger brother. Please go tell everyone to get out their sickles and start harvesting."

The village elder could tell from his tone that the Wayfarer was serious. Seeing the looks on the faces of the other masters standing behind the grand master, the village elder understood that they concurred, so he turned around and went off.

The Wayfarer of the Infinite had his colleagues and their disciple repair to a secluded spot outside the village to perform a special technique. As three of them took up positions around the top of a hillock, the Wayfarer of Pure Serenity explained to Wang Liping, "Observe that these clouds bring rain and lightning. When exercising rain-stopping technique, it is very easy to get hit by lightning, so the first thing to do is to avoid the lightning. The energy of lightning is in the category of fire, which corresponds to the heart organ in the human body. Thus the way to avoid lightning is to shut off the heart at the instant of the flash, to cut off any connection between the lightning fire and the heart. The energy of the lightning is enormous, but the fire energy in your heart is even greater. Silently recite this certain formula, and the electrical lightning energy will stop. At this time you have become the master of sky and earth. You are the ruler. The other is the minister and must obey you."

Having spoken, the Wayfarer of Pure Serenity made a hand gesture; suddenly his whole body shook, and a peculiar stream of sounds poured from his mouth. At the same time, there was a lightning flash, followed by a distant rumble of thunder. The Wayfarer pointed both hands in the direction of the lightning, making a gentle stroking motion. The clouds in the sky began to part, opening up a strip of pale light.

The Wayfarer of Pure Serenity then told Wang Liping to activate his inner energy so as to direct the universe outside his body by means of the universe inside his body—letting the universe within open up fully, letting the mind energy rise to the clouds, and using the hands to stroke the place where the mind meets the clouds.

Now the dense clouds slowly boiled, and the strip of light that had opened up grew wider and wider. The Wayfarer of Pure Emptiness also raised his hands, forming a triangle with the backs of the other three, whose hands were facing the sky. The clouds moved outward, like a herd of sheep scattering to the four directions. The clearing in the center grew larger and larger, becoming brighter and brighter. After a short while, the grey black cloud masses blew away from the men, toward the horizon. The center of the sky became unusually bright, a very deep blue, extremely beautiful. When the dark clouds had all flown off, the golden sun finally appeared in the east, lighting up the mountains with extraordinary splendor.

The four Taoists bathed in the sunlight, their vital spirits in a state of exceptional alertness. With a half hour's work, they had changed an overcast, threatening sky into a bright new world.

As for Wang Liping, he was unutterably happy—he'd learned something that day! On the way back to the village, his mentor, the Wayfarer of Pure Serenity, told him that it is not so hard to stop rain, but to make rain fall under conditions where there isn't a cloud in sight requires a higher degree of development. Harmonizing with natural law, obeying the Way of Nature, is a constant, invisible principle; the operation of higher powers to stop rain or make rain also has to be like this. Only when they benefit the people, furthermore, are such interventions permissible; they are not under any circumstances to be done arbitrarily or for the wrong reasons.

Seeing the clouds recede and the sky clear with such amazing rapidity, the village elder was more convinced than ever that these four travelers were not ordinary people. He brought the villagers to the barn to thank them, only to find that they had disappeared without a trace.

As it turned out, the grand master, the Wayfarer of the Infinite, had already packed all the gear, as well as what little provisions the villagers had afforded them, and was waiting on a mountain trail for the other three to come down. Then they all took off for who knows where.

Wang Liping understood, as his teachers had explained many times, that the most important issue for people who practice the Way is not the level of their own attainment; it is a matter of doing many good deeds, widely forming good relations, helping out all beings, carrying out the Way on behalf of Heaven. This means that cultivating essential nature is more than cultivating life. To do good deeds without expecting reward is for building up virtue; when virtue is high, attainment also rises.

After stopping the rain, the wizards knew the villagers would be coming to thank them, so they preferred to depart right away, to avoid burdening everyone and delaying the farmwork.

The Five Arts

During their years of travel, the three old wizards continued to take every opportunity they could find to teach their apprentice and transmit the Way.

Wang Liping was now beginning the seventh stage of his Taoist training, which is "developing knowledge." The main contents of study at this stage are the so-called Five Arts. These Five Arts are five kinds of traditional technology or art: medicine, divination, physiognomy, fortune-telling, and training.

These five arts originated in the experience and knowledge derived from the ancients' struggle for survival, adaptation, and balance. Later they were highly developed by Taoists cultivating them in the mountains, who used arcane symbolism to express their findings. Each art is permeated with the sweat and blood of generations of workers, crystallizing the experience and knowledge of the ages. If we can penetrate the outer terminological shell and extract the pure marrow, these arts could be a rare blessing for humankind.

To return to our story, the four Taoists were traveling by day and resting by night, still wandering the four quarters.

One day, they came to a remote spot in the mountains where they saw a clear spring. Sitting down beside the water, they washed off the dust of the road and took a rest.

All of a sudden, the Wayfarer of the Infinite shuddered slightly. Looking up, he said to one of his companions, "Go take a look—is there someone groaning?" The two younger Wayfarers had already heard the sound of groaning, so they followed it, with Wang Liping close behind.

Making their way through thickets of grasses, climbing over rocks and vines, at length the Taoists came to a mountain ridge and found the groaning man in the ravine below.

The man had gone up into the mountains to cut firewood, but had accidentally fallen into the ravine. He was about fifty years old, dark and emaciated, his clothes patched over and over. His right leg was already turning green and forming pus, and his eyes appeared to be unseeing. All he could do was lie there and groan.

Carefully examining the man's injury, the Wayfarer of Pure Emptiness knew that it couldn't have been sustained in the fall—it had to be snake-bite. Immediately, he took a silver needle from his pouch, held it with three fingers of his right hand, pointed it toward the sky, twirled it a few times in his fingers, concentrated his mind and focused his eyes on it, and then in a flash he jabbed it at the man's leg.

Wang Liping thought the thrust of the needle had been awfully violent. He hadn't expected the needle to stop two inches away from the surface of the skin, where his mentor made it vibrate as he listened for the response inside the woodcutter's body. Next the Wayfarer dotted a circle over the leg, then moved the needle down the leg, making the needle vibrate very slightly in his fingertips. At times he would stop at a certain place, whirl the needle, then move vigorously along. When he did this, sometimes he would make the needle bob like a boat going over a wave, then continue along. When the needle went around the kneecaps, it vibrated even more intensely. The Wayfarer twirled it, raised and lowered it, and guided it onward, as though he were deliberately inducing a malignant current to follow the course of the silver needle.

When the needle reached the spot of the snakebite, the Wayfarer made it vibrate lightly over the wound, closing his eyes and concentrating, focusing his whole body and mind on the tip of the needle, mumbling a secret formula. All of a sudden the Wayfarer pulled the needle up with lightning-like speed, whereupon black blood spurted from the wound. In a moment, the woodcutter opened his eyes and stopped groaning.

The Wayfarer of Pure Emptiness rose, put his silver needle back in his pouch, and told the woodcutter, "You'll be all right. The poison's been dispelled."

Now Wang Liping crouched over the man with his palms facing the woodcutter's injured leg and exercised his inner power to press down, so as to speed the man's recovery. The Wayfarer had already sealed off the points governing circulation above the knee, and the poison had already been ejected, so with just a few pushes of inner power by Wang Liping the black blood all flowed out and fresh red blood appeared. The swelling went down, and after a while the woodcutter could walk again. With tears in his eyes, the man tried to bow in gratitude, but the old wizard stopped him. Taking some medicine from his pouch, the Wayfarer handed it to the woodcutter, and they parted ways.

After the woodcutter had gone, Wang Liping was lost in thought about his mentor's unique art of using the silver needle. He was so amazed that he just stood there. The Wayfarer gave him a slap on the back and said, "What's the matter? Come on, let's go back!" Only then did Liping come to himself and head back with his two mentors.

The Wayfarer of Pure Emptiness knew that Wang Liping was thinking about the silver needle, so he talked about it as he walked. As it turned out, the wizard had three extraordinary silver needles, each of which had its own name. One was called the yin needle, one was called the yang needle, and one was called the large long-form needle. Although all three needles had been made by craftsmen, just like any other acupuncture needle, the extraordinary thing about them was that they too had to go through cultivation and refinement, which made them very different from ordinary acupuncture needles. When the needles were not in use, the Wayfarer would take them out and exercise them in tandem with the sky, earth, sun, and moon, inducing the true energies of the universe into the tips of the needles, so that they would then have extraordinary power when put to use.

As Liping learned, the methods of using the needles are also extremely exacting. There are large needle methods, small needle methods, long needle methods, skin needling methods, sectional needling methods, totalizing needling methods, infinite needling methods, and so on. The method that the wizard had just used was an infinite needling method. In this method, the needle is manipulated at a distance, without touching the patient, so one needle can perform many functions and can float spontaneously over the meridians, channels, and pressure points, stimulating each point and line. If the needle were thrust into the skin, then one needle wouldn't be sufficient; each needle, furthermore, would have to be placed in a specific spot and could not float, so the operation of energy would be impeded.

The first step in working with the needle is to do a test needling, which means to sense the quality and intensity of the energy inside after insertion. Wholesome energy is peaceful and calm; whereas unwholesome energy is turbulent.

The interior of the acupuncture points is also divided into three strata, "celestial, earthly, and human," and it is necessary to distinguish clearly in which stratum wholesome or unwholesome energy is flowing. Sometimes wholesome energy is flowing in the "celestial" stratum while unwholesome energy is subtly active in the "earthly" stratum; if these are not clearly distinguished, then it is not possible to use the needle properly and cure the ailment. When wholesome energy is found, then it is elicited in accord with its momentum. When unwholesome energy is found, it is stopped at key points and then forced out.

Listening to his mentor talking as they went along, Wang Liping reflected that it was no wonder the old wizard was called the foremost acupuncturist in the world. Acupuncture and moxacautery only qualify as higher arts, spiritual and sublime, when they are based on this degree of attainment.

When the three got back to where the grand master was resting, the Wayfarer of Pure Emptiness explained that someone had been bitten by a snake, but they had cured him. The grand master voiced approval then had everyone sit down to rest and take some refreshment.

As Wang Liping ate, he listened to the Wayfarer of the Infinite talk to him about medicine and healing. The Wayfarer explained that when someone is bitten by a snake it is necessary to determine whether or not the snake was poisonous. The bite of a snake without poison usually leaves a set of six wounds, four above and two below. Most poisonous snakes, in contrast, leave a set of four wounds; furthermore there is evident suppuration around the site, and searing pain is followed by paralysis.

Bites are usually on the hand or foot; swelling gradually creeps upward, accompanied by blurring of vision, difficulty in breathing, dizziness and vomiting, weak pulse, and high fever. When curing this, it is first necessary to exercise inner power to seal off the route of the poison and press it out.

Medicinal preparations may also be used; "Emergency Powder" and "Jade Essence Powder" will both do. Herbal ingredients normally used included Arisaema tuber, sileris, angelica root, Gastrodia rhizome, notopterygium root, and typhonium rhizome. The ingredients are used in measured doses, and the curing process must be approached analytically, not sticking blindly to a fixed routine.

In the analytic process, Dragon Gate Taoist healers are not like other physicians. The ancestral teachers of Dragon Gate Taoism worked out a total of nine methods, methods involving circulation, penetration of energy, induction of energy, meridians, channels, bone structure, the lymphatic system, inner gazing, and penetrating vision.

These nine methods, which yield rapid and accurate diagnoses, are also divided into three levels corresponding to "heaven, earth, and humanity." For example, the energy channels are more precisely defined as "soft, firm, or floating." These distinctions are also made in ordinary medical texts, but ordinary physicians only know how to take a "firm" pulse. Once the pulse floats up, the hand closes in very slightly on the patient's skin; this is "floating." This corresponds to upper level "heavenly" work with the pulse; people whose inner power is not highly developed cannot do it. Apart from the particular spots on the body, the brain and back of the head are both places where energy channels can be interrupted. In sum, there are endless horizons to this sort of work.

The ancients used to say that curing is not as good as caring, caring is not as good as diagnosis, diagnosis is not as good as prevention, and prevention is not as good as foreknowledge. The grand master told Wang Liping that since he was young he should start by learning to cure. To do this, he needed to be thoroughly familiar with Taoist medical science and actually heal people, using his whole heart, avoiding any wrong attitudes. He was not to reject or abandon the sick, and not to take from them, but to follow the rules of Taoism and create fortune and blessings for people.

When they had rested, the Taoist masters and their disciple set out on the road again. The old wizards saw that Wang Liping was very much interested in curing, so as they traveled along they talked of mountains when they encountered mountains, talked of waters when they came to water, talked of curing when they met with illness, and talked of medicine when they saw medicinal plants. They went to many places and saw many such herbs, each of which they discussed in detail for the edification of their young apprentice Wang Liping.

One day when the four had again come to a dense mountain wood, they stopped to rest their feet. It was just about noontime, and there wasn't a single human habitation in sight, so the Wayfarer of Pure Emptiness took Wang Liping to go look for wild fruits in the woods. Seeing the hour was still early and there was no hurry to get back on the road, after they had eaten the grand master took some time to teach Liping more about Chinese medicine and herbs.

The master explained that medical science is inseparable from herbology. Since people usually eat a mixture of grains, they are susceptible to illness. There are many methods of curing, but herbal preparations are the most commonly used expedient. *Shennong's Classic of Herbs* is the oldest manual, listing 365 medicinal substances, their number corresponding to the number of days in a year. These medicinal substances are divided into herbs, cereal, rices, fruits, woods, insects, fishes, animals, and minerals; they are also classified as higher, middling, and lower types.

There are 120 varieties of the higher type of medicinal substance. Called ruling medicines, they are used to nurture life and extend the span of life. They can be taken for a long time without harm. There are 120 varieties of middling medicinal substances. Called minister medicines, they are used to nurture essential nature, replenish lack, and cure illness. They should not be taken over a long period of time. There are also 120 varieties of the lower type of medicinal substance. Called assistants, they are mostly toxic and must be taken with care when used to cure illness. There are also many rules governing the preparation and combination of medicinal substances.

Devoting his whole life to research, the Ming dynasty worker Li Shichen wrote the fifty-two-scroll *Outline of Herbology*, which includes 1,892 medicine substances classified into 60 categories under 16 rubrics. This became the classic sourcebook of herbology, inclusive but not prolix, detailed but essential.

To give an example, in the section on water there are a total of 42 kinds of medicinal substance, classified into sky waters and earth waters. Among them is "year-end snow," which is sweet, cool, and free from toxins; kept in a tightly sealed jar in a shady, cold place, it keeps for decades without spoiling. Year-end snow is good for treating vegetables and grains, killing insects. When seed grain is soaked in it, the seedlings do not become infested. In brewing equipment the liquid can get rid of green flies; and storing fruit foods in it can prevent them from being worm eaten. It can disperse all sorts of toxins, cure seasonal epidemics, hangover, and childhood fevers, convulsions, fits, and so on. It also cures jaundice, but it has to be warmed a bit when taken for this purpose. Used to wash the eyes, year-end snow can get rid of redness. Used to make tea or gruel, it can dispel fever and stop thirst. It also has a remarkable effect when applied to rashes.

The use of water to cure illness also has its natural laws. People suffering from diarrhea and vomiting can be treated with yin-yang water. Yin-yang water is a half-and-half mixture of well water and boiled water, so it is very simple. According to *Historical Records*, when the great physician Hua Tuo saw a woman with a persistent fever, he had her sit in a stone tub while he doused her with cold water. Since it was winter at the time and the weather was very cold, people thought it was strange to douse her with cold water. After being doused seventy times, the patient was shivering uncontrollably, nearly frozen to death. But after she was doused eighty times, a warm vapor steamed from the patient's whole body. After dousing her a hundred times, Hua Tuo helped her out of the tub, rubbed her down, then wrapped her warmly and had her lie down. After a short while, she broke out in a sweat all over, and the fever disappeared. This sort of cure is of the kind that ordinary physicians dare not attempt.

On this leg of their journey the four Taoists had no idea how many days they spent passing through this dense mountain forest. All Liping knew was that during this period the three wizards had explained to him the essential points of numerous medical classics, and each one had also passed on his own unique arts. They also taught him over a hundred secret formulas, unknown to the world, which he was to memorize and not divulge readily. Recording everything he learned from his teachers in his memory, Wang Liping reached a high level of attainment in medical science.

It was now late fall, with winter approaching. Traveling through the mountains, the four Taoists saw the face of autumn grow old in a vast expanse of scenery. Wang Liping now had several more treasures in his traveling bag, rare herbs they had found along the way, as well as prepared pills and powders. Although he didn't have much of the medicinal substances, they are so rare that they were worth a great deal of money. The four Taoists had spent considerable time and energy collecting and preparing these medicines, but they weren't going to sell them or barter them; these medicines were for healing people in emergencies, in times of need.

One day, as they had just turned the bend around a mountainside trail, they saw several people staggering along. When the people got close, the Taoists saw that each of them had a sallow complexion and was dressed in tatters, like people fleeing famine.

When questioned by the Wayfarer of the Infinite, one of the men said that the group lived in a settlement not far from there whose inhabitants had been afflicted by an epidemic and were dying at a rate of a dozen a day. This group of people on the road now was going elsewhere for the time being, hoping to escape the epidemic. The man who spoke advised the four travelers to take a detour and avoid going through the settlement.

The Wayfarer of the Infinite smiled and said, "There's no need to detour. Please return with us. We will cure this disease."

The people had a look of doubt on their faces. The Wayfarer of the Infinite saw that one of them was a woman with a small child in her arms. The baby was pale, his lips were blue; his eyes were closed, and he was gasping weakly. The woman had a look of entreaty in her eyes. The Wayfarer reached out and rubbed the child on the head; then he said, "This little one's all right. Go home and feed him, and he'll get better."

The woman didn't believe him at first, but then the child's color improved, and she found he was no longer burning with fever. The child opened his eyes and cried, "Mama, I'm hungry!" Stupefied, the woman tried to bow in thanks, but Wang Liping hurriedly stopped her. The other people were also amazed. They wound up following the four travelers to the village, all the while trying to figure them out.

The village was desolate; not a soul was to be seen walking around outside, and there was not a single rooster crowing or a dog barking. All that was to be seen was blank paper hung on a number of doors, fluttering in the autumn wind.

The Wayfarer of Pure Emptiness took a look inside one of the houses, then turned to the Wayfarer of the Infinite and told him that it was undoubtedly an outbreak of cholera, requiring emergency measures.

Without taking a moment to rest, the four travelers immediately told the man who had led them there to have everyone who could walk gather in the village assembly hall, bringing the invalids along on litters. Wang Liping went ahead and cleaned up the hall, then closed the windows tightly. The Wayfarer of Pure Emptiness took out his silver needle, closed his eyes, and began working up energy. The Wayfarer of Pure Serenity collected firewood and piled it in the center of the room. The Wayfarer of the Infinite asked someone to bring paper and brush. Sitting on the ground, he drew a talisman, then fit it into the palm of his hand, placed it over his chest, then closed his eyes and activated the talisman, reciting a secret formula.

All the preparations completed, the whole village gathered in the hall. The Wayfarer of Pure Emptiness had them sit around the pile of firewood; those who could not sit up lay facing inward. The Wayfarer of the Infinite had Wang Liping first give each of those lying down a grain of a medicinal pill from his pouch. He also told Liping to light the firewood.

The firewood was not dry, so it gave off a lot of smoke as it burned. The Wayfarer of the Infinite burned the talisman he'd made in the fire.

Now the doors were shut, so the smoke filling the room choked the people, making them cough louder and louder. Then some people vomited, and chaos ensued. The smoke and the stench filled the room with foul odors, while sounds of coughing, retching, and moaning filled the room with noise.

In the pitch darkness, the Wayfarer of Pure Emptiness held a needle in both hands and performed a field-effect mass acupuncture treatment in the air, mentally thrusting the needle into certain special points, so that all the patients there simultaneously felt an effect. After the Wayfarer of Pure Emptiness had performed the acupuncture, the Wayfarer of Pure Serenity then proceeded to give the whole group a field-effect therapeutic massage, which was also distinctly felt by all the patients.

After about an hour, the room quieted down; there was no more coughing, retching, or groaning to be heard. Those who had been seated began to feel comfortable; while those who had been lying down began to sit up. All of them felt well.

Now the Wayfarer of the Infinite told Wang Liping to open the doors and windows, letting in light and fresh air. The Wayfarer of the Infinite said to the villagers, "You can all get up and go home now. Eat little for a few days, rest quietly for a few days, and you will gradually recover your physical strength."

Hearing this, the villagers all looked at one another. All of them felt as if they had been placed in a dream world, yet when they got up and walked off, to their amazement it was all very real. When the people looked for the four "strangers," it turned out that they had already packed up and gone. The man who had first brought them to the village shouted after them to wait, and that woman with the child also called out her thanks. The four travelers kept on going, however, young Wang Liping alone turning his head to wave good-bye. The villagers were all in tears.

After leaving the village, for several days in a row the Taoists used long-distance remote massage to heal the most seriously afflicted of the villagers. These patients recovered very quickly, to the great joy and gratitude of all the people. There is something missing from this story of curing the cholera epidemic, something that needs to be added. When the Wayfarer of Pure Serenity first sat down in the hall with the villagers, he exercised an art known as "the clothing of Nature, without any seams," meaning that he first enveloped the entire village securely in an enormous field of inner power. After the grand maestro had worked the talisman and the other master had worked the needle, he then performed therapeutic massage by properties of field-effect from a distance. The three wizards all used things with form and substance to transmit formless yet substantial impressions, simultaneously treating a whole group of patients in order to finish their task.

For nearly the entire population of a village to be afflicted with cholera at the same time was something the three wizards had rarely seen in their many years of medical practice. There were so many sick people, and the symptoms were so serious, that there was no leeway for hesitation. They had to assemble all the patients and administer unique arts, medicines, talismanic science, acupuncture, and massage, all on the same occasion.

Drawing a talisman on paper, activating inner power on it, and then burning it, thus curing illness, is called "ceremonial moxacautery." There are many kinds of talisman: there are "prescription talismans," "sunlight/moonlight talismans," and "five element talismans," as well as "heaven, earth, and human talismans" and "universe talismans."

It is not true that a talisman can be used once it is drawn. After it is written, the talisman has to be activated and operated; this is done by specific methods that require a very high level of inner power. For example, to activate a "sunlight/moonlight" talisman, it is necessary to learn how to gather energy, and also to be able to transfer the energy onto the talisman. When it comes to even higher level varieties like the "heaven, earth, and humanity" talismans, these are already beyond the middle three realms, and require the harnessing and deployment of even higher level powers before they will work.

These higher level powers are not visible to ordinary human beings, and there are those who even doubt their very existence. Then again, there are those who believe in their existence but consider them to be incomprehensible mysteries. And what about the reality? This sort of "power" does exist, as seen in the earlier story about stopping rain and this story about curing illness.

~~~~~

Chinese medical science originated with shamanic healing. In antiquity, curing and shamanism were united; later they gradually separated. Some people regard this as historical progress, but some people also consider this progress to contain regression within it. Which of these points of view is correct? It would appear that there is no ready conclusion to this question, but one thing is for sure: if Chinese medical science is removed from its overall context in Chinese culture, if it is separated from the foundation of the yin-yang and five elements theories, if it is abstracted from the pragmatic basis of inner work, then it has lost its living source.

Experience is indispensable in the development of Chinese medical science; Western medicine also has some elements in it that could shed light on the development of Chinese medicine. Neither experience nor Western medicine, however, can be a foundation for the development of Chinese medicine; that would be confusing root and branch.

Chinese medicine is divided into three levels, corresponding to heaven, earth, and humanity, just as experience also has these three levels. The experience of which ordinary people speak is not beyond the domain of the lower three realms; if Chinese medicine were limited to this framework, its development would suffer tremendous constraint. Taoist medical science has no such limitations; it enlarges the domain of experience to reach the middle and upper three realms, where there are numerous useful techniques that can be applied, and numerous powers that can be employed. The precondition upon which these methods and powers can be used is the healer's own personal cultivation of inner work. Here is where curing and shamanism are united; this is superior to ordinary Chinese medicine, and even more superior to Westernized Chinese medicine. This premise is the original basis and proper tradition of Chinese medicine;

only by following this can there be even greater development.

Here is a simple example. Several years ago, Master Wang Liping lectured on Taoist medicine to professors from a number of Chinese medical schools. When he explained how pulses are divided into three levels corresponding to heaven, earth, and humanity, and talked about how to take a floating pulse, the professors understood the principles, saying that they had heard of them from their own teachers, but they did not know the reason for them, and so had never practiced them, had never employed them, and could not find the floating pulse on the upper, "heaven" level. Master Wang Liping told them that it is naturally impossible to find it by using ordinary methods. This pulse has dozens of signs, he went on, with very minute distinctions among them; without inner work, one cannot even understand what is written in medical texts, let alone apply it.

This is stated in reference to normal nursing methods. Chinese medicine does not cause the patient more pain and suffering, but can diagnose, prescribe, and give treatment based on external manifestations. Western medicine, in contrast, can hardly take a step without instruments; when it comes to afflictions of the internal organs, or ailments below the surface of the skin, Western medicine needs to perform biopsies or exploratory surgery to make accurate diagnoses, thus bringing the patient even more pain and suffering. Western medicine also lacks a consciousness of the totality and cannot practice dialectical treatment: when the head hurts, the head is treated; when the feet hurt, the feet are treated—regardless of what side effects the medicines employed may have. Often it happens that when one illness has been eliminated, another ailment arises. This way of going about things may seem advanced, but in reality it is primitive.

Taoist healing goes back to simplicity, eliminating a number of intermediate processes, looking directly into the source of the ailment and removing its cause directly, with extraordinarily good results. Ordinary people who witness the healing process consider it quite marvelous, but it really isn't strange. Master Wang Liping says that whereas ordinary physicians have to take pulses and perform examinations, he can understand an ailment just by looking. Whether or not the person is even present, Master Wang can "see" sickness with his eyes.

Why does Taoism insist so firmly on the foundation of personal self-cultivation? There are reasons. First, without refinement of thought to a high level, the marrow of ancient culture cannot be understood. Second, without a very high degree of inner power, many techniques cannot be made to work, and nonhuman powers cannot be harnessed. Third, according to the theory of the unity of Nature and humanity, the natural body of the universe is in the process of evolving, so the human body, which corresponds to it, is also in the process of evolving. New problems arise, which require people of later times to study and try to resolve them. In terms of medical science, the medicinal nature of some medicinal substances has changed, so the methods of compounding and prescribing must also change, lest they lose their therapeutic effect. This is a task for physicians of future generations.

In sum, the development of Chinese medicine is inseparable from its traditional cultural background, particularly traditional philosophical thinking. It is also inseparable from cultivation of inner power on the part of physicians themselves. It also needs to absorb nutrients from everyday experience and Western medicine. All three of these things are necessary, but it is important to distinguish the basic from the subsidiary so as not to abandon the root to pursue the branch, inverting the proper order of things.

10

Transcending Time and Space

When we speak of transcending time and space here, we mean it in a narrow sense, that of thought transcending time and space. The method of transcendence is the study of traditional cultural arts of divination, physiognomy, and fortune-telling.

Divination, physiognomy, and fortune-telling are all studies of prediction and foreknowledge. What is nowadays referred to as prediction was in ancient China called divination, physiognomy, and fortune-telling, which are several methods of prognostication.

If we say "prediction," people will accept the term, even without pursuing the question of whether prediction is accurate or not. If we say "divination," "physiognomy," or "fortune-telling," however, people are unlikely to accept the terms, because their minds have already been taken over by the common idea that these are "superstitions." If relatively good results, or accurate predictions, are obtained by use of these methods, people say it was coincidence and do not ask how the "coincidence" could happen.

This is a kind of obstacle preventing the development of learning; it is not an appropriate attitude for unearthing the treasures of traditional culture. Once we remove this barrier and change our mode of thinking, our eyes will become clearer, so we can perceive the jewels buried deeply in the ground.

Though we call them jewels or treasures, really these are tools. Although tools for prognostication are of relatively minor importance, as long as they are useful, why not use them? If their use does not obstruct the Great Way, why abandon them?

Prognostication is indispensable for human life and society. Whatever the time or place, people want to know the future in advance. Prognostication and foreknowledge may be more or less, relatively deep or shallow, crude or detailed, having distinctions of time, space, and content. Prediction and foresight, in response to which appropriate measures can then be based, are aspects of human wisdom.

Prognostication requires understanding of the natural laws by which events and phenomena operate. To give a small example, everyone knows that some hours after the sun sets it will again rise in the east; so everyone can make arrangements to do daytime tasks in daylight and nighttime tasks at night. When it comes to the timing of solar and lunar eclipses, however, people cannot calculate them without scientific instrumentation, based on which predictions can be made.

Prognostication requires collecting elements or information relevant to a given matter and analyzing them before it is possible to draw conclusions and make predictions. If the information is not accurate, then there is no way to make an accurate prediction.

This is common sense. People will not accept what is beyond the boundaries of this domain.

For example, what constitutes relevant information? Is it possible to cast a few coins, observe the images, and from that tell what is going to happen? What do these events have to do with coins? How is it possible to tell a person's destiny from his face, hands, and back? How can someone's whole life be predicted from the time of birth? Most people would say that these two kinds of information are either too remote or basically irrelevant.

Traditional culture, however, has its philosophy; and this philosophical basis, namely the theory of the unity of Nature and humanity, has never been effectively challenged.

In this stage of "developing knowledge," the three old wizards taught Wang Liping quite a few things. It was on this process that they spent the most time and effort.

The reader must remember that after Wang Liping had experienced death, though still a member of the lower three realms he was already different from people of the lower three realms. The practice and knowledge the wizards were teaching him after his death were not the same as before; the contents and methods of their transmission were now taking place on a higher level. Our own thinking now has to rise accordingly to a higher level before we can understand certain things.

On one occasion, the grand master asked Wang Liping if he could recite the twenty-first chapter of the Tao Te Ching, which the master wizard had taught him earlier.

Liping recited from memory: "For the countenance of great virtue, only the Way is to be followed. As a thing, the Way is abstract and elusive: elusive and abstract, there are images in it; abstract and elusive, there is something there. Recondite, hidden, it has vitality therein: that vitality is very real; it has information therein. From ancient times to now, its name is the undeparting; thereby are seen all beginnings. How do I know all beginnings are so? By this."

The grand master asked, "Do you know the meanings implied?" Wang Liping replied, "Not too clearly. Please point them out to me."

The old wizard explained, "The Way is immaterial and formless, yet it permeates matter and form. Heaven, earth, humankind, and all things and beings are united in the Way. Since all things contain the Way, the trail of their evolution can be followed. How do we look? All things have images: the things are yang, the images are yin; one is the counterpart of the other. There is a vital essence in beings, a vital essence containing information. The methods of observing changes in the universe are called apprehending information and apprehending images. To look directly into the vital essence in beings and the information in that vital essence is the method of the higher vehicle. To apprehend images to observe things, matching yin to yang, is the method of the middle vehicle. Ordinary people observe changes in things based on experiences; this is the method of the lower vehicle."

The grand master then gave a detailed exposition of the methods of the middle and higher vehicle, and taught Wang Liping a number of methods one after another.

The methods of the five arts are all inseparable from a number of major elements: heaven, earth, and humanity; yin and yang; water, wood, fire, earth, and metal. These also produce the sky and earth "stem and branch" parameters of the calendrical system, as well as the eight trigrams and nine chambers. Among these, yin and yang are the most fundamental elements. "The Way produces one, one produces two, two produces three, three produce myriad things." The "two" is yin and yang, the "three" is heaven, earth, and humanity. Heaven, earth, and humanity also contain the five elements, each of which has yin and yang. When primordial chaos first began to open up, there was a single energy, undifferentiated and still; the energy contained yin and yang and had both cloudiness and clarity. The clear energy swirled to the left and rose to produce water, then turned into fire when it had climaxed. The cloudy energy swirled to the right and descended to produce metal, then turned to water when it had climaxed. Between yin and yang, at the hub of rising and descending, the centered energy became earth. So yin and yang are the governing order of all things, the parents of evolution, the origins of vivifying and killing, the seat of spiritual illumination.

As for the calendrical stems and branches, there are ten "sky" stems and twelve "earth" branches. In combination, they make the sixty-year cycle. These stems and branches are all divided into yin and yang. They have correspondences in time and space, which are essential to calculating techniques used for prognostication.

The eight trigrams are constructed by spatial and temporal changes in positions of broken yin and solid yang lines. Three lines make a trigram, six make a hexagram. A trigram is divided into three positions representing heaven, earth, and humanity, with a distinction between yin and yang line positions. A hexagram is also divided into three positions representing heaven, earth, and humanity, and yin and yang positions are also distinguished. The permutations of the eight trigrams produce the sixty-four hexagrams, which are used to represent myriad things.

The "nine chambers" is a notation device used to complete the spatial arrangement of the eight trigrams in the four cardinal and four intermediate directions, which otherwise leaves a space in the middle.

Using these basic elements of calculation, based on their mutual production and their extension, the natural laws of evolution of myriad things are investigated, using the present to examine the past, using the present to figure out the future. These are the tools used by the ancients for purposes of prognostication.

There are two important charts of relevance here: one is the chart of the five elements, the other is the chart of the eight trigrams and sixty-four hexagrams.

The five elements chart is most simple, yet extremely important. Heaven, earth, humanity, and all things and beings are contained therein; all of them can be explained by means of this chart. This is a very important part of traditional Chinese culture.

The basic relationships among the five elements are mutual production and mutual overcoming, used to understand changes and developments in heaven, earth, humanity, and myriad things. "In learning, you add day by day; for the Way, you reduce day by day." In the context of using images to categorize things, containing the natural laws of the evolution of the universe and everything within it in a simple chart, by "reducing" it all to yin and yang and the five elements, simplicity and ease are combined with loftiness and profundity.

The eight trigrams and sixty-four hexagrams are also a kind of simple chart, but its permutations are extremely complex.

There are many ways of arranging the eight trigrams and sixty-four hexagrams; the I Ching or Book of Changes represents one type. The text of this book has been transmitted in full, and there have been many commentaries and interpretations made in the more than two thousand years that it has been current. The development of learning proceeds from the simple to the complex, then from the complex to the simple; then it is possible to employ the complex by means of the simple, with endless potential for change and evolution.

The five elements and eight trigrams charts are tools for taking images to clarify ideas and understand the Way; the subtlety of their function lies in the mind.

Chinese medicine, one of the five arts, is incomprehensible apart from yin and yang and the five elements. Since Chinese medicine has been used effectively for thousands of years, that is ample proof of the conformity of the yin-yang and five elements theories with the Way.

Like Chinese medicine, the arts of divination, physiognomy, and fortune-telling are based on the same principle, come from the same source, and all have some utility for people of the world.

Methods of physiognomy are based on symbols of visible things, organized into categories, used to figure out things underlying events and phenomena at a deeper level, or changes and developments across time and space. Heaven, earth, humankind, all phenomena, and all beings have form and substance, so they all have images and signs. People ordinarily stop at observing the surfaces of things, without thinking about what their images represent, what information they have to offer, how they have evolved, and how they will develop. Scientists do make this sort of effort, seeking more knowledge in hopes of arriving at answers to questions.

Physiognomy, or observing signs, requires good eyes and an active brain. This active brain, furthermore, requires the guidance of philosophy. If the philosophy is right, it will lead you to think in the right direction; if the philosophy is incorrect, it will lead your thinking into bias, or lead you to an impasse. There were a number of great expert physiognomers in ancient China. Jiu Fanggao, for instance, is considered one of the all-time best judges of horses. It is said that he could see right into a horse's bones. Bai Luo was another expert horse physiognomer; he even wrote a book on the subject, which is unfortunately lost. At farmers' markets where livestock is traded, there are also some people who know how to read the features of horses and oxen. When livestock is paraded in front of them, they first examine several key places, see how old the animal is, and then give an evaluation. They are all physiognomers in a sense, although there are differences in the levels of their skills.

Speaking in terms of such a low standard, everyone is a physiognomer; everyone evaluates relevant people, events, and things of all sorts, making choices among them; so how could we do this without examining appearances, looking at signs? If you want to get married, for example, you have to see who would be best, who would be most compatible. And when you go to the market to shop, whether or not you know anything about the product, you have to look at the item and be satisfied with what you see before you decide to purchase it. But in this you still remain at a low level, and cannot be a real physiognomer, a specialist in a certain field.

From this perspective, the arts of physiognomy are quite practical and not at all mysterious. Of course, people still have a negative image, thinking of physiognomy in the same terms as superstition, thus losing something useful.

There are many kinds of physiognomy, of which analysis of human features is one. This is not limited to facial features; every part of the human body can be "read." The most developed arts in traditional physiognomy, however, are generally of five kinds, dealing with the features of the face, hands, feet, back, and head.

There was an expert physiognomer of the Song dynasty known as the Hemp-Robed Wayfarer, and a method of physiognomy named after him has come down through tradition. Master Chen Bo learned physiognomy from the Hemp-Robed Wayfarer, who passed on his art directly to Chen without the use of words. Later he wrote *Ode to Spiritual Marvels*, *Ode to the Golden Key*, and *Song of the Silver Spoon*. Chen Bo's accounts of his teacher the Hemp-Robed Wayfarer also go into detail about physiognomy.

The art of physiognomy is an important part of Chinese medicine. *The Yellow Emperor's Classic of Internal Medicine* distinguishes people into five conditions with reference to yin and yang: major yin people, minor yin people, major yang people, minor yang people, and people in whom yin and yang are balanced. The classic also explains that people can be differentiated in terms of the five elements, and that the permutations of the five elements and the five yin-yang types result in a total of twenty-five human types.

Wood type people, for example, "are of pale complexion, small head, long face, large shoulders and back, erect body, small hands and feet; they are talented and hardworking, but lack strength and have a lot of trouble with things. They are all right in spring and summer, but not fall and winter. In fall and winter they are sensitive and susceptible to illness." Wood people are further subdivided into several subtypes.

Fire type people "are of ruddy complexion, broad back, sharp face, and small head. They have good shoulders, backs, sides, and bellies, with small hands and feet. Their walk is steady, but when in haste their action is unstable. Their shoulders and back are fleshy; they are mettlesome and care little for material wealth. They trust little and worry much. They see things clearly and put on a good face, but tend to rush and are likely to die violently before their time. They are all right in spring and summer, but not fall and winter, when they are susceptible to illness." Fire people are also subdivided into several types.

Earth type people "are yellow of complexion, with a round face, large head, fine shoulders and back, large abdomen, beautiful limbs, small hands and feet, lots of flesh, and upper and lower body in proportion. Their walk is steady, their step is light; steady in mind, they are altruistic, unambitious, and generous. They are all right in fall and winter, but not spring and summer, when they are susceptible to illness." Earth people are also further subdivided into several types.

Metal type people are "square of face, with white complexion, small head, small shoulders and back, small hands and feet, lightboned, nimble, hasty, calmly ruthless, bureaucratic. They are all right in fall and winter, but not in spring and summer, when they are susceptible to disease." Metal people are also further subdivided into several types.

Water type people are "dark of complexion, with uneven face, big head, wide jaws, small shoulders, big bellies, active hands and feet, unsteady movements, long buttocks and spindly back. They are irreverent, good at cheating people, and likely to die by violence. They are all right in fall and winter, but not spring and summer, when they are susceptible to illness." Water people are also further subdivided into several types.

The general classifications of body types are associated with seasonal conditions to make it easier to predict the occurrence of sicknesses and to effect cures. Thus physiognomy is very useful in the healing arts.

The art of fortune-telling physiognomy comes from the same source, but it is even more detailed in its analysis of parts of the body. Its function is in predicting human affairs, the major events of an individual's lifetime, or the trend of development and evolution over the years.

For example, traditional face-reading physiognomy divides the center line of the human face into thirteen positions, and also dissects the whole human face into twelve departments: life, money, siblings, property, children, employees, spouses, sickness and calamity, movement, profession, blessings, and looks. There are also other ways of analyzing the face, special study being made of the eyes, ears, nose, and mouth. Wrinkles, moles, brows, eyes, ears, nose, mouth, lips, tongue, teeth, hair, shape, color, bone, flesh, voice, mood, and spirit are all treated in great detail.

From a modern scientific point of view, traditional Chinese physiognomy seems quite thoroughgoing in its research in this area. From a philosophical point of view, it can also be seen that traditional Chinese physiognomy is not a crude and arbitrary invention, but is pervaded with the traditional Chinese philosophy of the unity of Nature and humanity, as well as the doctrines of yin and yang and the five elements. When it comes to practical application, however, there is a vast range of differences. There are plenty of mountebank physiognomers who only know one or two things about the art; they read faces without having done any deep research, actually doing no more than giving a performance. Some people make a living this way. Nevertheless, there are people who are highly expert in this art, people who can read others' faces and tell things about them with proven accuracy.

In his *Ode to Spiritual Marvels*, the Hemp-Robed Wayfarer wrote that the hardest thing to determine by physiognomy is whether someone will live a long time or die early; this is not in the human domain alone, and is only determined with certainty on a spiritual level.

When the Dragon Gate wizards taught Wang Liping physiognomy, they taught him to read not only faces, but also hands, feet, abdomens, backs, and heads. In sum, there is an art of physiognomy for every part of the body. The arts taught by the wizards were different from ordinary physiognomy in two major respects: one is the detailed treatment of each individual part; the other is the practice of analysis followed by synthesis. An issue seen in one place has to be rechecked in another; then a total picture is assembled before a judgment is made.

Speaking in terms of hand physiognomy, most physiognomers focus on the palms, or on the shape of the hand. The method the old wizards taught Wang Liping has quite a bit more to it. Not only is the hand examined from the wrist to the fingertips, front and back; it is diagnosed on five levels, from outside to inside—prints, skin, flesh, bone, and marrow. On the surface of the back of the hand, for example, one examines pores, vertical patterns, and horizontal patterns, discerning therefrom people's relationships with their ancestors. This is not a common art in physiognomy, and these patterns cannot be seen by the eyes of ordinary people. Only those with lofty and profound inner power can see so accurately and with such penetration.

Nowadays, people have accepted the possibility of inferring the condition of the whole body from the condition of one of its parts, thus diagnosing and treating disease in this way. This is none other than the modern theory of the hologrammatic universe.

The basic principle of Chinese ear-acupuncture healing is to view the ear as a whole body, with the individual pressure points on the ear corresponding to particular organs of the human body. If an organ develops an illness, therefore, this is reflected in the corresponding spot on the ear; a specific point on the ear is then given acupuncture to treat the ailment. The ear is thus a hologram of the whole human body. This is a major discovery made by the Chinese. In the mid-1950s, Chinese ear-acupuncture treatment aroused interest around the world, becoming the subject of lively discussion in the medical world.

In 1980 a Chinese named Zhang Yingqing published an extraordinary paper entitled "The Hologrammatic Rule of Living Beings," which caused an uproar inside and outside China. Mr. Zhang later continued to publish on this subject, treating the matter in detail. He writes, "Each part of the hologram that is a living being has a corresponding position in the whole, or in another hologram. Each part of a hologram, plus its corresponding locus in the whole, or a noncorresponding locus in another hologram, is of a size comparable to the biological entity in the corresponding position. The laws of distribution of each part in a hologram are the same as those in each corresponding part of a whole, or of another hologram. Each hologram contains the special biological information proper to each part of a whole, as well as each point in another hologram. This is similar to the way in which each fragment of a hologrammatic photo contains the information for the whole picture."

In 1973 Zhang Yingqing discovered an orderly set of new acupuncture points beside the second palm bone, which could be used to diagram and treat illnesses of the corresponding parts of the body. Although the second palm bone does not have as many points as the full hologram of the whole body contained in the ear, for rough diagnosis it is more practical and more popular. What is of particular importance is the fact that in both cases the theory rests on the same basis, namely the hologrammatic law of living beings.

From the theory of living beings as holograms to the notion of the whole universe as a hologram is but one short step, soon proposed by Chinese people, whose cultural background is based on yin-yang and the five elements as a holographic plate of all events, all beings, and all things.

Lao-tzu says, "The Way is great, heaven is great, earth is great, and humankind is also great." Also, "Humankind is modeled on earth, earth is modeled on heaven, heaven is modeled on the Way, the Way is modeled on Nature." To be modeled on something means to imitate it, to resemble it; it means to embody the totality of its information, as in a hologram.

If the eyes contain information about the internal organs, and the ear is like a miniature human form containing information about the whole body, can it not be said that people's faces and hands, and indeed other parts of the body, likewise contain information about a person's life?

Physicians diagnose illnesses from observation of specific body parts; physiognomers diagnose developments in human affairs. Simply put, it is all a matter of information, but "The humane see humaneness, the wise see wisdom." When the eyes used are not the same, the information drawn from data is not the same, and the conclusions drawn are not the same.

Among the five arts, the easiest for people to understand and accept is healing, next are physiognomy and training; the hardest to understand are fortune-telling and divination.

Training refers to common methods of development; in a narrow sense, it refers to martial arts. Since the martial arts, both soft and hard, have set courses that can be observed, people believe in them.

Of course, healing, physiognomy, and training have to be accepted as compatible with science, on the level of the lower three realms of persons, events, and things in order to be understood and accepted. Once this level is transcended, however, to rise to the levels of the middle three realms of heaven, earth, and humanity, people will become uncertain. For example, the infinite needle acupuncture, long-distance massage, and using talismans to cure disease appear to ordinary people to be incomprehensible mysteries. To see to the bones is a level of practice that ordinary physiognomers cannot do, so most people would probably think it is a bunch of nonsense. Ordinary martial arts are simply a matter of strength and technique; authentic operation of inner power, combined with the application of esoteric methods, results in effects unattainable by ordinary strength and techniques, so this is also hard for most people to understand.

Now when we talk about fortune-telling and divination, the moment we begin people will be full of doubts and suspicions. Most people consider fortune-telling to be synonymous with coincidence; no one grasps its relationship with inevitability. The thinking of the ordinary person stops here.

Fortune-telling and divination are both arts of prognostication. Prognostication, or prediction, is something people have to use all the time in the course of everyday life. It may be said that as long as there is thought there is prediction; but methods of prediction differ, theories differ, and results also differ.

Traditional Chinese fortune-telling is mainly used to predict the trend of evolution of a person's lifetime; whereas divination is mainly used to predict something that is going to happen in a particular time and place, or a currently emerging event.

The theoretical foundation of fortune-telling is the traditional Chinese philosophy of unity of Nature and humanity, and the doctrines of yin and yang and the five elements. This art regards the development of an individual human life as a miniature reflection of developments in the universe, so the evolution of the universe determines the evolution of human life. On this point, the perceptions of science and fortune-telling concur. If we stopped at this general level, however, fortune-telling would not emerge, and controversy between fortune-telling and science would not occur.

Under the guidance of traditional Chinese philosophy, the intellectuals of ancient China applied their brains to this issue, searching for how a human life relates to the evolution of the universe, and how it could be predicted what would happen in a lifetime.

One of the ways of arriving at answers found by the ancient Chinese is the so-called Four Pillar method of calculation. Beginning its calculations from the time and place of the individual's birth, this method constructs a number of different models of change and development, in order to foretell the course that the individual should pursue in life. Here is where controversy arises between fortune-telling and science; fortune-telling considers it possible to predict this sort of thing, whereas science considers such predictions to lack grounding.

In the economically developed countries of the West, people's level of conventional culture is relatively high, and scientific concepts have already entered deeply into the average person's brain, but science has no way to answer many questions within the domain of convention. Some intellectuals have already sensed that science is facing a crisis, and are beginning to seek wisdom in culture outside conventional science, looking for some kind of resolution to these questions. Fortune-telling is one avenue they are exploring.

Although scientific thinking is quite influential in China, since education is not developed, the influence of traditional culture remains very great, and among the populace there are a great many people who believe in fortune-telling. This is the current state of the culture; needless to say, whatever angle you view it from, fortune-telling is not an element to be sold cheaply.

Chinese fortune-telling is generally traced back to the Warring States era, but the Four Pillar technique was not completely systematized until the Tang and Song dynasties. The key figures in this were Li Wuzhong of the Tang dynasty and Xu Ziping of the early Song dynasty. Mr. Li based his calculations on the year, month, and day of an individual's birth; Mr. Xu added another element, the hour.

In traditional Chinese calendry, the year, month, day, and hour are all figured by the system of sky stems and earth branches. Four figures are arranged horizontally, with the sky stems above and the earth branches below, forming four pillars; there are eight characters altogether, so this is also called the eight-character calculation method of fortune-telling. Since the sky stems and earth branches represent time and also represent location, containing within them yin and yang and the five elements, they comprehend the complex relationships of changes in heaven, earth, and humanity. In modern scientific terms, these eight characters define quality and quantity, so they can be used to carry out extrapolations.

The eight-character calculation in fortune-telling known as "Ziping's Fortune-telling Technique" is a kind of format; there is also the "Building Star Calculation," which is another kind of format. This Building Star Calculation is relatively complex, arraying symbols of stars into a circle, used to predict the course of an individual's life in some detail. In modern scientific terms, each of these charts is an independent holographic plate; in theory, there is no question that is is completely possible to use them to predict a lifetime. So where is the problem? The question is how to employ these formats to accurately predict something is going to happen at a certain time and place. Once we speak of certainty and concreteness, science will express opposition, because science considers "coincidence" to be unpredictable.

Whether or not we can make this step is one issue; whether or not everyone who uses these tools can make this step is another issue. These two issues are not to be confused.

The fortune-telling the three wizards taught Wang Liping involves employment of several kinds of prognostication tools at once. His mentors told him that fortune-telling is a methodology by which the ancients understood humankind. Everyone has a destiny: destiny is birth, aging, sickness, and death; destiny is the ups and downs of the individual in society. Social changes have natural laws that can be traced; the developments in an individual's life also have natural laws that can be traced. Some of these changes have forms: some are formless. The issue fortune-telling needs to investigate is how to grasp what has form to perceive the formless, to see the present and predict the future.

The Building Star Calculation and other methods require careful reading. Using the Four Pillars method, it is possible to determine the highlights of someone's life, one's fortune through several major stages of development and change. Using the Building Star Calculation method, the positions of the sun, moon, and earth at the time of birth are figured, as well as the angle and direction of the five major planets vis-à-vis the Earth; by calculating these relationships in a future year, one predicts important events of that year and the relationships of those events to someone's life.

The three wizards spent a great deal of time and effort teaching Wang Liping divination. The bases of divination are also yin and yang and the five elements, but there are many concrete methods of making calculations. The basic course of study is the eight trigrams.

Confucians and Taoists both respect the I Ching or Book of Changes. Confucians esteem the philosophical principles contained in the I Ching. Over a period of more than two thousand years, several thousand Confucian commentaries on the I Ching were written, most of them expounding philosophical principles. Taoists esteem the tools and methods of cognition provided by the I Ching, making it even more practical.

The three old wizards followed Taoist tradition in teaching Wang Liping the I Ching, differentiating the I Ching into seventy-two varieties, all of them based on the fundamental format of the sixty-four hexagrams. Among them are plant *Changes*, animal *Changes*, human *Changes*, and so on. All events and all things and beings can be classified in terms of the sixty-four hexagrams, in order to observe and predict their developments and changes. Actually, the eight trigrams and sixty-four hexagrams should also be considered a hologram of the universe, with the evolution of all things proceeding according to the same natural laws.

A special feature of the use of the eight trigrams as taught to Wang Liping by his mentors is in regarding them as a sphere, rather than as a plane as ordinarily understood. The heaven and earth trigrams are the extremes, so they can be removed; the remaining six trigrams correspond to above and below, left and right, front and back, thus forming a three-dimensional structure. All things and all beings, all entities that have form, are inseparable from this sphere.

Another peculiarity of the method of using the I Ching Wang Liping learned from his Taoist mentors is that when divining a matter by means of a hexagram, one directs questions about the matter to the hexagram; so there is a host-guest relationship, which must be correctly defined in order to obtain a correct answer. The hexagram is the host; the self is the guest;

when the self asks the host about something, it is necessary to place the sixty-four hexagrams outside, the sixty-four hexagrams forming a large sphere surrounding the self. This is the correct relationship. If the self is regarded as the host, and the sixty-four hexagrams are set up in one's own mind, then the answers to questions are all subjective, all in one's own mind—then how is it possible to question things? When using the eight trigrams for divination, the difficult point is in so-called broken changes, when a basic hexagram and a changed hexagram both come out, requiring interpretation in order to understand what is being said. Interpretation requires learning, experience, and the power of associative thinking, so that one may eliminate impossible answers and choose a feasible answer.

There are also other systems of divination, including the notorious "Concealment in the Door of Luck," one of the secret arts of traditional Chinese culture. This prognostication technique is very deep, impossible to learn by individual study without an enlightened guide to give the personal instruction necessary to make it actually useful. From ancient times, therefore, many have known the name of the art but few have mastered it; those who have been able to employ it were all great people in history, people who accomplished great works with its help.

The basic format of Concealment in the Door of Luck is also a universal hologram; including heaven, earth, humanity, and spirits in one array, observing the various relationships of yin and yang and the five elements, with it good and bad luck at particular times and places are discovered to guide people's actions. This system is pervaded by the philosophy of union of Nature and humankind; what it deals with are questions of necessity or inevitability. When people should adjust to conditions whose occurrence can be predicted, this is an issue of inevitability and necessity, not of coincidence.

Chinese fortune-telling also has a very popular book called *Iron Board Spiritual Calculations*, of which there are numerous different versions. This is attributed to the famous Song dynasty scholar Shao Ying, because it uses a special method of calculation published by Shao Ying in another famous work. In reality, the *Iron Board Spiritual Calculations*, with its very complicated contents, is not the work of a single author. A complex construction, this book is a compendium of knowledge, techniques, terminologies, and methods of many facets of traditional Chinese arts of prognostication. Some of the statements in it are worded very elegantly, others simply and crudely. The method of consultation is very difficult, and the cryptic manner of expression is very hard to understand without considerable training in classical literature and history. For these reasons, *Iron Board Spiritual Calculations* is very widely known, but people who are able to use it are rarely seen.

As the three old wizards taught Wang Liping each of these arts of developing knowledge, they also admonished him that these five arts are all to be practiced by means of the Way, using the arts to help people, using the arts to support the Way, using the arts to communicate the Way—this is basic. The arts are outgrowths: the Way is the main body. When one develops on the Way, intelligence opens up, and it is not hard to learn techniques. When the Way is lofty, techniques are also lofty; this principle becomes all the more evident in work on the higher vehicle.

Wang Liping understood what his teachers meant. Even though he was very interested in learning the arts, and he spent a lot of time and effort on them, to the end he never departed from the basic essence of the Way. Later on, Wang Liping would prove the truth of his teachers' admonitions in actual experience. When dealing with patients who are seriously ill, or when treating difficult cases without precedent, a high master instructed him in dreams, teaching him extraordinary arts and telling him how to cure the particular illness. By this time, of course, Wang Liping already had the capacity of spiritual communication.

After developing knowledge, the three wizards taught Wang Liping to "refine the spirit."

11

Deliberate Dreaming and Refinement of Spirit

"Refining the spirit" was the eighth stage in Wang Liping's life as a Taoist apprentice. At this stage, vitality, energy, and spirit have already been sublimated to a higher level. The term "energy," in particular, is different here. Actually, "energy" is understood differently in each of the lower, middle, and upper three realms.

For example, everyone and everything casts a shadow under a light. Is this shadow empty or substantial? On the level of the lower three realms of persons, events, and things, people say it is empty: if you break the shadow up, that has no effect on the corresponding solid object. In reality, however, breaking up the shadow actually does have an effect; only persons, events, and things cannot feel this because they are not sensitive enough to do so. When you get to the level of "heaven, earth, and humankind," however, it is not the same; here, a shadow is perceived as substantial. For example, a person's shadow corresponds specifically to each individual part of the person's body; if middle-level energy, or an object, acts upon the person's shadow, that is equivalent to acting on the person's body.

When Wang Liping had developed to this point while in the process of "cultivating the triple realm," when his mentor broke up his reflection in water, Liping felt something in his body. This sort of sensation can only be detected when inner work has successfully progressed to a considerably advanced degree. Now then, at an even higher degree, if a needle pierces a certain part of a person's shadow, that is equivalent to thrusting a needle into the person's body. Ordinary people do not feel this at all, yet in reality it has caused an effect; this is the nature of curing disease by performing acupuncture on a shadow.

In sum, at this stage of our story the reader's thinking needs to change. If you keep on applying the original meaning of a given concept beyond a certain point, it will cease to work effectively.

Now the three wizards trained Wang Liping in deliberate dreaming. From the point of view of ordinary people, a dream is something that has form but no substance. When they go to sleep, they arbitrarily dream all sorts of strange dreams, most of which they don't remember. Some dreams leave a deep impression, but people don't understand what they mean.

The wizards and Wang Liping view dreams in a different way from that of ordinary people. Simply put, on the level of "persons, events, and things," dreams have form but no substance, but on the level of "heaven, earth, and humanity," dreams have both form and substance. On this level, people do not dream passively, but actively; they perform tasks in dreams. To reach this level it is necessary to go through special training, and it is necessary to have quite high attainment in inner work. This inner work is special training of vitality, energy, and spirit.

After the wizards had taught Wang Liping to develop his own vitality, energy, and spirit to a very high state, they then taught him how to make specific use of vitality, energy, and spirit to dream deliberately.

The wizards began by explaining that the spirit is divided into two kinds; people have a yin spirit and a yang spirit. The yin spirit is the lower soul, the yang spirit is the higher soul. Wang Liping felt he didn't understand what they meant, as he hung around day after day asking them to explain more clearly. At first the wizards had virtually poured their teachings into their apprentice, but later on, once they saw that Liping was on the Way, they started avoiding him. Wang Liping could still always find one of them, however. All of the wizards were teaching the same thing, but each had his own individuality.

So how do you dream deliberately on the level of "heaven, earth, and humanity"? There are two kinds of dreams. One is operated within the body; this kind is formally the same as the dreaming of an ordinary person, but it is different in that you can control the contents of the dream. For example, you set a particular topic, an issue you want to think about, or a question for which you are seeking an answer; then you go to sleep, and the answer to the question will be there in a dream.

According to Master Wang Liping, when he goes out to give lectures or run training sessions, he never writes a draft of his speech; he doesn't even draw up notes. Every day he sits for several hours; when he goes to sleep at three or four in the morning, he first determines a topic, namely what he is going to say in his lecture the following day, and then he does dreaming. The contents of his lecture come to him in his dream. Usually he sleeps for two or three hours.

After he gets up, his mind is perfectly clear, and he can start lecturing at once. He can talk about what he has seen in his dream for hours on end, even for a whole day or more, without exhausting it all.

Another kind of dream is not really a dream, but is actually beyond what ordinary people call dreams. This is the yang spirit, the "external traveling" of the yang spirit.

For the yin spirit and the yang spirit to go through an aperture and travel outside is already a very high attainment. Quite a few people do not believe that we have a yin spirit and a yang spirit, much less that these spirits can travel outside. This is a very serious methodological issue, one that is very significant for humankind as well as the universe, and one that is well worth profound investigation.

How is this second type of dreaming done? Master Wang Liping explains that the wizards taught him to take vitality, energy, and spirit and separately make each the "director." The spirit may be in the vanguard, with vitality as the director and energy behind it as the propelling force. Vitality may also be in the vanguard, with spirit as the director and energy behind it as the propelling force. Then again, spirit may be in the vanguard with energy as the director and vitality behind it as the propelling force.

For example, when the yin spirit emerges, if spirit is the director, vitality envelops spirit, and energy envelops vitality, then form is manifested. If spirit is the director, energy envelops spirit, and vitality is outside, then form is not manifested. Manifestation of form is called the "art of reproducing the body," and can be accomplished even without dreaming. Nonmanifestation of form can also be accomplished when not dreaming. In dreaming, however, it is mostly the yin spirit that is projected, not the yang spirit.

When doing this second kind of dreaming, projecting the spirit to operate across time and space, dreams have both form and substance; there is nothing empty or illusory about them.

According to Master Wang Liping's practical experience, human dreams as we presently know of them can generally be divided into two major categories. One is spontaneous dreaming, which people cannot control. The other is controllable dreaming, which can be manipulated by people to become a useful tool. The first kind of dreaming is that of ordinary people; the second kind is the dreaming of those who have risen to the level of "heaven, earth, and humanity."

Ordinary dreams have been the subject of inquiry since ancient times. Discussion of dreams has become even more lively in the twentieth century, with the West producing a number of influential thinkers like Freud and Jung. China has also recently produced a major thinker in this area, Professor Liu Wenying, who spent years researching references to dreams in Chinese literature, presenting a "new Chinese dream theory." This new theory appears in his latest work, *Superstitions about Dreams and Investigations of Dreams—A Facet of Ancient Chinese Religion, Philosophy, and Science*. The following citations on ancient Chinese theories of dreams, excluding explanatory remarks, come from Professor Liu's work.

The first mention of classification of dreams in ancient Chinese literature is seen in the *Zhou Rites*, which gives a categorization proper to the people of the pre-Imperial era. In this classic of rites, dreams are divided into six types: "First is accurate dreams, second is startling dreams, third is thoughtful dreams, fourth is wakening dreams, fifth is joyful dreams, sixth is fearful dreams." This is how official dream interpreters of the Zhou dynasty classified dreams. Official dream interpreters used to determine the good or ill omen of the six types of dreams according to the sun, moon, stars, and planets. This type of classification is mainly based on the contents of the dream and the psychological state of the dreamer.

During the Eastern Han dynasty, Wang Fu classified dreams into ten categories in his *Treatise of a Hidden Man*: "Generally speaking, dreams may be direct, or they may be symbolic; they may involve vitality, thought, personality, feelings, or the times. In them may be reversal, sickness, or sexuality." Wang Fu says, "These ten elements are the general parameters of dream interpretation." He also classifies dreams into those that have validity and those without validity. However, he also says, "Extraordinary dreams mostly have a reason; few are meaningless."

From this we can see that people of ancient times viewed the study of dreams quite seriously and did not regard different sorts of dreams as the same. In particular, they took "extraordinary dreams" seriously, hoping to "read" from them some useful information about life or society.

The distinctions among types of dreams delineated in Buddhist scriptures is even more advanced. For example, the *Grove of Pearls in the Garden of the Teaching* cites an earlier source distinguishing dreams into four types: dreams resulting from a physical indisposition, prescient dreams, dreams connecting the supernatural with humanity, and dreams coming from thoughts. It would not be appropriate to try to figure these terms out literally; it is very difficult to say exactly what they mean. In the case of "dreams connecting the supernatural with humanity," however, this evidently refers to dreams in which there is sense and response between Heaven and humanity, having the nature of foresight.

The Buddhist *Treatise on Transcendent Wisdom* also classifies dreams into five kinds: "In cases of disharmony within the body, if there is fever, one will often dream of fire, seeing yellow or red. If there are chills, then one dreams of water, seeing white. If there is palsy, one dreams of flying, seeing black. Also things one has seen or heard appear in dreams if one thinks about them a lot. Celestial beings may also grant dreams to inform people of future events." The first three categories here correspond to physical indisposition; the fifth is the same as the aforementioned category of "dreams connecting the supernatural with humanity." The latter type involves communication with spirits in dreams, by which one may know the future; so these are considered nonordinary dreams.

Regarding nonordinary dreams, there is comparatively little relevant literature over the ages, and there is even less adequate research. This is one important reason why people have not made any great breakthroughs in their perception of dreams.

Master Wang Liping considers Taoist theory and practice dealing with dreaming to present the basic nature of the existence of the universe on a higher level.

Firstly, dreams are divided into passive dreams and active dreams. Passive dreams may be individual expressions of people's subconscious, or they may be stimulated by external influences; in any case, they are not the results of the subjective will of the dreamer.

External forces, in this domain, are forces that science has yet to deal with distinctly.

Then there are human vitality, energy, and spirit as found by Master

Wang Liping in his own practice. Cultivated and refined vitality, energy, and spirit can be controlled and employed deliberately. They can even be used to control the unrefined vitality, energy, and spirit of ordinary people in such a way as to create dreams. The passive dreaming has active dreaming within it; for the ordinary person it is passive; for the cultivated practitioner it is active.

Active dreams are also of two types. First is that just mentioned, where one uses one's own inner power to involve another person in a dream. The other is when one sets up a topic to dream on, then finds the answer to questions in dreaming.

Secondly, temporal and spatial relationships change tremendously in dreams. In the dreams of ordinary people, space seems to be shifting around, with all images as insubstantial as clouds, water, and air, shifting from one scene to the next, impossible to get a grip on. There is a sense of time, but there seems to be no accurate sense of time.

In contrast, in the active dreaming practiced by Master Wang Liping, the situation is quite different. The scenes in dreaming are so much like real scenery that it is hard to tell the difference. Some might say there is no difference, that the dreamer could be said to actually be there.

Here we touch upon a significant controversy: what is the fundamental nature of dreams? The modern Western dream researcher Freud believed that dreams are expressions of subconscious psychic activity. On the lower level of "persons, events, and things," this is an important achievement in dream theory. But Taoists consider it insufficient to remain on this level, and they seek to investigate more deeply. This leads us back to vitality, energy, and spirit.

In their basic nature, dreams are related not only to spirit, but also to energy and vitality. This is true not only of the dreaming of ordinary people, but also of the dreaming of cultivated people. That is because dreaming is a kind of mode of existence in which vitality, energy, and spirit operate in concert: its form of manifestation in time and space is extremely fluid and free; this is how Taoist practitioners use dreams to awaken mental power, to relate to other people, and to transcend the barriers of time and space.

Third, regarding the meaning of dreams, this is the question that has been investigated most over the ages. Taoists, maintaining their idea of the unity of Nature and humanity, explain the basic nature of dreams in terms of the balance or imbalance of vitality, energy, and spirit, recognizing profound meaning in both passive and active dreaming.

As with the hexagram images of the I Ching, so in dreams, when there is a thing there is an image, and when there is an image there is structure, and when there is structure there is reason. This reason is not obvious, but concealed. The mode of expression of dreaming is moving pictures, not abstract language; the pictures represent the relationship between humanity and the universe even more directly. Expression in abstract language is often limited, especially after words have been frozen by fixed cultural concepts, when this limitation is particularly evident. Since dream states, in contrast, are not bound by time and space, they have tremendous versatility and much more freedom of expression. Because people are bound by the restrictions of immediate actualities, particularly by culture, their vital spirit and physical body are often in suppressed states; dreams are one way of liberating them.

Finally, regarding the interpretation of dreams, Taoists regard the meaning of active dreams as self-evident, needing no interpretation. As far as passive dreams are concerned, where the meaning is clear there is no interpretation needed, while those whose meaning is concealed need to be interpreted based on their images. The tools for interpretation have to do with the sources of dreams—vitality, energy, and spirit—and the principles of yin and yang and the five elements. What is important here is to elevate thinking from the level of "persons, events, and things" to the higher level of "heaven, earth, and humanity" in order to understand.

The active or deliberate dreaming mentioned before in which dreams are induced in other people, traveling across time, is in reality no longer "dreaming" but actually "projection of spirit."

The basic condition for projection of spirit is to have a sufficiency of vitality, energy, and spirit, and to train them in such a way as to get them to operate freely. What the three wizards taught Wang Liping was methodology for training vitality, energy, and spirit.

The yin spirit is like an infant: first it is slowly nurtured and developed inside the abdomen; then it is transferred to the nirvana chamber in the brain. As the yin spirit develops, it must be carefully protected. It is particularly important to be careful about climactic changes and not work on projecting the spirit in bad weather. This is like the case of a baby, which can leave the mother's body after it is fully developed, but as a newborn is still helpless and needs to be nursed and carefully minded to enable it to grow up healthy. After it has grown strong, then it can be taught to walk, and gradually allowed to move around.

When projection of spirit is first practiced, it is only made to act in the immediate vicinity, and it is recalled very quickly. Later it is made to act out of doors, and returned along its original route. After long-term training, when the yin spirit has become powerful and can enter and exit freely, then it can be allowed to travel a bit further, and it can also be projected several times in a day. Because it is the traveling of vitality, energy, and spirit, after this capacity has been developed it travels as fast as the speed of thought itself. By different uses of vitality, energy, and spirit, it is possible to manifest form or not manifest form; herein lies the secret of the "art of reproducing the body."

After Wang Liping himself had learned to project spirit, he went through the same experience he had had after fasting, undergoing suspended animation, and dying. He experienced this several times, but now there were two differences from his death experience. One difference was that he didn't have the same extreme pain as he had had at the moment of death. The other difference was that now Wang Liping could not only hear others talk in his vision; he could also talk back to them. Before he could only hear and not talk.

The visions Wang Liping had on these occasions were so much like mythical fables that they would be incomprehensible from an ordinary point of view.

12

A Mountain Treasure Hunt

Traveling over mountains and rivers through the heat and cold, before they knew it the three wizards and their apprentice had been on the road for nearly two years.

The Wayfarer of the Infinite, Zhang Hodao, was now eighty-eight years old; the Wayfarer of Pure Serenity, Wang Jiaoming, was seventy-eight years old, and the Wayfarer of Pure Emptiness, Gu Jiaoyi, was seventy-six. Ordinary people who reach such advanced ages have mostly run out of fuel, and their movements have stiffened. A few people maintain their physical health, but most of them cannot take any stress; they need to take it easy to live out their years. How could they endure hunger, exposure, and the other miseries of wandering at large? But the old wizards had merged their bodies and minds with the Way. Although they were traveling around to avoid trouble, they were still innocent as children—bathing in the natural world like fish cavorting in water, they did not seem to suffer, but actually appeared to have fun and enjoy themselves.

Ragged clothes aside, their complexions had a ruddy glow, and their spirits were ever more extraordinary. If they were mixed in together with ordinary people, even the most unperceptive person might be able to spot them by their faces and spiritual atmosphere, might be able to see that these four were people who had attained the Way.

The four were together every day. The task of the three old wizards was clear; they had to bring their young apprentice along, transmitting practices and teachings to him step by step. Because of the exigencies of the time, Wang Liping was not able to learn the Way in the normal manner; he could only take whatever opportunities arose in the course of their wanderings to make progress in his practice.

When they were traveling in the wilds, if they managed to find some food they would eat their fill; if there was nothing to eat, no one would utter the word "hungry." All four of them were aware that whoever revealed such a thought would be "caught" by the others and told to go find something to eat. At first Wang Liping didn't understand that this was a kind of contest of wits practiced by his teachers. Being young and not hesitant to speak, he was always the one to blurt out that he was hungry. So time and again he was the one who wound up making long trips trying to figure out how to find something for everyone to eat.

Often it happened that there wasn't enough food to go around, and there was no way to divide it up evenly. At such times, they put the food in the center and sat around in a circle, each putting forth his own idea for the consideration of the others. If they could all agree, then they'd divide the food according to the method suggested. If their opinions differed and no one would defer, then they kept on deliberating.

Later Wang Liping understood that it was not hard to go along the road begging for alms; the issue was who was going to be trapped into doing such chores. So he had already been beaten in the contest of wits. Now Liping began to exercise his brain to think of a way to "catch" his teachers.

Once The Wayfarer of Pure Emptiness was "caught" by the others in an inattentive moment, so he went off to find something to eat. He had to go a very long way. When he finally came back with some dumplings made of grain and vegetables, everyone sat down and began to discuss how to divide them.

Stroking his whiskers, the grand master spoke up first: "I'm the oldest one here. I'm not as strong as you all, so I should have a little more."

Wang Liping spoke next: "I'm still growing, so I should get a little more. You old fellows should take care of a youngster!"

The Wayfarer of Pure Emptiness said with conviction, "I walked a long way. These dumplings were not easy to obtain. Based on the principle of reward according to achievement, I should first get half, and the rest of you can divide up what's left."

"What are you talking about?" The Wayfarer of Pure Serenity wouldn't back down. "I took care of your knapsack for you, so we both have some merit in this, not just you. Let's divide the food into three parts: Jiaoyi and I will take two, and the grand master and Liping can divide the remaining portion."

Seeing that none of the three mentioned the word "old," the old master saw it was no use to debate. So he backed off and suggested, "How about if we divide it equally among the four of us?"

"No, no!" The other three all disagreed. "An equal division is the least interesting, and there's no logic to it." But no one could think of a compelling reason to divide the food another way.

Seeing everyone at an impasse, The Wayfarer of the Infinite came up with a plan. "All right," he said, "don't argue anymore. I have a way that is fair. If you all agree, let's do it this way."

"Please tell us what your plan is."

"Put the dumplings here, and let's all eat them at once, so everyone has an equal chance. Isn't that the fairest way?"

"Fine!" Everyone agreed.

The grand master found a rock and put the dumplings on it. All at once the four of them stretched out their necks to grab the dumplings in their teeth, as if bobbing for apples. The dumplings were not very big, and all they managed to do was bump heads.

The Wayfarer of Pure Emptiness was the first to pull back. "It's no use," he said. "I can't take this! The rest of you go ahead!"

The grand master laughed and said, "Just as I figured! You care about the skin on your forehead. We care about the dumplings!" The three began to laugh, each wolfing down a dumpling. Finally the Wayfarer of Pure Serenity also withdrew, leaving only two. The grand master picked up the last dumpling and split it with Wang Liping.

Now the Wayfarer of Pure Serenity saw that the Wayfarer of Pure Emptiness had turned away, and realized there was some reason for it. Sneaking up behind him, he saw him eating a yam. Without a word, the Wayfarer of Pure Serenity snatched the yam, broke it in two, and shared it with the Wayfarer of Pure Emptiness.

A dumpling and a sweet potato isn't enough to satisfy a man, but the dividing of the food made mealtime plenty interesting. Out in the wilds, from time to time the laughter of the Taoists filtered through the mountain glades.

Thus time flowed by in a sort of simple, unaffected atmosphere unbound by any restrictions. The teachers and their apprentice spent their time hatching schemes and setting up traps for each other in a friendly way to stimulate their wits and develop their intuitions. Whenever any one of them got taken in, the others would have a great laugh.

These three old wizards were, after all, innocent children who never grew up. Chaotic as the times were, in the world of these four Taoists there was no suppression or constraint of any kind, no front or back, no right or left, no distinction between north, south, east, or west. Their minds were bright as the sun and clear as the moon, their thought like flying clouds and flowing water, unpolluted, transparently pure, thoroughly genuine, natural and spontaneous, lively and active, serene and at ease. The Way of Heaven, the Way of earth, and the Way of humanity merged into one.

This period of practicing the Way on the road was an unforgettable time for Wang Liping. This was the second peak of his life.

During this time, the three wizards taught Wang Liping the workings of the movements of the celestial bodies, the principles and patterns of social change, the techniques of fortune-telling, healing, physiognomy, divination, and physical culture, as well as the art of projecting the spirit and doing deliberate dreaming. While Wang Liping was in the process of practicing the Three Immortalist Exercises from the *Ultimate Teaching of the Spiritual Jewels*, the three wizards also transmitted their individual extraordinary skills to him.

Now Wang Liping finally understood what his life's task was. His duty was to live up to the wizards' teaching and fulfill his own mission honorably. He had already attained deep understanding of the principle of the unity of heaven, earth, and humanity and had attained the means to unite the human mind, the mind of heaven, and the mind of the Way. In the eyes of the old wizards, their protégé had gradually matured from childhood to adulthood.

The Taoist masters and their apprentice traveled along freely, talking and laughing, their hearts clear of the troubles of the mundane world, intoxicated with the merging of their bodies and minds into Nature.

One day they came to a broad roadway through the mountains. Sometimes a truck would go whizzing by them. The grand master lifted his foot and saw that his shoes were worn out. The Wayfarers of Pure Emptiness and Pure Serenity knew what was on his mind and silently indicated their readiness. Wang Liping watched a truck disappear ahead of them, then turned around just in time to see another one on the way.

As this truck approached, the three old wizards took a flying leap onto it. Startled, Wang Liping began to run after them at full speed; the truck was already several dozen yards away, and the old men were laughing at

Liping from the back of the truck.

Wang Liping realized that he had been outfoxed by the old men. In a burst of energy his inner power rose, and he ran over a hundred yards at lightning speed, finally leaping lightly onto the truck. The three wizards laughed and laughed.

The driver drove the truck at full speed, his whole attention up ahead, altogether unaware of what was going on in back. Suddenly hearing the sound of laughter, he thought it very strange. Not many vehicles took this route through the mountains, and there were few travelers. The driver didn't see anyone. Where did the laughter come from? It seemed close by. Could there be someone on the truck? But he had no assistants. How could there be voices? Looking into the rear-view mirror, he saw there were indeed people on the truck, and they were old men, too—how very, very strange! The driver stopped the truck, intending to find out who they were. Stepping out of the cab and into the back of the truck, the driver was astonished to find no sign of anyone at all.

Just as he was wondering what in the world was going on, the driver suddenly heard someone say, "Thank you, sir, for letting us hitch a ride." Turning around, the driver saw four men standing in front of the truck, three of them old and one young, joining their palms in a gesture of gratitude. The driver wanted to question them and find out who they were, but before he knew it they had already taken off up the mountainside.

In fact, the four Taoists had used their power of invisibility when they noticed the truck stopping; they got off, so the driver naturally didn't see them.

The wizards and their apprentice continued on their way until they came to the foothills of Flower Mountain. They saw the mountain was extraordinarily huge, with an unusual atmosphere, like a giant standing with his head in the skies, with an air of majesty and grandeur.

Flower Mountain has always been known for its steep precipices. There are five peaks on the mountain: the eastern peak is called Morning Sun, the western peak is called Lotus Blossom, the southern peak is called Alighting Goose, the northern peak is called Five Clouds, and the central peak is called Jade Woman. The five peaks are a splendid sight. The mountain peaks stand like sheer walls, sharp as knives, extremely difficult to climb. There is a famous poem about this mountain that goes,

Only the sky is above it;
no other mountain can match:
raise your head, and the red sun's near;
turn around, and the clouds seem low.

Another special feature of Flower Mountain is its location, standing in the middle of the great dividing line between eastern and western China, which form two natural economic zones.

Taoists appreciate all the unique characteristics of Flower Mountain. They have not only observed the lay of the mountain, but they have also observed what accumulates and circulates here, namely energy in the form of wind.

Over the ages, Flower Mountain has been a place where Taoists cultivate energy, where they cultivate the wind. When Wang Liping and his teachers journeyed to Flower Mountain, this was their main objective.

The four Taoists followed a steep mountain trail upward. The first wave of the "Great Cultural Revolution" had already been through, and the traces left by the "Horizontal Broom" of the "Red Guard" were still clearly evident. There were very few pilgrims there, and quite a few famous sites were in ruins, weeds covering the broken tiles and scattered bricks. Liping's teachers, who had been to the mountain before more than once, were shocked by what they now saw.

The Taoist masters and their disciple climbed up the mountain by the steepest and most dangerous route. Here the stone stairway is nearly vertical, with iron chains for safety, and it is so narrow that it can fit only one person at a time. The steps are so steep that the person below can see the soles of the feet of the person ahead. If you look down, the feeling is like being on a ladder suspended in the sky; you cannot help being frightened.

Halfway up the mountainside, one of the mentors had Wang Liping stop and gaze at a number of cave openings barely discernible on a distant peak. The mentor explained that this was where Hao Datong, one of the Seven Real People of the North, the Taoist Master of Eternal Reality, had cultivated realization and attained the Way.

This Taoist had journeyed to Flower Mountain and dug out a cave in a cliff wall in which to do his practices. Once the cave was completed, however, another Taoist came to him with a cushion and said he had no place to sit and wanted to borrow the cave. So the one who had dug the cave let the other have it, and went off to dig another cave for himself.

Now when the second cave was done, again another Taoist came asking to borrow it. The man who had dug the cave again let the other have it, and again went off to dig yet another cave for his own use.

Believe it or not, the same thing happened when the third cave was finished, and the fourth, fifth, and sixth caves. Day in and day out, month after month, year after year, Hao Datong kept digging caves in the cliff to meditate, but every time he finished one cave, someone else would come and ask to be allowed to use it. By the time he had finished digging the seventy-second cave, this man, later known as the Master of Eternal Reality, had finally attained the Way and accomplished realization.

The four travelers came to a halt by a ruined pavilion. The grand master told Wang Liping that this was called "Chess Pavilion" and was the site of a famous chess match between Chen Bo and the first emperor of the Song dynasty a thousand years ago. The emperor bet two prefectures on the match, hoping to beat Chen Bo. As it turned out, the emperor lost. Chen Bo had no wish to become an official, so he asked the emperor to eliminate the burden of taxes from the peasants of these two prefectures. The emperor gladly acceded to his request. As for Chen Bo, he remained on Flower Mountain practicing Taoism; he is especially famous for his mastery of sleeping meditation.

The plank path of Flower Mountain is the most frightening place of all. Halfway up a sheer cliff, someone dug a series of small holes, into which were inserted wood bars; on top of the bars were then placed narrow wooden planks. This is the plank path of Flower Mountain. Seen from a distance, the plank path looks like a thin belt stretched across the middle of a sheer cliff wall. Looking upward from this plank path, all you see are green cliffs overhanging, blocking the sky, making you gasp for breath.

Looking downward is even more terrifying. Below, misty clouds roil thick and thin beneath your feet, rising and falling, making you feel as if you were in a billowing sea. If you were to lose your footing and fall, you would plunge into the abyss to a certain death. Everyone trembles with fright when they get here.

When Wang Liping and his teachers arrived at Flower Mountain, it was late spring, when winds gather around Flower Mountain from several directions and pass through there. So it was a good time for refining energy and cultivating the wind.

Near evening, before the four Taoists had reached the plank path, they heard the mountain winds whistling in their ears and felt wave after wave of cold air in their faces. When they climbed an enormous boulder right in the wind corridor, a tremendous gale blew, sending sand and pebbles flying. In the ravines there seemed to be innumerable dragons coiling and swirling and dancing about. The sand and stones hurled by the whirlwind into the cliff faces made such a noise that, combined with the whistling of the wind, an enormous wave of sound thundered in the air.

It was late spring, and the wildflowers of the southern foothills were already in full bloom, and the trees were clad in emerald. Beyond the northern ridge, however, the plants and trees were just starting to return to green again, with new buds slowly unfurling. The northern ridge acts like a natural barrier stopping the warm moist air from the south, so the energy of spring lingers here and has a hard time crossing to the north. Since Flower Mountain is right at the tail of two great mountain chains, it forms a natural passageway, through which a vast stream of warm wet air steams upward to nourish the life of the northern regions with moisture.

The sky has five movements, six energies, and eight winds. The energy of spring causes plants and trees to grow; and wood is associated with wind. The south is associated with fire, and the air from the south is full of fiery energy; its fiery nature must be subdued, making it warm but not burning, containing yin within yang. A warm, moist air current from the south swirls around within the five peaks of Flower Mountain, losing much of its burning heat, so that it has become clear and cool by the time it has left the mountain; with moisture in its warmth, it helps everything grow and develop.

The four Taoists climbed the plank path with the mountain wind bearing down on them from above, clinging tightly to the cliff face as they made their way along. Darkness was already falling; the crescent moon hung in the sky. All around were pitch black mountain peaks: below was an abyss. The wind hitting the cliff wall whirled around and ricocheted, nearly blowing the travelers off the plank walk. From time to time a cold wind also rose from below, nearly lifting them into the air.

The grand master was in the lead: it seemed as if he were floating in the air. Nimble as a mountain lion, he moved from one place to another in a flash. As for Wang Liping, for the first time he got an experience of the rhythms of the winds on Flower Mountain, and the need to resolve the changing forces of the winds coming from all directions to achieve equilibrium. The two mentors, for their part, walked along the plank pathway as if they were walking on even ground.

Having made their way across the plank path, the four came to a level spot. Here the power of the wind suddenly diminished; there was only a gentle breeze, relaxing and pleasant. The grand master said that they should sit here. The mentors then taught Wang Liping the breathing and energy induction methods needed to sit in this place. Doing as they instructed, Wang Liping suddenly felt it was very different from his former experience in sitting; here was a whole new heaven and earth.

The mentors also taught Wang Liping how to cultivate the winds on Flower Mountain, how to call the wind, transmitting esoteric methods and secret teachings to him. Finally the grand master also taught Liping an esoteric method for sitting atop the main peak of Flower Mountain and watching the changes of the winds and clouds all over the land.

The south peak, Alighting Goose, is the main peak of Flower Mountain. By the time the three Taoist masters and their apprentice had scaled this peak, it was already late at night, the stars twinkling brightly, the moonlight silently splashing the mountain ranges. The sky was crystal clear, without a single cloud. The mountain peaks below were like a layer of light silk. Clusters of trees were enveloped in a dusky glow, appearing increasingly vague and diffuse the further away they were. At the summit of this peak is a spring-fed pond, called the Taishang Spring. The surface of the water is smooth as a mirror. The stars and moon penetrate the depths of the pond.

The three wizards and their apprentice sat around the pond, merging into oneness with the stars and the moon, the mountains and rivers, the plants and trees, the pure, clear spring. The four rapidly expanded the "field" of the universe within their own bodies, gradually covering the whole of Flower Mountain.

In a trance, Wang Liping felt the peaks gradually disappear before his eyes. In front of him was a solid expanse of shining, bright water, from which there emerged a piece of dry ground. Now he seemed to be floating way up high in the sky. Looking down, he saw bodies of water everywhere, of different shapes and sizes. Between the bodies of water were thick masses, some light, some dark, giving off different colored glows—there were gold and yellow ones, grey and white ones, crimson ones, and multicolored ones. Some places resembled deep, dark caverns.

Now another scene unfolded, like a level plain below the mountain, not very clear, but vaguely discernible. It was an ancient battlefield. On one side was a square battle formation slowly moving forward with a powerful, vigorous air. In the battle lines there appeared to be banners flapping, war horses neighing, swords flashing. On the other side was a huge army roiling like an ocean tide, not wearing regular uniforms, but wielding sticks and hoes, in a state of great agitation, with a tragic, pathetic air about it.

When the two forces joined in battle, the men and horses in front collapsed one after another, and more men and horses emerged from behind. Once the battle had begun, the square formation lost its integrity; while the motley ocean tide of the other side roared in unstoppably, pressing the enemy hard. Dust filled the air so that it was no longer possible to see the action clearly. Liping could only hear the shouting of men and the crying of horses, the clanging of swords and spears clashing. Before long the square formation crumbled, and the oceanic force rolled over it.

Momentarily the countless soldiers and horses seemed to be battling in the air; some of them finally turned upside down and floated past like fleeting shadows, flitting past, changing endlessly. Then when a clear breeze blew through, all of these scenes and images quickly dissolved and dispersed.

From the dark vagueness another scene appeared. The mountains were green, the rivers gleaming; the birds were chattering, the flowers fragrant. In the dappled light of a bamboo grove, by the side of a gurgling spring, there appeared a corner of a roof, with upturned eaves and decorative beams. A dark smoke with a penetrating smell was rising into the air. On the mountainside were several enormous old wisterias of haunting beauty, intricately knotted and twisted. Under the wisterias lay a man of distinguished aspect, dressed in an ancient style, with long unkempt hair, sound asleep with a fan in hand: he had not wakened in a thousand years.

About two hours later, the four Taoists all stopped this exercise. Now all there was to be seen were the bright stars in the clear sky, with the natural pond there as before, smooth and clear as a mirror.

Wang Liping was still absorbed in the scenes he had just witnessed; an indescribable feeling welled up within him.

The grand master asked him, "Did you see the old master Chen Bo?" Wang Liping replied, "Was he the sleeping wizard under the wisterias?"

The grand master smiled and said nothing. Liping understood what he meant. Hm! he thought to himself.

Some people might explain the foregoing phenomenon hypothetically in the following terms. Accepting that the magnetic field of Earth and the ionosphere are capable, under certain special conditions, of recording events occurring in society at corresponding times; then two conclusions follow. First, when the Earth's magnetic field and ionosphere are in normal states, events will not be recorded, so this results in significant "lacunas" in the record. Second, the special conditions of the Earth's magnetic field and ionosphere must coincide precisely with events spatially, or else they cannot make a recording.

This hypothesis might explain certain extraordinary phenomena, but it cannot explain the various phenomena produced by advanced Taoists when they cultivate their practices, how they can view events of other times and places when the Earth's magnetic field and ionosphere are in a normal condition.

It would seem that this theory needs further development; it needs a new view of time and space, investigating deeper levels of material existence.

Let us analyze the memory function of the brain. Whatever we experience through our senses leaves a memory in our brain. This memory may be deep or shallow, and it may remain in the brain for a longer or shorter period of time. Many personal experiences eventually fade into oblivion. The brain remembers and also forgets; this opposition shows that the brain power of ordinary people is limited and can only retain a certain amount of memory. However, modern brain research has found that the human brain has over ten billion neurons; if all of them were used to store information, it would be possible to record many things indeed. Many scientists say that 90 percent of the human brain is not put to use; so there are glorious prospects for the development of human intelligence.

Information left in the brain by past events may seem to be lost or forgotten, but really it is not. The information lies silently hidden in the brain. If it is not retrieved, or if there is no means of retrieval, this information cannot be made conscious.

Taoist inner work is applied to vitality, energy, and spirit. When the work is accomplished, then it is possible to retrieve information hidden in the subconscious. As seen earlier, when Wang Liping practiced recollection back to infancy, he was able to recall scenes from childhood. And when he practiced fasting, especially while in suspended animation and after dying, scenes of his whole life reappeared within a very short span of time. At this point forgetfulness no longer existed; his memory had reached an unprecedented level of activity.

This is looking at the storage, recollection, and loss of information only in terms of the microcosm of the human brain. What if we observe the whole universe in terms of the unity of Nature and humanity? The same conditions will pertain. When one mode of existence in the universe changes into another mode, no matter what kind of change it is, it must leave some information, depositing this information in a sort of information repository. Furthermore, the transition from a substantial form to an information deposit is also a kind of change. The "information repository" certainly does exist; we cannot yet say for sure, but it may be that this is also true of all natural phenomena, including mountains, rivers, and human beings. Where this information exists is inaccessible to the five senses of the ordinary person, but people who are trained and refined are able to retrieve it. This is also a sort of hypothesis, but this hypothesis has the support of practical experience in Taoist training, so it is the most hopeful source of a whole new theoretical system.

Through systematic training in the exacting methods of Taoism, Wang Liping had now risen to a new level, at which the universe he saw, felt, and conceived was very different from that of ordinary people. When ordinary people come to a new location, they may make superficial observations of the surroundings. Most will do no more than a routine scientific survey of the flora and fauna, the climate, the characteristics of the waters, and the quality of the soil, to determine whether or not the location is suitable for human habitation, work, study, pleasure, construction, industry, mining, and so on. Wang Liping, in contrast, would go even deeper, using his body to "sense" the sky above and the earth below, apprehending even subtler elements to determine the influence of this place on the human body and its activity, only then finally deciding what this place is suitable for doing and what it is not suitable for.

This is the difference between those who have risen to the level of "heaven, earth, and humanity" and those who remain on the level of "persons, events, and things."

Not long after the Taoist masters and their apprentice stopped their exercise atop the south peak of Flower Mountain, the predawn light gradually delineated the outlines of the distant mountains and nearby woods. The mountains were so graceful and peaceful. Where the four stood on the ridge peak, they didn't feel the slightest trace of wind.

In this magnificent setting, surrounded by this scenery, the Wayfarer of the Infinite couldn't help recalling a poem from the Song dynasty:

> *Cold wind shook the blue darkness all night.*
> *When the wind stopped, fine snow sprinkled,*
> *giving the appearance of the heaven of Jade Purity:*
> *in the white clear light I recite*
> *the Classic of the Yellow Court.*

When the four Taoists came to the central peak of Flower Mountain, called Jade Woman, they also took the time to sit there before the sun rose, quietly examining the subtle changes in the four surrounding peaks.

Wang Liping steadied his spirit and listened clearly. He seemed to hear the mountain breathing, pulsating very, very subtly. All around was utter quiet, yet there was a silent operation and evolution going on without cease. Heaven and earth were so closely joined, man and mountain were so thoroughly merged, everything in the universe was carrying on a kind of mystical communion in the midst of this peace, engaging in wordless conversation, the beautiful and the ugly, the good and the bad, coming into being all at once. As he was sensing this, apprehending it, grasping it, Wang Liping was to see, within this peace and quiet, changes dramatic enough to overturn heaven and earth.

On the peaks all around Liping saw a thin mountain vapor like clouds, like fog, like smoke, like a glow, moving slowly, floating upward. As this vapor rose, it gave a clear, light feeling of lucidity and freshness. Then, as it rose higher, it gradually became somewhat opaque and unclear, turning dark and dense. As it rose yet higher, beyond the mountain heights, the vapor, now denser and darker, was suddenly tinted with dark red, blue, and violet lights. There wasn't the slightest breath of wind, but this mass of mist enshrouding the mountaintop, now light, now dark, seemed to be chased by something, leaping and bounding, clustering and massing, wrapping and enveloping, roiling and surging, whirling and curling, stretching and expanding, a wild chaos of countless forms.

Wang Liping also sensed in his heart a slight tremor of a kind of chilling anxiety.

The Wayfarer of the Infinite had been watching for a long time; he closed his eyes, looking somewhat troubled.

"The four forms are out of harmony. The atmosphere of the mountain is inauspicious. The chaos reigning all over the land will hardly settle down for some time," said the Wayfarer of Pure Emptiness, by way of explanation.

The Wayfarer of Pure Serenity asked Wang Liping, "Did you get a reading?"

Knowing his mentor's meaning, Liping nodded.

At that moment, the peace and silence of early dawn was broken by a long whistle. A train thundered by the foot of the mountain, billowing smoke. This night on Flower Mountain had come to a conclusion.

As crimson light appeared on the eastern horizon, everything became clearly visible. An ocean of clouds churned, an endless vastness; the blood red orb of the sun rose to the juncture of the sky and the clouds, conveying a sense of tragic beauty.

The famous old Tong Pass was in view; the endless Yellow River made a sharp turn to the east. Even the Yellow River could not wash away the troubles of the world. The strategic Tong Pass, which has seen so much grief and distress, still stood there by its side.

After seeing the wind of the night before and the vapors of the morning, now facing these mountains and waters, in these circumstances, in the midst of this scenery, the Wayfarer of the Infinite could not help recalling another ancient poem, lamenting the instability of human society and the ups and downs of worldly affairs:

> *The peaks are densely clustered,*
> *the billowing waves are roaring;*
> *mountain and river surround*
> *the route through the Pass of Tong.*
> *Gazing toward the Western Capital,*
> *my thoughts hesitate;*
> *heartrending the place*

where armies came through;
myriad palace rooms
have all turned to earth.
When the state rises,
the peasants suffer;
when the state falls,
the peasants suffer.

When the master had finished reciting this verse, the travelers all headed down the mountain.

The Taoist masters and their apprentice headed along the northern foothills of the Qin mountain range fanning out to the west, avoiding populous places and only traveling on mountain roads, occasionally passing by a mountain village. The villagers they saw were all simple and unaffected, with something of an air of ancient times remaining about them.

Revisiting this area, the Wayfarer of the Infinite couldn't help thinking of ancient times when their spiritual ancestor Changchun cultivated reality and transmitted the Way in this region.

Before many days had passed, the Taoist masters and their apprentice had reached the top of Mount Zhongnan. Zhongnan is also called South Mountain, and it is also referred to as Earth Lump Mountain. In ancient times it was given several different names. One of the main peaks of the Qin range, for Taoists it is one of the so-called Rich Earths they seek for special practices. According to Changchun's book, *Journey to the West*, the mountain begins in Khotan and ends in China, so it is called Zhongnan, "Ending the South." There are beautiful sites there, such as the Gold Flower Cavern and Jade Spring Cavern, Sun and Moon Crags, and so on. Masters Zhongli, Lu Dongbin, Liu Haizhan, and Wang Chongyang all practiced the Way here.

Proceeding farther west from Mount Zhongnan, one comes to Tower Observatory in Zhouzhi prefecture, which is one of the famous sites of Taoism. According to tradition, this was the abode of the Keeper of the Pass in the reign of King Kang of the ancient Zhou dynasty. He built a tower from which he observed the stars and atmospheric phenomena, so it came to be called the Tower Observatory. This was the first Taoist cloister in history; over the ages, it has been reroofed and rebuilt repeatedly.

According to the classic *Historical Records*, "Lao-tzu cultivated the

Way and its virtues, learning to conceal himself and be free of labels and names. After living in Zhou for a long time and seeing the deterioration of the Zhou dynasty, he eventually left. When he reached the pass, the Keeper of the Pass said, 'Since you are going to disappear, please write me a book.' So Lao-tzu wrote a book consisting of two sections, telling of the Way and its virtues in somewhat more than five thousand characters. Then he left; no one knows where he ended up." So according to tradition it was here at Tower Observatory that Lao-tzu, the ancestor of Taoism, expounded and wrote the Tao Te Ching, which has been hailed as the King of Classics.

The Tao Te Ching, also called the Lao-tzu, is composed of two sections, the first called "The Course of the Way," the second called "The Course of Virtue." The whole book is divided into eighty-one chapters.

The wording of the Lao-tzu is quintessentially simple, while the principles it elucidates are as vast and profound as can be. Historical documents show that this book already circulated widely before the Qin dynasty (247–206 B.C.E.); many famous thinkers were well versed in this text and absorbed its ideas. Later on, the influence of Lao-tzu's book expanded and deepened even further; politicians, military scientists, philosophers, natural scientists, writers, and physicians all knew about Lao-tzu and his book, and so did everyone else, from the emperors and kings down to the peasants. All literate people read it and understood that every word and every phrase contains deep principles; even illiterate people draw nutrition from the common proverbs originating in the Lao-tzu, intuitively realizing the principles of natural creation and evolution, thus understanding the basis of what it means to be human.

Lao-tzu has melted into the very blood of the Chinese culture, rooting in the hearts of the Chinese people. The modern thinker Lu Hsun said, "The roots of China are wholly in Taoism."

There is also someone named Zhang Musheng who wrote a new analysis of Lao-tzu published in 1946; in his own preface to a 1988 reprint, he wrote, "China has two books most worthy of attention: one is the Confucian *Analects*, the other is the Taoist Lao-tzu. These two books should be read by every literate individual; one need not be a specialist to study them. This is because the Confucian *Analects* discusses ordinary principles of social life and human affairs, while the Lao-tzu discusses the highest principles thereof. One deals with the way things are, the other deals with why things are the way they are. As members of society, when we deal with tasks like self-cultivation, family structure, orderly government, and world peace, we need to know not only how things are but also why they are as they are; only then can we consider ourselves lucid and accomplished. The *Analects* of Confucius and the Tao Te Ching of Lao-tzu have these two major functions; that is why we have to read them."

The reason Taoists revere the Lao-tzu is that it expounds the highest principles of the evolution of the universe, the development of the individual, and the ordering of society.

During the era of the Warring States, someone named the Man on the River wrote the first commentary on the Lao-tzu; emphasizing self-cultivation and physical health, this commentary came to be a classic on Taoist life hygiene.

Let us quote some passages from the Lao-tzu:

"The Way can be expressed, but not as a fixed path; terminology can be designated, but not as fixed labels. Nonbeing is called the beginning of heaven and earth; being is called the mother of all things. Therefore constant nonbeing is used to observe the subtle, while constant being is used to observe that which comes about. These two come from the same source but have different names. Both are called mysteries. The mystery of mysteries of the gateway of subtleties."

"The Way is at the profoundest depths of all things."

"The Way produces one, one produces two, two produce three, three produce all things. All beings bear the negative and embrace the positive, with a mellowing energy for harmony."

"The sky is clear by virtue of unity, the earth is stable by virtue of unity, spirits are effective by virtue of unity, valleys are full by virtue of unity, all beings are alive by virtue of unity; rulers are right for the world if they attain unity."

"Humanity follows earth, earth follows heaven, heaven follows the Way, the Way follows Nature."

"The open spirit undying is called the mysterious female. The gateway of the mysterious female is called the root of heaven and earth. Continuously on the brink of existence, its use is not strained."

"The Way of heaven wins skillfully without contest, responds skillfully without words, and comes spontaneously without being called."

"Return is the movement of the Way, pliability is the function of the Way.

"All things in the world are born from being, being is born from nonbeing. Those who know others are intelligent, those who know themselves are enlightened. Those who overcome others are powerful, those who overcome themselves are strong."

"Great completion seems lacking; its function does not deteriorate. Great fullness seems empty; its function is inexhaustible. Great directness seems constrained, great skill seems inept, great eloquence seems inarticulate. Activity overcomes cold, stillness overcomes heat. Clear calm is a rectifier of the world." Knowing without presumption of knowledge is best; presuming to know without knowledge is sick. Only by regarding sickness as sickness is it possible not to be sick.

"Trustworthy words are not prettified, prettified words are not trusted. The good are not argumentative, the argumentative are not good. The knowing do not generalize, generalists are not knowers."

"The reason that rivers and oceans are kings of all valleys is because they can lower themselves to them; so they are able to be kings of all valleys. Therefore, if you want to be above people you must lower yourself to them in your speech; if you want to lead people, you must put yourself after them."

"The softest thing in the world drives the hardest thing in the world." Govern a large country as you would cook a small fish.

"A wise leader has no fixed attitudes but is mindful of the wishes of the people."

"Unruliness in a populace is due to ulterior motives on the part of their leaders."

"If you want to contain something, you must first let it expand. If you want to weaken something, you must first let it grow strong. When you want to get rid of something, you must first let it be promoted. When you want to take something away, you must first concede it. This is called subtle enlightenment. Softness overcomes the hard, yielding overcomes the strong. Fish should not be taken from the deep, the effective tools of a nation should not be shown to others."

"Hold fast to universal images, and the world goes on; it goes on without harm, in great security and peace."

Wang Liping and his three teachers paid respects to the memorial tablet of the ancient master Lao-tzu inside the Taoist observatory and recited the Tao Te Ching on the traditional site of its first declamation.

Farther in, below a mountain cliff, is a deep and wide stone cavern. The grand master told Wang Liping that this was the cavern of Ancestor Lu Dongbin. Lu Dongbin, whose given name was Yan, is titled Master of Pure Yang. He is one of the Eight Immortals of folk tradition. When he was young, he studied Confucianism and Moism. Failing to obtain a master's degree in the civil service examination, he finally took to wandering. Meeting Master Zhongli in Changan, after being tested ten times he was taught life-prolonging arts. Later he also met the Realized Master of Bitter Bamboo, who transmitted to him the method of combining solar and lunar energies. After a long time he finally traveled to Mount Zhongnan, where he met Master Zhongli a second time and learned the alchemy of the gold liquid. He finally attained the Way when he was fifty years old. When he was over a hundred years old he still had a youthful appearance and an agile walk.

In this mountain cavern at the Tower Observatory, Ancestor Lu plunged his mind into practice of the Way, completing his spirit and refining his energy, seeking understanding of hidden patterns, finally attaining a body of pure positive energy. He originated many new methods of practical cultivation. Some of these practices are part of the esoteric tradition of the Dragon Gate sect; quite a few others have not been transmitted. Ancestor Lu compiled the principles in books, which he concealed in four special places.

Ancestor Lu had met Master Huolong, who transmitted to him a sword art known as "Escape into Heaven." Ancestor Lu reformed the art of the sword into "cutting through psychological afflictions, cutting through sensual desire, and cutting through greed and anger." He also changed material alchemy into inner work; he considered the path to attainment of the Way to be compassionate liberation of society. He once said, "If people can be loyal to the nation, respectful at home, faithful to friends, humane to subordinates, honest with themselves, free from hypocrisy, effectively altruistic, and naturally and unassuming as they conceal their virtues, then other people will love them, ghosts and spirits will respect them. At this moment, they are the same as I am; even if they do not meet me, they still see me."

The method of natural energy circulation, which forms an important part of the Spiritual Jewel inner arts of developing mental capacities, secret teachings of Complete Reality Taoism, was invented by Ancestor Lu when he journeyed to Mount Zhongnan.

In cultivating the natural energy circulation method, the practitioner is required to join the mind, spirit, energy, attention, and vitality intimately, and carry out refinement of the universe within one's own body in the process of regulated movement. When practicing this exercise, the practitioner is maintaining a relaxed, calm, natural walking posture; attention and thought, mind and spirit, join into one. The self is a universe; as the universe goes through myriad changes, all beings invariably act, their action producing effect. As the body moves, the attention gathers and releases, seeking stillness in movement, producing spirit in stillness, mind and spirit conjoining, breath and attention together, ethereal and fluid.

The training technique of the "natural energy circulation method" is different from the way ordinary people take a walk. When ordinary people walk, they do not focus their attention; mind and spirit are not focused on the body, so mind, spirit, attention, breath, and movement are not combined. Thus no inner "work" is done; the mind scatters, the spirit flies, and energy is expended uselessly.

There is a common saying, "Walk a hundred steps after meals, and you will live ninety-nine years." But it is possible to achieve this result only if the mind is relaxed, almost as if one were meditating, and the practice is continued regularly for a long time.

The "natural energy circulation method" emphasizes intimate coordination of physical movement, mind, spirit, energy, and vitality. It emphasizes merging of the microcosm with the macrocosm, arrives at higher results through regulated, graded exercises.

Those who are experienced in the practice of the natural energy circulation are able to expand or contract the microcosmic "field" of their bodies as well as their auras, joining them with the field of the natural universe and the auras of all beings, interacting with them in all sorts of ways, with mind, spirit, attention, breath, and movement working together, the universe of the human body and the universe of the celestial bodies becoming merged into one.

Having gone through this training, a practitioner can absorb and project ethereal substances from all beings in order to diagnose and cure illness in others, to transmit messages and give guidance, to spread energy into specific arrays, to operate refined energy to foster effects in others, bringing them along in inner work.

People who work with their brains usually are not in command of their own spirit or will, vitality or body. Eventually their vitality dissipates, their energy deteriorates, and their spirit wanes away. By means of the method of natural energy circulation, it is possible to "unite mind and spirit, enlivening the spirit and returning spirituality to the mind. When the mind is released, spirit is there, and when the spirit is there, the mind resorts to it. When vitality is full, the spirit thrives; when the spirit thrives, energy returns to it." Thus one can attain the aims of tuning the breathing and nurturing the spirit, strengthening the brain and increasing intelligence, eliminating illness and preserving health, extending one's years and increasing the span of life.

The natural energy circulation method is divided into three vehicles and nine methods, sometimes called three parts and nine practices.

The first part consists of practices to eliminate illness and extend life, to attain health and ease. It is subdivided into three practices: breathing combined with walking, holding the breath while walking, and absorbing substance while walking.

The second part consists of practices to realize the return of all things to the root and the immortality of the universe. It is subdivided into three practices: expelling substances while walking, spreading energy while walking, and arraying energy while walking.

The third part consists of practice to realize mastery of adaptation, both conventional and unconventional, and assimilation of Nature and humanity. It is subdivided into three practices: closing and opening energy channels while walking, ethereal transmission while walking, and becoming invisible while walking.

This too is a course of development progressing from lower to higher states, encompassing the three levels of "heaven, earth, and humanity."

Birth and death, death and birth, returning to eternity, has been the main subject of Taoist investigations over the ages.

As an individual, there is no way to choose or control one's birth, and there is obviously nothing one can do to escape one's inevitable death. In the interval between birth and death, which is "life," it seems that the brain is clear and alert and has some sort of autonomy. In reality, however, it is subject to control by numerous forces other than itself; in the face of those forces, one is after all slight, weak, powerless, and unable to master one's own fate.

Humanity exists between heaven and earth, life exists between birth and death. Birth and death are the two extremes of human life; people experience most and know most about life; whereas birth and death, the two extremes of life, are experienced for the briefest time and are the least known.

Taoists spend equal effort investigating birth, life, and death. The depth and breadth of their investigations, furthermore, are inconceivable to ordinary people.

Why are people born? Why is a particular self born at a particular time and place? What kind of changes occur at the moment of birth, and what kind of influences do they have on subsequent life?

Why do people die? What does the moment of death feel like? What sort of changes take place? Do people exist in some form after death? Is death the final end of the individual?

This is birth and death.

After people die, can they return to life? If people have been dead for a short while, it may be possible to revive them. But what if the period of death stretches to a year or two, or a decade or two—then is it possible to come back to life? After people die and their original physical body no longer exists, can they return to life in another form? Are such things possible?

This is death and birth.

Is it possible for people not to die? Or if we have to die, is it possible to live a little longer? People ordinarily consider this possible. But to transcend the limits of a single time frame, say, for example, one, two, or three centuries, or even longer, is this possible? Is a life beyond time and space possible?

This is birth, death, and life.

This is the problem in the lower three realms. So then from the higher perspective of the middle three realms, where does humankind come from? Is humankind going to perish? Where is the future destination of humankind? Going even higher, what about the birth and death of the earth and the solar system? And what about the birth and death of the universe?

When we extend these questions a step further, there is no way to accept them within the domain of ordinary human knowledge; so they are considered nonsensical.

Taoists, however, do not accept these constraints; not only do they come up with even deeper questions; they even use their own bodies as objects of experimentation to see whether such possibilities exist.

Taoists firmly believe that the philosophical basis of Taoism, the unity of Nature and humanity, is not mistaken. They believe that the universal truths and the ways to perceiving these truths presented by the Lao-tzu and the I Ching are not mistaken.

This has given Taoists great wisdom and courage.

No matter how society may develop, from the human point of view heaven and earth are still heaven and earth; the sun and moon are still the sun and moon; eternity exists within change. Birth is like an eternal mystery, which bothers us and also bothered the people of old as well. Death is like an ungraspable ghost, which haunts us and also haunted the people of old.

Nowadays we use all sorts of instruments to study the questions of birth and death. Taoists, in contrast, use the human body to study the human body, and use natural methods to study Nature. Which of these two ways of researching questions is closer to the nature of the human body and the universe?

We cannot now return to the womb and reexperience birth. Everyone, however, has experienced the sensations of being a fetus to being an infant; these sensations surely must have been deposited in the memory, but have unaccountably been forgotten. These memories might be revived if a method of doing so could be found. Is it possible? Taoists have made their own inquiry into this question, and they have their own answer.

As for death, to know that it will inevitably occur and to actually experience it are two different things. The only way to get the experience is to die.

This is what Lu Dongbin did; he performed a grandiose, fearless test of death.

Death opened up the great truths of the universe to him. Death bestowed great wisdom on him.

In order to grasp the process of cultivation in which by going through death one sees clearly into the universe and transforms it so that it can be controlled, Lu Dongbin led his disciples along the road of search into the mysteries of the universe and human life, carrying out tragically heroic experiments along the way. Out of three thousand disciples, eight hundred died; so the cost was very great. The results they obtained, however, were extremely valuable; the practical methods, having been put in order, have been transmitted secretly without interruption for eleven hundred years by teachers within the Dragon Gate school of Complete Reality Taoism.

Those eight hundred precursors are now nameless—there is no way to find out who they were. But their successors never forgot their work.

Even now, however, the Dragon Gate school has not completely resolved the question of dying and reviving. When Wang Liping practiced fasting and died, the grand master and his mentors were not in complete control of whether or not he would live through it.

Wang Liping has no hesitation about this at all; he accepted questioning calmly. He continues to hold to the belief that dying is worthwhile as long as it enables one to understand something.

By fasting and dying, reaching death and then returning to life, beginning the flight upward from the lower three realms of person, events, and things to the middle three realms of heaven, earth, and humanity, the ascent is begun to a whole new realm.

This course of exercise is the art of inner work founded by Ancestor Lu. An important structural element of the inner work is the cultivation of six lines of inner work within the human body.

The ancients' study of the human body began with what has form and substance, then came to what has form but no substance, finally considering what has neither form nor substance. Medical science began with shamanism; inspired by dreaming, the ancients conceived of the existence of mysterious "worlds" inside and outside the human body, worlds that are formless, immaterial, and unfathomably profound. Over the ages, unlocking the mysteries of the human body became a sacred task.

The remarkable thing about Chinese medical science is having found the existence of energy channels in the body, based on the theory of yin and yang and the five elements. We now have no way of knowing the process of this search and discovery.

Modern people using scientific methods still have not perceived the existence of the energy channels in the human body. Taoists can see the channels by means of two methods. One is to see them by inner gazing, which is possible after having reached a certain degree of cultivation of inner power. The other is to ingest alchemical elixir after having established a basis of inner power through inner work; by this means, it is possible to see the network of parallels and meridians clearly on the surface of the human body.

In the course of his training, Wang Liping ingested alchemical elixir three times. The first time has already been described earlier. The second time was for the purpose of experimental viewing of the parallels and meridians of the network of energy channels of the human body.

After the experiment was done, Wang Liping sat in a huge container filled to the level of his lips with hot water. Sitting there in the water, by the power of inner work he slowly ejected the alchemical elixir from his body. When enough of the elixir had floated to the surface, then he stopped the work and got out of the water.

———

There are six main lines of inner work in the human body.

The plumb line from the top of the head to the genital region was termed by Master Chongyang the "line of severance." When people who practice inner work without the guidance of an enlightened teacher easily produce distortion, it comes out in this line; when they get fired up and become demonic, that too comes out in this line.

The line from the "point where all meet" on top of the head to the perineum is called the "line of reflection." When one begins to cultivate this, it is in front of the spinal column; then gradually it shifts to within the spinal column itself. The line of reflection also used to be called the "central vessel" in ancient times. Practitioners do inner gazing through it. It is sometimes hidden and sometimes manifest; for people whose inner power is pure and deep, it is manifest when in use and hidden when not in use. There are also two vessels on either side of the spinal column, referred to as the left and right vessels.

The horizontal line through the three points known as the "heaven," the "eye," and the "opening" is in the head; this is called the "line of essence." The opening of the eye to heaven was originally called the heart of heaven, and also called the stem of heaven. When people are just born, there is a seam between the eyebrows; later on, as they grow up, only a single hole remains. This hole is different depending on the individual; some are long, some are short. The heavenly eye opening is properly called the opening of the eye to heaven. The "opening" is in front, the "eye" is in the middle, and "heaven" is in back. The "opening" can be treated with acupuncture, the "heaven" can reflect, the "eye" is the nirvana chamber. The end of the line of essence is the "jade pillow pass" at the back of the head.

The line from the solar plexus to the midspine is called the "line of power" or the "line of strength."

The line running back from the center of the umbilical area is called the "line of preserving life." To the left and right of this line are the kidneys; this is the region of the "gate of life" or "door of fate."

From 1.2 to 1.5 inches below the navel, running inward toward the coccyx, a line can be drawn when practicing cultivation; this is called the "line of cultivating life."

In each place where the line of essence, the line of strength, and the line of cultivating life pass through is an elixir field. These are the upper, middle, and lower elixir fields. The three lines go through the elixir fields, and the three lines face the three passes. When cultivating refinement, one draws out the three lines; when energy goes into motion, it easily breaks through the three passes.

Among these lines, the two vertical lines are bright lines visible to inner gazing, while the four horizontal lines are hidden and yet actually existent routes. Besides these, there are two lines in space at the edge of the external universe.

On the level of "persons, events, and things," people have an upper mysterious pass, a central mysterious pass, and a lower mysterious pass. The upper mysterious pass is the opening to the eye to heaven, which is also called the ancestral opening; this is the spot through which spirit and energy pass in coming and going. The five patriarchs of northern Taoism called this the North Star Opening. Because this opening is between the two eyes and two eyebrows, in ancient times it was represented by three dots, which stood for the sun, moon, and North Star. What Ancestor Lu worked out with his three thousand disciples—eight hundred of whom died in the process—was precisely this point, the opening of the eye to heaven.

Ancestor Lu said, "The opening to the eye to heaven is the mystery of mysteries, the opening of openings, the way to join inside and outside. The wise open it, the foolish close it. Those who open it live long; those who close it are broken off short." He also said, "Maintaining sincerity is subtle activity; there is an even subtler marvel of marvels, which is when all ruminations are set aside."

When refinement reaches the level of "heaven, earth, and humanity," there are mysterious passes everywhere. When one reaches the even higher level of "universe, time, and space," then the opening to the eye to heaven is no longer inside the body, and yet it is not outside the body either; it opens up spontaneously when used. Ancestor Lu said, "Whatever you see is not it. When you want what is not anything, then there is a permanent opening up. But the practical method is in the two words 'maintaining sincerity.'"

The opening to the eye to heaven is the route by which the light of spirit goes out and comes in. When people unconsciously have hallucinations, images, and intuitions, or when they consciously construct specific thought images, they may come up with the question of whether or not such erratic, ungraspable images in the brain can be stabilized in some way in order to make them controllable. Taoists have pursued this line of thought in their investigations and practices. Through cultivation, they take control of the "rating" of these images in the brain, then project them outside the brain to observe them clearly, finally withdrawing them. The route of this projection and withdrawal is the opening to the eye to heaven.

The method of training the opening to the eye to heaven is also called "drawing the line of essence." The way this is done is as follows: after collecting the mind, quiet sitting, adjusting the body, and tuning the breathing, one holds up the head and gazes forward, slowly bringing in distant scenery by means of the light of spirit, bringing it in to the "opening," then further into the "eye," then even further into the "heaven." Then one uses the light of spirit to send it quickly back out, projecting it as far as possible, sending it to the very horizon. This is repeated twice; then the light is finally gathered to the place of the "heaven." The "heaven" is also called the "mirror of the temporal" and is a reflective surface; the light of spirit is reflected from here.

After that, one can practice deliberate structured thinking in the brain, deliberately thinking of a scene, an object, something beautiful and fine.

The thing one has constructed in thought has form but no substance. Then one closes the eyes and looks ahead, actually projecting the image outward through the opening to the eye to heaven, propelling it by refined energy. When one first begins to practice this, it seems like there is nothing going on; there is no form and no substance, nothing visible at all. Eventually images gradually appear. As inner power increases, these images also gradually become more complete, clear, and sharply defined. They can also be shifted, further away or nearer, and can be magnified or reduced in size. Although the images are there, if you try to grasp them you will find nothing.

After the line of essence is drawn out and the opening to the eye to heaven is developed, then it is possible to project and take in forms, and to project and take in light; thoughts and vital spirit can thus be sent outside the brain into the universe outside the body, thus infinitely expanding the range of activity of thought and spirit. At this point, people's capacity to sense the external world is not the same as before; they can sense things that cannot be sensed by the five sense organs of ordinary people. Penetrating vision and inner vision are examples of capacities developed by this sort of training. When practitioners reach this stage, the world they perceive is quite different from the world perceived by ordinary people; their manner of thinking and speaking are also obviously different. The way that Taoist practitioners see the universe is richer, more complete, and more profound than that of ordinary people; their perceptions are also closer to the fundamental nature of things.

At this level, practitioners realize that there are actually four modes of existence of the universe, and that these four modes interchange. There is existence with both form and substance, with form but no substance, with substance but no form, and without either form or substance. In the view of Taoist practitioners, the ordinary person's limitation of the universe to the domain of the perceptions of the five senses is quite narrow-minded; even if they have greatly expanded the sensible world with the help of modern scientific instruments, it is still limited to the confines of a narrow framework.

Thought can be transformed from being formless and immaterial to having form without substance. It can even be made to have both form and substantiality.

Thought can be projected without the use of speech, literature, or other ordinary media, by means of the light of spirit. People can thus sense across space and time.

Leaving aside extraordinary capacities manifested spontaneously by the human body, according to the history of the Dragon Gate sect of Complete Reality Taoism, the process of conscious ascent to this stage by cultivation of the human body was formulated into a complete system of principles and practices at least a thousand years ago.

Human civilization is evolving, but while it has progressed in some ways, it has regressed in others. People of later times have not necessarily surpassed people of earlier times in every way. Zhang Guo, one of the Eight Immortals, deeply understood this pattern; he used to ride backward on a donkey so that he would be facing backward rather than forward, indicating his aim of learning from people of the past who had reached higher attainments and greater accomplishments.

Wang Liping practiced sitting in the cavern of Ancestor Lu to find the exact location of the lower elixir field in the human body when in this place. After several days of experimental observation, all four of them clearly felt the life cultivation line slowly rise, settling at a position 1.3 inches below the navel. When they practiced in Wushun, the lower elixir field was a little bit lower. Wang Liping had already realized the correspondence between the human body and the earth. He also realized how deep the philosophy of the union of Nature and humanity is; with the use of methods of practical cultivation, it is a simple way to unlock the secrets of the human body and the mysteries of the universe.

~~~~~~~

During the days at the Tower Observatory, Wang Liping learned a big lesson. His teachers in this class were Lao-tzu and Ancestor Lu. Wang Liping now had an even deeper understanding of the Great Way.

The Way is the greatest treasure of the universe and human life.

13

Skies Beyond the Sky

L eaving the Tower Observatory, the Taoist masters and their disciple went over the Qin Range, across the Han River, and through the Granary Mountains into the Four River Basin of Siquan.

All along the way, the mountains were high and the rivers deep, the paths were dangerous and the roads steep, but this was no difficulty for the four Taoist travelers. They only saw the soaring peaks, the rushing rapids, the cliff-hanging pines, the birds calling, and the monkeys chattering. It was as if they were outside the world; they all felt very much opened up in mind.

After entering Siquan, they continued to follow the mountains southwest. After a few days, they arrived at Green City.

Green City Mountain is so called because green mountains join on four sides, making the form of a fortified city wall. It is one of the ten major Open Skies of Taoists, called the Open Sky of Nine Rooms of Precious Immortals. Spiritual immortals over the ages, like Zhang Daoling, Fan Changsheng, Sun Simao, Du Guangding, and others all cultivated themselves in seclusion here. The four travelers visited famous locations such as the Observatory of Long Life, the Cavern of the Celestial Masters, and the Valley of the White Clouds, but they didn't meet up with any other Taoists, so they left Green City and headed for the sacred Mount Omei.

Viewed from far off, Omei is deep green, hazy in the mist, enshrouded in a kind of sacred atmosphere. It has three beautiful peaks, standing out distinctly, making an extraordinary impression. The name "Omei," which means "Beautiful Brows," comes from the sloping form of the mountain, delicate and long, gorgeously beautiful. Omei is one of the thirty-six Open Skies of Taoism; it is entitled Open Sky of Immaterial Spirituality, and also Mound of Spirit, Sky of Wonder. It is also one of the four special mountains of Buddhism, known in that tradition as Mountain of Radiant Light.

Taking the path up the mountain, the four travelers found that all the temples and shrines had been pillaged and were deserted, a total mess. The three elders felt pained as they viewed the destruction. The grand master told Wang Liping that Omei was a sacred ground of Buddhism, with a hundred great and small temples and shrines on the whole mountain. The mountain is a site of the responsive manifestation of the famous Buddhist bodhisattva Samantabhadra, the Universally Good Enlightening Being. There had been quite a few highly accomplished monks and Chan masters in the temples, with considerable wisdom and enlightenment, who had practiced Buddhism very deeply. In the past, the grand master said, he had once brought his disciples the Wayfarer of Pure Serenity and the Wayfarer of Pure Emptiness to this place and discussed Buddhism and Taoism with the abbots to polish and improve themselves, and found they were very much in accord. Now that disaster had befallen this place, he had no idea where the great Buddhist masters had gone, or whether or not they were safe.

Ever since the founding of Complete Reality Taoism, sectarianism was eliminated, and emphasis was placed on the union of the three teachings of Confucianism, Taoism, and Buddhism. Later Taoist works include quite a bit of Buddhist vocabulary. Both Taoism and Buddhism, as Eastern cultures, have principles and doctrines in common; the higher the level to which one rises, the smaller the differences are between them.

Since they were on Buddhist ground, the grand master taught Wang Liping a little bit about Buddhism, to introduce him to the subject for deeper study later on.

"Buddha" means "Awakened One." "Awakening" has three meanings: self-awakening, awakening others, and fulfillment of awakening and action. One who has reached these three kinds of awakening is called a Buddha. Attaining Buddhahood means having awakened understanding of everything in the universe and human life.

Buddhism began 2,500 years ago in India, founded by Shakyamuni, whose name means "Sage of the Shakya Clan." Born in a royal family, Shakyamuni was the crown prince, talented and intelligent. He also had a wife. He had all the pleasures of life, including glory, wealth, rank, repute, and natural pleasures, but he knew that all these were no more than temporary phenomena, which would inevitably disappear and could not last forever. He wanted to understand the cause and reason thereof, in order to find a way to get rid of afflictions and pains so as to transcend birth and death. For this purpose he abandoned wealth and status, fame and gain, authority and rank, emotional attachments—all those things that usually keep people in the grip of anxiety—and left home at the age of twenty-nine to practice spiritual cultivation, going through various ascetic disciplines. After six years, he finally sat under the bodhi tree to meditate quietly, searching deeply until he awakened and attained enlightenment. Buddha spoke of four truths—suffering, its cause, its extinction, and the way to extinction. Nirvana is the highest ideal state to be attained by cultivation.

After Buddha passed away, Buddhism spread widely and divided into many sects, the main ones being Theravada Buddhism and Mahasanghika Buddhism. Later on Mahasanghika Buddhism split again, into Mahayana Buddhism and Hinayana Buddhism. Hinayana Buddhism emphasizes individual cultivation to reach the state of the arhat transcending birth and death. Mahayana Buddhism considers the teachings of Buddha to be boundless and says all believers can become Buddhas, who are numerous as grains of sand in the Ganges River. Mahayana Buddhism also divided into schools of emptiness and schools of being. A sect of Mahayana Buddhism combined with Brahmanism produced Esoteric Buddhism, which is distinguished from the exoteric teachings by its secrecy.

Buddhism entered China by two routes during the first century of the Common Era. One route went west from India through Pakistan, into Afghanistan, then into China's Xinjiang region, from there into the Chinese heartland, and from China into Korea and Japan. This is the Chinese canonical tradition. Another route was from India to Nepal, on into Tibet, and again into the Chinese heartland, forming the Tibetan Buddhist tradition, also known as Lamaism.

Southern Tradition Buddhism went from Sri Lanka to Thailand, Burma, Laos, Vietnam, and other countries, including the region of Yunnan in China. This is the Pali canonical tradition.

From the nineteenth century onward, Buddhism has filtered into Western countries.

As Wang Liping listened to the grand master talking about the history of Buddhism, he was reflecting on how familiar the old Taoist wizard was with the subject. Ever since he had been studying the Way with the three old wizards, Liping's ears had been filled with Taoist doctrines. On the road, the three masters had also systematically elucidated the sources and process of development of traditional Chinese culture, mainly based on the Taoist canon.

The Taoist canon, in over five thousand scrolls, contains seventy-two fields of learning, including astronomy and geography, writings of various masters, philosophy and history, politics and military affairs, agriculture, crafts, chivalry, arts of calculation, shamanism, medical science, divination, physiognomy, and so on. Whatever the field or subject, of course, of whatever dynasty or era, the grand master and the mentors could quote freely, explaining inexhaustibly based on the canonical scriptures and classics, relating everything to the Way. Some of the most important works all three wizards could recite from memory, with astonishing fluency. Wang Liping thought it absolutely incredible that the brains of these three old men could actually contain such a vast wealth of information; they were vast as oceans, immense as the sky.

On this particular occasion, Wang Liping listened as the grand master continued to talk about Buddhism.

After Buddhism entered China, it mixed with Chinese mysticism to gradually form eight major schools: the School of the Essence of Things, the School of the Characteristics of Things, the Tiantai School, the Huayan School, the Pure Land School, the Esoteric School, the Discipline School, and the Chan School.

Of course, whatever country Buddhism entered, it metamorphosed considerably, but its basic vital spirit continued on.

Suffering, its cause, its extinction, and the path: these are the four Truths of Buddhism. "Suffering" is a general critique of human life as painful. Humans may be superior to other beings, but their status in the universe is not high, and they cannot escape the misery of the cycle of birth and death. Buddhas and all living beings are divided into ten domains, four of them saintly and six of them ordinary. The four saintly kinds are Buddhas, bodhisattvas, pratyeka buddhas, and arhats. The six ordinary kinds of beings are angels, humans, monsters, animals, hungry ghosts, and hellions. There are higher existences than the human. Human beings are born in a cry and die amidst the crying of others. Eight pains come along with the course of human life: the pain of birth, the pain of aging, the pain of sickness, the pain of death, the pain of separation from loved ones, the pain of contact with enemies, the pain of unfulfillment, and the pain of the energy of the five clusters. The five clusters are matter, sensation, conception, action, and consciousness; these form the basic constituent elements of the human being. The human being is, however, fundamentally empty, as everything in the universe is empty, all things being the products of combined causes and conditions. If there is combination, there is existence; otherwise there is none—this existence is causally conditioned. Combination has no inherent nature of its own, no basic substance—it is ultimately empty. The meaning of the truth of "suffering" is to teach people not to cling to external things.

The truth of the cause of suffering points to the source of pain and misery in human life. When people have no enlightenment and do not understand things and their patterns, and do not recognize that everything in the universe is void, then their desires and cravings are insatiable, so they find affliction for themselves. Suffering arises from this. Without clarifying the cause of suffering, there is no way to comprehend the realm of emptiness.

Extinction means the process and methods of elimination of psychological afflictions, emancipation from suffering, transcendence of compulsive routines and attainment of emptiness. By following a course opposite to that of ordinary human life, it is possible to attain extinction and thus reach Buddhahood. The essentials in this process are three forms of learning: discipline, concentration, and wisdom. When mind and objects are both forgotten and not a single thought stirs, that is called discipline. When awareness is complete and clear, inwardly and outwardly lucid, this is called concentration. Responding to things in accord with conditions, subtle function inexhaustible, is called wisdom. These three learnings complement and foster one another, being as substance and function to each other. Through cultivating discipline, where emptiness has nothing to empty, concentration produces wisdom, thus bringing one to transcendence. By long-term practice one gradually awakens, but the basic nature of the universe is an indivisible whole, so when one arrives at a certain key, one then experiences a great awakening, sudden enlightenment.

The path is the realm at which one arrives after "extinction." By way of nirvana, people transcend birth and death, eliminate all the vexations and miseries in compulsive routines, and enter into the Pure Land of Infinite Bliss.

This process is described by Guanyin:

First in the midst of hearing, enter the stream and forget the object.
The entered is thereupon silent; the duality of movement and stillness
no longer arises.
Gradually progressing in this way, when hearing the heard is ended,
ended hearing does not remain.
When aware that what you are aware of is empty, empty awareness is
ultimately complete.
When emptiness and what is empty are extinct, birth and death are
nil.
Perfect peace then appears, suddenly producing transcendence; in the
world and beyond, a round light pervades the ten directions.

Having explained this much, the grand master looked at Wang Liping, then continued, "You already have experience of the state referred to in these last few lines; you have already been to the realm of Infinite Bliss spoken of by the Buddhas. That highway of light you saw after you died is in fact the road to the paradise of Infinite Bliss. You are already awakened in Buddhism; in our Taoist terms, we call you a 'living dead man.' You now know there is such a resort in this universe, but when you finally resort to it, you still should continue to cultivate refinement."

Finally the Wayfarer of the Infinite recited a verse:

If you want to know past causes,
see them in present effects.
If you want to know future results,
see them in present acts.

The explanations of the grand master were crystal clear to Wang Liping; he made no remarks and asked no questions. The principles of Buddhism and Taoism concur; with his own practice Wang Liping had already proved these principles simply, clearly, and penetratingly. Now he knew Buddhist doctrine as well as Taoist doctrine. Once he had listened openly and heard clearly, there was no use saying any more; the essential thing in study is practical application. Whether it be Buddhism or Taoism, the topics of research are similar: to transform the temporality of human life into the eternity of the universe, to transform the finiteness of human life into the infinity of the universe. What is the nature of the universe? Buddha concluded it is "emptiness," Lao-tzu concluded it is the Tao or the Way. What is the highest ideal state for humanity? Buddhists say it is entry by way of nirvana into the "world of Ultimate Bliss,"

Taoists say it is cultivated realization of the "higher triple realm" to "attain immortality." One is just as good as the other.

This one talk by the grand master unfolded a whole new world for Wang Liping, a sky beyond the skies!

In two years of traveling, Wang Liping had witnessed wonder and learned a great deal, opening up his eyes and developing his knowledge. The teacher's talk on Mount Omei about Buddhism increased Wang Liping's sense of the immensity of the universe and the vastness of wisdom. Who knows how many jewels of wisdom there are in the world awaiting discovery, how many mysteries there are to be solved!

Most of the earth's surface is covered with water; is there a lost continent under the sea, one which hosted brilliant civilizations long ago?

What secrets do the pyramids of ancient Egypt conceal? Why are Christian cathedrals domed?

Did humankind evolve from apes or crawl out of the water onto the earth?

A number of religions say humankind was created by God. Is this myth or reality?

The world is quite marvelous. Questions like these were profoundly absorbing to Wang Liping. He wanted to unlock the mysteries of the universe and of human life.

<hr>

After half a day in front of the shrine talking, the four Taoist travelers finally rose and continued on their way up the mountain. The three elders did not follow the route they had taken in the past to climb this mountain. Instead they chose an extremely steep and inaccessible place to start their ascent.

Wang Liping figured that the grand master and the mentors were deliberately avoiding the scenes of desolation in the temples and shrines along the pathway. Here, where people never went, the natural condition of the environment was still intact, and this was a help to their hearts and spirits.

He had a funny feeling that something was about to happen. The three elders, meanwhile, were already climbing up nimbly, so Liping followed them without having time to think too much.

Making their way through woods, up cliffs, and across ravines, before too long the four made it to the middle of the mountain. Here the trees gave dense shade, the mountain brooks gurgled, extraordinary flowers were in full bloom, and fragrant grasses abounded. A group of monkeys had gathered here to escape the heat, some frolicking about, some climbing trees for fruits and nuts, some swinging and sailing around in the high branches, some sitting picking lice, some wrestling and chasing each other. This was their world.

Suddenly a branch shook very obviously, and a dark shadow flashed past. Suddenly startled, the monkeys quickly gathered around their elders, the young taking to the bosoms of the mothers. Quieting down, they looked to see what was going on. The head monkey saw that humans were coming. Baring his fangs, he gave a sharp cry and headed for where the humans were. The other monkeys also came, clustering around him.

Seeing the monkeys coming at them, the Wayfarer of the Infinite couldn't help laughing. Turning to his companions, he said, "We're lucky to have monkeys for companions on our trip to Omei, but we'd better not provoke them." Agreeing, the others tied their backpacks tightly.

Seeing the four men, the group of monkeys boldly surrounded them, closing in on them with hoots and howls. Using their lightness technique, the four Taoists suddenly jumped away from the approaching monkeys, landing on a huge boulder yards away. Taken aback for a moment, the monkeys hurriedly pursued the men, but how could they catch them?

Wang Liping saw the monkeys were very playful; he tossed a handful of pebbles, which cascaded over the side of the boulder. Thinking they were under attack, the monkeys screamed even more sharply, bounding wildly forward.

As the monkeys approached, the four Taoists leaped up into the trees and started moving from tree to tree. The monkeys also scrambled up into the trees—they were, after all, monkeys—to continue the chase. But now the four humans were nowhere to be found!

Seeing the monkeys stymied, the four Taoists laughed and laughed. Presently they observed the monkeys finally getting tired out and acknowledging defeat. Then the four men went on their way.

Before long, they came to the foot of a sheer cliff hundreds of feet high, with some trees sticking out halfway up, and some vines trailing down. The four of them climbed right up the face of the cliff, using the vines, trees, and weeds to pull themselves up. When there was no vegetation, they made their way upward clinging to seams and protuberances in the rock.

Halfway up, the travelers suddenly heard someone say, "Here I have visitors, but I've failed to go out and meet them!" The voice boomed like a huge bell, echoing in their ears.

Looking up, Wang Liping saw a man of the Way standing there facing the wind, Taoist garb fluttering, looking very much like one of the immortals. The wind on this mountain whirls from below upward, so anyone who could project his voice against the wind here must be an extraordinary individual.

In the time it takes to tell, the four travelers had reached the peak. The mountain Wayfarer invited them into his cave, where they paid their respects and sat down.

It turned out that this was not an ordinary man, but a mountain Taoist permanently secluded on Mount Omei, respectfully known as the Cloud Roaming Wayfarer. At that time, he was one hundred and eighteen years old; at the time of this writing, he is a venerable old man of one hundred and thirty-nine years. Every three years now, Master Wang Liping takes time off to go visit him.

The Cloud Roaming Wayfarer had not left the mountain for fifty or sixty years. He told Wang Liping that people used to come to the mountain on horseback or carried by porters, but now they are transported on legs sprouting circles. As he said this, he depicted a circle with his hand; Liping realized he was talking about the wheels of trains. Wang Liping invited him down the mountain to have a look, but the old man firmly refused, insisting that he could not leave the mountain.

The old Taoist, cut off from society, secluded deep in the mountains, paid no mind to the chaos and turmoil going on in the world, but just practiced the Way with all his heart.

Lao-tzu said, "For learning, you gain daily; for the Way, you lose daily. Losing, and losing even that, until you reach noncontrivance, then even though you do not strive nothing fails to get done." Intellectual learning is a matter of accumulating knowledge to become widely learned. Cultivation of the Way requires serenity and unity: "Close the mouth, shut the eyes," getting rid of random thoughts. When there is no longing and no rumination, your essential nature is inherently complete and clear, calm and tranquil—then you see the effect of the work. In this state, the mind is like a clear mirror, or like the bright moon, reflecting and illumining the subtle principles of heaven and earth and all things. From there, you "know everything in the world without even going out the door, seeing the course of Nature without even looking out the window."

There are mountains beyond the mountains!

Vast as the world is, there certainly are people of high attainment.

Great directness seems restrained; great skillfulness seems awkward; great eloquence seems mute; great knowledge seems like ignorance.

There are also people whose eye of insight recognizes reality and who brave long and difficult journeys to call on realized people on remote mountain peaks and inquire about the Way in cavern headquarters. This too is a case of beings clustering according to kind, people dividing into groups.

The first time the Cloud Roaming Wayfarer saw Wang Liping, he was very happy. The ancient told the youth about something that had occurred in the past. It was several decades earlier, when the nation was in turmoil, without a bright spot on the horizon. This is just the sort of time when new people emerge to unfold far-reaching plans.

Even as competing powers rose and fought each other day in and day out, Mount Omei remained aloof from the clamor of the world, still an abode of peace and tranquility. Every day the priests could be heard chanting, the ancient bells booming, fragrant billows of incense rising from the temples, pathways lined with pilgrims.

The Cloud Roaming Wayfarer remained sequestered in his cavern headquarters. Knowing the disturbance in the world was going to last for quite a while yet, he spent his days calmly cultivating himself, going deep into the mountains in his spare time to gather unusual flowers, plants, medicines, and wild fruits. On rare occasions when a sudden storm arose, he would pick a spot to quietly gaze upon the unique violet halo of Mount Omei. Roaming freely on the mountains without a fixed track, the Wayfarer was seen by few people and known to none.

One morning at dawn, there was a clear, gentle breeze blowing. The clouds on the mountain thickened and thinned, and the sunlight appeared and disappeared, sometimes shining through, sometimes blocked by the clouds.

The Cloud Roaming Wayfarer had already had a peculiar intuition while sitting the night before; he knew two important people would be coming to call on him that day. He also knew it was a matter of destiny, so he could not refuse to see them.

That morning the Cloud Roaming Wayfarer was standing in a wood practicing breathing exercises, when all of a sudden someone came up the slope. The old Taoist knew the first of his visitors had arrived. Neither concealing himself nor paying attention to the man, he remained stock still with his eyes closed, absorbed in the spirit.

The visitor was a mature man in his forties, with a massive physique and a distinguished air. He was dressed very simply, yet he gave the impression of great power of clarity.

Seeing an aged man with the face of a child and dark hair practicing energetics in this uninhabited place, the visitor knew this was not an ordinary old man. Walking straight up to the Wayfarer, he addressed him respectfully.

The Wayfarer opened his eyes slightly, revealing a spiritual light, an uncanny glow, and said with a smile, "You've come a long way, a hard road."

Hearing this, the visitor involuntarily shuddered in his heart. He gave no outward indication of this, however. "Are you the Cloud Roaming Wayfarer?"

"Yes."

"May I trouble you to speak about the affairs of the nation?"

"The rise and fall of nations are responsibilities borne by ordinary men. I am untalented and hide deep in the mountains. I am unfamiliar with worldly affairs. How could I talk about the nation?"

"The nation is in a crisis, and all the people are troubled. You have lived through so many changes in the world, so many ups and downs. You have seen a lot, and your knowledge is vast, encompassing the heavens and the earth. Your heart has penetrated the inner workings of things. Everyone has heard of your name, and all the world respects you. Please do not be so deferential, but tell me a thing or two."

"The east is not bright; the west is bright. When it has blackened in the south, there is the north. The northwest is viable; the northeast is penetrable. With your heroism, ability, and strategy, a vast plan can be unfolded, a great work can be accomplished. Don't bother me for details."

A Taoist immortal schooled in the mountains and a great man of the world—here at dawn on the top of Mount Omei the two of them took a look into the timing of heaven and the movement of earth, into the future of the nation, the prosperity and decline of the people. Just presenting the main essentials, the ancient wizard spoke right to the point. His visitor laughed with delight, a laugh that was refreshed and clear.

Finally the man said to the old Taoist, "Your instruction has been of great benefit, but I have so much to do that I will have to leave now." Folding his hands in a farewell salute, the man departed. The Cloud Roaming Wayfarer saw him off with his eyes.

The Wayfarer then went to another spot in a quiet glen to nurture his spirit, when suddenly another man showed up. This man was nearly fifty years old, with a tall and imposing frame, his back straight as a ramrod. Dressed in military garb, he had a stern, severe air, with an overpowering gaze. This man had lived below the mountain for a long time and often used to climb the mountain to roam around and see the sights. On this particular day, he too had purposely come to call on a Taoist immortal, though he had no idea he would run into one in this place.

The two men exchanged polite greetings. This visitor also asked the Cloud Roaming Wayfarer to tell him something relevant to the national emergency.

The Wayfarer asked the man, "How do you think the nation is to be governed?"

The man replied, "In my opinion, the essentials are in the classic Great Learning. The path of great learning is in clarification of enlightened qualities, in closeness to the people, and in stopping at the optimum good. Everything has a root and branches; all events have a beginning and an end. Know what comes first and what then follows, and you will be close to the Way. Make knowledge objective, make your intention sincere and your heart straight, cultivate yourself, take care of your family, and govern the land. The most essential of essentials is to find out the patterns where things begin, to look into subtleties when the mind and attention first stir."

"Fine. The nation has an existing science, the union of Nature and humanity; Confucianism, Taoism, and Buddhism complement each other, but this is the basis of all of them. Sun Yat-sen's doctrine of Three Democratic Principles is also derived from this, even if it is a new current of a particular era. The course of Nature has a Way; those who follow it thrive, while those who violate it perish. This is an immutable principle. As for the affairs of the nation, what has long been united inevitably divides, and what has long been divided inevitably unites; this is the mode of its operation."

"Mencius said, 'There are not two suns in the sky, there are not two rulers for a people.' Is this the principle?"

"Division makes two, union makes one. Change and evolution are in flux, flowing everywhere. That which is softest in the world drives that which is hardest in the world. Know the masculine, preserve the feminine, be receptive to the world. Know the glamorous, yet watch over the little thought of; be open to the world."

The visitor realized that the Wayfarer had thoroughly assessed his short-comings. He didn't have the heart to listen any further, so he said, "Could you please tell me about the future?"

"Fire rages in the south, but if there is much water, it will still be viable." The visitor saw that this conversation didn't work for him, so he bade the Wayfarer farewell and went back down the mountain.

Coming to this point in his recollection, the Cloud Roaming Wayfarer said, "For two people to come calling in one day is itself extraordinary. I told them about the logic of natural mechanisms, and it all subsequently turned out as I had said. After that I concealed myself and never showed my face again. And I never went down from the mountain anymore. I couldn't say any more, because one inevitably makes mistakes if one says too much. Now this present tidal wave has come in with a thunderous roar, but it too will eventually dwindle away to nothing."

Listening to this centenarian speak of the course of events, Wang Liping was filled with admiration for the old Taoist.

The Wayfarer of the Infinite said, "Those two men each took command of one region, resulting in a temporary peace. Now the chaos going on at the present time is, in my view, of a magnitude rare in the history of China. Ever since the first emperor unified the nation, order and disorder have alternated over and over again. When we observe times of flourishing, we inevitably find wise leaders and intelligent rulers, as well as new laws and strict regulations observed by the officials and obeyed by the people; business flourishes, peace is maintained, and sanity prevails. If this is managed in a regular way, disorder naturally does not occur."

Now Wang Liping asked the grand master to talk about the way of government. The Wayfarer of the Infinite said, "There are various sorts of government—by people, by laws, by principles, and by the Tao. As for government by people, in the beginning human nature was quite pure and simple, and human desires and wishes were also extremely simple. In those times, when there were sages who were monarchs, leading the people to be responsive to heaven and earth, then a nation was naturally peaceful.

"As for government by law, when society had developed to the point where there was a division of labor, a social structure divided into different occupational classes, a variety of ideologies in circulation, and a mixed population living interdependently, desires and ambitions increased, and human nature was no longer innocent. The only way to govern them was by law, regulating things by legal measures.

"When there is government by law, the laws have to be reasonable; laws have to be such that they are both respected and trusted, and the law must be rigorously applied. The law is the same, furthermore, for government officials and ordinary citizens; there cannot be a dual standard. Lao-tzu says, 'That which is at rest is easy to hold; that which has not occurred is easy to plan for. What is frail is easily broken, what is vague is easily dispelled. Do it before it exists; govern it before there's disorder.' When society reached this stage it was already so complex that continuing with government by people was no longer a practical guarantee against disorder; and yet government by law was not necessarily always completely effective either, so government by principle had to develop as well.

"Government by principle means having both rulers and ruled understand the principles by which people can live and nations can thrive, considering these principles as law rather than taking a legislative approach to law. Then a nation is easy to govern.

"Government by the Tao, or the Way, is on an even higher level, nurturing the people by means of the Way, returning to naturalness and going back to reality, assimilating humanity to heaven and earth, taking no artificial law as law, but being orderly without being managed. Lao-tzu said, 'The sage says, "Since I contrive nothing, the people are spontaneously civilized. Since I like calm, the people are spontaneously upright. Since I have no interests, the people spontaneously prosper. Since I have no desires, the people are spontaneously innocent."' Government without artificiality is government by the Way. This is the highest level of social development, and the highest attainment of government."

Stroking his long whiskers as he listened, the Cloud Roaming Wayfarer added, "Domains governed by the Way exist only in the realms of wizardry. Before the mundane world is governed by the Way, who knows how much time must pass, and how much calamity and hardship our nation and our people must endure."

Listening to the two ancients talk about government, and thinking of his own personal experience, Wang Liping realized how deep the insight of the elders was, and he strengthened his own resolve to cultivate refinement even further.

14

The Dream of the Universe

The Taoist masters and their disciple stayed on Mount Omei for several days, talking about Taoism with the ancient wizard. When Wang Liping and the ancient first met, there was more than a century's difference in their ages, but both were children in Taoism. The ancient took a liking to the young apprentice and showed him all over the mountain, bringing him to special inaccessible places and teaching him methods of self-cultivation. There was no "generation gap" between the two, and young Liping eagerly sought instruction from the ancient Taoist.

After a number of days at Mount Omei, the four travelers reluctantly bade farewell to the Cloud Roaming Wayfarer and headed down the mountain. Making their way east, as before they avoided crowded cities; taking the back roads, they visited all the unusual mountains and bodies of water along the way. Cultivating Taoist practices, doing charitable deeds, and seeking out Taoist adepts as they traveled, they had many experiences on the way.

Finally, after a journey of thousands of miles, at last they arrived at Mount Lao, the cavern headquarters by the sea where the three old wizards had been stationed before they sought out Wang Liping. They had been gone for seven years.

The mountain and sea were the same mountain and sea, the waves slapping the foot of the mountain, breakers roiling, mountain winds echoing in the woods, wave upon wave of pines. Everything was so familiar to the three old wizards. Now, however, they didn't feel the same excitement they had in the past; instead they were shrouded in a sort of emotional chill.

The Mansion of Supreme Purity no longer had the magnificence of before, and the Taoist priests had disappeared to who knows where. The

Nine Mansions and Eight Observatories all presented scenes of desolation following depredation. Even in the mountain caverns where people hardly ever gain access, they couldn't find any trace of fellow Taoists. From all this they saw something of how widely the wave of oppression had reached, and how profound its effect had been.

Coming to the Cavern of Eternal Spring, the four found numerous vines and creepers hanging over the mouth of the cavern. The inside of the cave was dark and shadowy. All four went inside. The Wayfarer of Pure Serenity lit a lamp and brushed the dust off the implements inside. He told Wang Liping that this was a place where their spiritual ancestor Qiu Changchun had practiced cultivation, and where they too, Liping's three Taoist teachers, had also practiced. Wang Liping helped his mentor clean the place and straighten things up. As the three old wizards looked around the cavern, seeing it as before, they were flooded with feelings, recalling how they had left seven years earlier to go looking for a Transmitter. Within the space of a few years, they had undergone untold vicissitudes and hardships, including the difficulties of teaching an apprentice while facing the changes going on in the world. Disaster had fallen upon the populace, Buddhism and Taoism were persecuted, and the nation had reached the brink of destruction. The only thing they had to offer as solace to the spirits of their ancestors was the fact that in the midst of all this chaos and misery and while enduring a fugitive lifestyle they had managed to locate and train the eighteenth-generation Transmitter to inherit, disseminate, and bring to light the treasures of knowledge accumulated over a thousand years by the Dragon Gate branch of Complete Reality Taoism. This was the bright spot in the darkness.

Keenly aware of the mood of his teachers, young Wang Liping bowed to each of them and suggested that they all go outside for a change. Outside the cavern, he brushed off a flat rock and politely offered the senior master a seat. One of the mentors chided Liping for being so uncharacteristically formal, as if he were some sort of grandee. Everyone laughed, dispelling the clouds of sadness that had been hanging over them.

As the masters bathed in the sunlight and sea breeze, reclaiming their old haunt, the Wayfarer of Pure Serenity said to Wang Liping, "We're going to let you see one of the heirlooms of the Dragon Gate sect." He pointed to the mouth of the cave, and in the blink of an eye, a pure white turtle came crawling out.

Liping's eyes brightened. He wanted to pick the turtle up, but the mentor stopped him, saying, "Don't move it."

The turtle was small, about the size of the palm of the hand, but it could crawl quite fast. Heading straight for the Wayfarer of the Infinite, the turtle started to climb up his robe. The Wayfarer extended his hand, and the turtle crawled right into his palm. Once in the Wayfarer's hand, the turtle lay still, just sticking out its head, nuzzling the old wizard's palm very affectionately.

The Wayfarer of the Infinite put the turtle down, and it crawled over to the Wayfarer of Pure Serenity; he greeted it with his hand, whereupon the turtle crawled right into his palm. The Wayfarer brought the turtle up close to his face, and the turtle nuzzled the old wizard's face, seeming to be whispering in his ear. Delighted, the Wayfarer of Pure Serenity put the turtle down, and next it crawled over to the Wayfarer of Pure Emptiness. The Wayfarer seemed to have a brief conversation with the turtle, then put it back down on the ground. The white turtle now lifted its head and looked at Wang Liping, then hurriedly crawled up to him. The turtle climbed up on Liping, nosing around as if it were looking for something. Wang Liping too extended his hand, and the turtle crawled into his palm and remained there motionless, as if they were old friends.

The three old wizards nodded approvingly when they saw this scene.

The Wayfarer of the Infinite said, "Spiritual turtles have intelligence. Even though this is the first time you've been here, this turtle knows you are a member of the family and is treating you like an old friend."

The grand master had Liping put the white turtle on a flat rock and watch it carefully. To all appearances, the white turtle lay quietly on the rock unmoving, as if it were practicing meditation.

The grand master said, "See where the sun is. Which direction is the turtle's head facing?"

Wang Liping looked and saw that the sun was in the southeast, and the turtle was facing southeast.

The grand master now told Liping to change the turtle's orientation, so that it was facing northwest. The turtle slowly turned back by itself until its head was facing southeast as before. He tried this several times, and each time the turtle turned itself to align its direction with the sun. Wang Liping told himself this turtle really was intelligent.

The grand master told Wang Liping, "This turtle is older than all four of us put together. It's already an ancient, over six hundred and eighty years old."

Liping gasped involuntarily. Now he viewed the turtle in a new light. "This is a treasure of our Dragon Gate," continued the grand master. "It has been handed down from our spiritual ancestors for twelve generations now. For six hundred and eighty years this turtle has been absorbing the essences of the sun and moon, obtaining the ambrosia of heaven and earth, merging into unity with Nature, harmonizing with the Way that circulates throughout the universe. It has a method of longevity and a way of communicating intelligence. Responding to the changes of sky and earth, sun and moon, it is a very special treasure, through which people can discover quite a few truths."

Even as the grand master spoke, Wang Liping saw the white turtle adjust its position very slightly, so as to keep its head directly facing the sun.

The grand master continued, "The turtle had been working for three hundred and sixty years before it could follow the sun, but it could still only turn half a circle. It will be able to turn a full circle when it has been working for seven hundred and twenty years. Our predecessors kept meticulous records of this spiritual turtle's development; when it is passed on to you in the future, then it is up to you to continue the research. This is one of the responsibilities we are giving you."

Wang Liping nodded gravely.

The Wayfarer of Pure Emptiness pointed to the turtle's back and told Wang Liping to look carefully and see if there were anything special about it.

Looking very closely, Liping saw that the pattern on the turtle's back was indeed extraordinary. On examination, it proved to be an outline diagram of the eight trigrams. "Is this eight-trigram pattern natural or man-made?" Liping couldn't help asking.

The Wayfarer of Pure Emptiness said, "What would be extraordinary about a man-made pattern? The remarkable thing about it is that it grew naturally corresponding to the eight trigrams. This makes us reflect deeply on the reality of the inspiration of Nature underlying the invention of the eight trigrams. Let us also ask how the eight-trigram pattern came to be on the turtle's back. Here we have to think of the evolution of an even greater space; in actuality, this is a reflection of the force of space. Space has six directions: above and below, before and behind, left and right. Each direction has force existing in it; and therein are change and combination, harmony and opposition, benefit and harm. When we include the sun and moon as powers for forces influencing all beings, the number adds up to eight. When these forces are impressed upon a flat surface, they form the eight trigram pattern. That is why our understanding of the eight trigrams must be cubic and not planar, three-dimensional rather than two-dimensional. This is the way to go into study of the I Ching." The mentor also gently picked up the turtle and turned it over to show Wang Liping its underside, saying, "See how its underside is made of exactly twelve plates forming a single whole. This totality can be interpreted numerically, taking the number twelve to correspond to the twelve calendrical earth branches, the twelve months, and twelve main energy channels. This also has a profound background, originating in the universe itself. In this respect, we are both students of the grand master. Ask him to explain it for you."

The grand master laughed when he heard this. He said, "We're all students of the white turtle. Why not ask it instead of me? Isn't it said that those who were born before us must have heard of the Way before us? Since we have this spiritual turtle here, we should learn from it attentively."

The grand master then put the turtle on his hand, looked at it very closely, and said, "The Cloud Roaming Wayfarer was right; it looks like the country is going to be in chaos for several more years. We shouldn't stay here; let us continue traveling."

"What about the white turtle?" asked Wang Liping. "The turtle can take care of itself. It's safer than we are!" "Let's take it with us. I'll have another teacher!"

"All right." Even as he spoke, the grand master handed the white turtle over to Wang Liping. The young apprentice was delighted.

Now they had another companion on the road, a six-hundred-and-eighty-year-old spiritual turtle. They descended from the mountain and headed north. As they traveled along, no matter what the external conditions, the white turtle remained motionless inside a cloth sack, quietly practicing self-cultivation. When the men rested, they would let the turtle out, and it would frolic with them. The turtle did not eat or drink, and it did not eliminate waste; it appeared to be practicing fasting for longevity.

Within a few months, the travelers had come to Cinnabar Cliff Mountain on the northern tip of the Shandong Peninsula.

Cinnabar Cliff Mountain faces the sea. It is not very high, but it is exceptionally beautiful, surrounded by clouds and mist. It faces Long Mountain Island over the sea, and to the east is an endless expanse of ocean. When the morning sun rises in the east, the ocean water shining like crystal, the sky deep blue, water and sky merging into one color with the red sun hanging in between, it makes a gorgeously magnificent sight. On windy days, the seawater ripples, lightly brushing the sand and rocks below the cliffs, as gently as a mother caressing her child. The cliff walls are sharp as swords; when the north wind blows, as it hits the cliff walls the wind rushes straight upward; and yet the wind is only felt slightly on top of the cliff.

There is a pavilion on top of the cliff called Penglai Pavilion, a very famous place. Against the background of the sea and sky, it stands out quite distinctly. Sometimes it is wrapped in sea mist, giving it an otherworldly air. When one climbs the pavilion and gazes out into the distance, the sea breeze refreshes the lungs and massages the face, giving a sublime feeling of openness, joyfulness, and lightness. The world and all its honor and disgrace forgotten, one seems to become transformed into an immortal beyond the mundane.

Below the southeast cliffs is an ancient naval station. Constructed by a leading admiral of the Ming dynasty, the walls retain their original form even after hundreds of years.

This region was very prosperous in the Tang dynasty. In the Ming dynasty, it was an important naval base. In modern times, its status is lower, but the beauty of Penglai Pavilion endures undiminished, a place of resort for travelers. When the three wizards and their disciple came here in the course of their journey, however, they had come to see sights other than those viewed by the ordinary tourist.

Because of the Cultural Revolution, the mountain temples had been closed. The four Taoists did not go to any of the temples, and did not climb up Penglai Pavilion either. Instead they chose a spot on the summit of the mountain, sat there facing the azure sky and aquamarine sea, and began to practice gazing.

From the human perspective, the oceans are an eternal, unfathomable mystery. In this gazing, the Taoists were seeking to see mysterious visions over the sea.

The four sat in a row. Eyes closed, they solidified their spirits and worked up their inner power. Gradually opening their eyes, they slowly extended their hands toward the sea, raising them upright very gradually; their whole bodies vibrated very slightly, almost imperceptibly. In these movements, they sent an extraordinarily great, unique force toward the surface of the water in the distance.

The Wayfarer of the Infinite began to operate a secret formula mentally, also marshaling a kind of extraordinary power. The spiritual turtle lay quietly beside Wang Liping, not moving; it too was waiting for changes over the surface of the ocean water.

At first, the surface of the sea showed no peculiar change. Waves were not rising, but an ocean vapor steamed up, like clouds and fog, covering a vast expanse. Before long, the fog on the sea began to swell and expand, gradually forming a massive wall of fog. Then things gradually began to move inside the wall of fog, delicate shadows that seemed to form images of things, the scenery now light, now dark: there were mountain peaks, there were buildings, there were chariots and horses, and there were people. Everything floated by so airily, now seeming illusory, now real, like a dream or a hallucination, changing inconsistently.

The four Taoists began to steady their spirits and focus their eyes, carefully examining the details of this vision, watching how it changed and developed, using their minds to sense it, using their spirits to read it.

The vision was pretty at first, like an ancient Chinese landscape scroll.

Then there was a change in the wind and clouds; whereupon a cluster of steep and dangerous mountain peaks appeared. Suddenly the mountains inverted, and human beings surged forth like an ocean tide, crushing each other, then flipped over like the mountains had, hanging underneath chariots and horses. The mountains gradually turned into a number of tall, narrow towers, drifting and swaying, then suddenly crumbling and dissolving. In a moment another cloud bank rose, and a ship slowly sailed out from it. Around the ship there were no ocean waves—there appeared to be herds of sheep, with people driving them along. The ship sprouted two wings—one was long, and the other was short, as if it had been broken off. This was very strange.

All of these images flowed past, and then a whole new scene appeared, a vision of southern China, with its rice paddies, tiled houses, oxen working in the fields, children playing in the villages, a wave of energetic imagery conveying peace and tranquility. Then, in the blink of an eye, the houses turned into a locomotive and train, which leaped into the clouds and went off into the distance, floating off to who knows where.

The wizards and their apprentice stopped their exercise, and the visions on the sea disappeared without a trace. The surface of the ocean was calm and unruffled as before; the sky was clear blue as before. The sunlight poured down, shimmering on the ripples of the water.

The old wizards' expressions were very serious. Wang Liping alone had not seen the true sense of vision transmission; he looked at his teachers with questioning eyes.

The Wayfarer of the Infinite took the spiritual turtle into the palm of his hand and quietly looked at it for a while. Then he looked up again and gazed at the ocean, falling into deep thought. He seemed to be trying to remember something, looking for a thread of interpretation.

The Wayfarer of Pure Serenity said, "Should we gaze once more?" The Wayfarer of the Infinite nodded.

All four began the exercise again. Mist rose on the ocean, and visions again appeared; vaguely, indistinctly, shadowy and willowy, appearing and disappearing, the shifting illusions never remained steady. There were mountains, rivers, and lakes; trees, fields and meadows; villages, houses, and tall buildings; people, birds, and animals. There also seemed to be some sort of scenario, some vignettes woven in. There also appeared a crowd of people upside down, buildings leaning obliquely, and flowing water like clouds. As they watched the apparitions, the three elders discussed the vision among themselves, gradually clarifying the meaning. Listening to them talk, Wang Liping learned something about gazing at visions.

What these visions actually convey is a kind of natural mechanism, information about future changes and developments in society. Now the reader will have seen that "visions" is a sort of code word, referring to what people usually call mirages.

The scientific explanation of mirages is purely physical and stops at the level of what Taoists consider the lower three realms. According to the scientific analysis of the necessary conditions for a mirage, from the point of view of optics, the moisture in the air has to be evenly distributed, the droplets have to be spherical, and so on. So there are very strict atmospheric conditions that must be present before distant objects can be reflected through a mist. Thus from the point of view of physics, a mirage does not appear easily; for every image that appears, furthermore, there must be a concrete reality. Otherwise, mirages are inexplicable.

Taoists are not "explaining" mirages; what they want to do is "make" them.

What they seek to interpret are the meanings of these visions.

Master Wang Liping says that the old masters go to the sea almost every year to make visions and gaze on them, sustaining them as long as they need. These are not rare marvels; they can be performed at any appropriate time. The meanings shown by visions can only be read and interpreted with the help of abundant knowledge and experience.

When the three masters taught Wang Liping the method of producing images over water back in his hometown, he used to work on it by the waterside under the sun, but the surface of the water was not very large, so it was hard to carry out the practice fully. The vision images he produced were not very clear, so even if he could see them, he could not be sure others could see them. Now by the sea, with the vastness of the ocean water, it was like a dragon taking to its natural environment; here the practice could be fully exercised, bringing out psychic powers to the maximum degree. With the three masters and their apprentice all doing the exercise at once, it was not hard to produce visions.

Recently we asked Master Wang Liping why mirages, which from the ordinary point of view are purely physical phenomena, can contain and present secrets of social developments. Master Wang laughed and said, "They are dreams of the universe."

This is a startling statement, but it penetrates the essence of the question. The universe has its own thought, intelligence, and millions of unique languages.

This Earth is as small as a grain of sand; and this universe is as small as a drop of water. Both are living mechanisms and have their own brains. These brains are dreaming waking "dreams." People have human dreams; the universe has dreams of the universe. People with developed inner power can see into other people's dreams, and they can also see into the dreams of the universe. They can interpret human dreams, and they can interpret the dreams of the universe.

Taoists observe things by seeing where everything begins, just as the branches and leaves of a tree all grow from the same root. They also see everything as interdependent, not existing in isolation. So there is self in other, other in self; "this" and "that" are interconnected. Nature and humanity correlate: nature and humanity are one. So it is possible to observe waters from mountains, to find mountains in waters, and to see humanity in mountains and waters.

Taoists want to see the extraordinary in the ordinary; that includes seeing changes in society with the sea mist.

15

The Way Follows Nature

After their vision gazing over the sea, the four travelers took a boat to Lushun, then headed northeast from the eastern part of the Liaoning peninsula. The cold winds of late autumn blew harder and harder, filling the mountains with fallen leaves. The Taoists had now entered the vast domain of Everwhite Mountain. One day, when they came to a large birch grove, they suddenly heard a howl in the wind. Following the sound, they came to a rocky hillside, where they found an enormous birch behind a boulder; the ancient tree had split at the base, opening a deep cavern. The sound was coming from here.

The Wayfarer of Pure Emptiness said, "This is a wolf lair. There's a cub inside waiting to be nursed."

Wang Liping found this most interesting. He crouched down and put his ear by the opening to listen. The wolf cub, being cautious by nature, didn't make a sound. Hearing nothing, Liping thought of using a stick to probe, but the Wayfarer of Pure Emptiness hurriedly stopped him. Creeping up to the mouth of the cavern, he signaled to the others to back off. The Wayfarer suddenly made two short, sharp cries, imitating the sound of a wolf calling its cub. Immediately there was a stir inside the cavern. Before long a grey wolf cub emerged; looking around, seeing that its mother was not there, it hurriedly turned around and tried to scramble back into its lair with a cry. Wang Liping, swift of eye and quick of hand, caught hold of the cub and picked it up. Delighted, he held the cub in his arms and didn't want to let it go.

The grand master looked at the two mentors and said with a smile, "Now it's up to you two to watch out for Liping!"

The mentors were thinking the same thing. They called Wang Liping away from the wolf lair. Then all four exercised their ability of lightness, and in the blink of an eye they were out of the birch woods, leaving it far behind.

Crossing two mountain ridges and a freezing cold river, the four travelers came to a wide open level area. Seeing a lumber truck coming down the road, the Taoists surreptitiously jumped onboard, to go wherever it would take them. An afternoon on the back of the truck took the Taoists a long way. Finally, at a signal from the grand master, the four jumped off. Landing lightly on the ground, they headed for the high fastness of Mount Chong, Lofty Mountain.

Reaching a comparatively level spot on the mountainside, the four Taoists found huge cedars growing together with sturdy pines, as well as a dense grove of deciduous trees. It was dusk, and the four sat under a huge pine tree to rest.

As the men took out some provisions, the wolf cub cried with hunger. Since it was just a baby, Wang Liping chewed the food himself first before feeding it to the cub, mouthful by mouthful.

Suddenly there was a piercing howl. On the alert at once, the four men saw a massive grey wolf bound out of the woods. Observing a group of humans, the wolf stopped a dozen yards away, fangs bared, her eyes fixed on the cub in Wang Liping's arms; breathing roughly, teats swaying, she watched for a chance to attack.

Wang Liping inwardly mobilized his energy, preparing to fight with the mother wolf. The grand master commanded him not to hurt the mother wolf, and to release the cub back to her at once. Liping obediently set the wolf cub lightly on the ground; whereupon it bounded toward its mother. Without waiting, the mother wolf leaped forward, grabbed the cub by the scruff, and disappeared into the woods.

Just as Wang Liping was about to sigh with relief, he saw that unexpectedly the wolf had retraced its steps and reappeared before him, even more ferocious than before. Lowering her muzzle to the ground, she let out a long, low howl, which was answered by several clear cries from a distance. Sweeping the area in a glance, the four Taoists saw that they were already surrounded by grey wolves looking for an opportunity to attack.

"Climb a tree!" The moment the grand master gave the command, all four men leapt off the ground and scrambled up a tree. At that instant the wolves attacked, nearly catching Wang Liping.

As the four men sat in the tree branches, the pack of wolves paced around below, baring their teeth and howling. Wang Liping asked the masters what to do.

The masters laughed. Liping was puzzled.

"You're the one who brought these wolves here," said the Wayfarer of the Infinite to the youth. "You think of a way to get rid of them. Why ask us? I'm old and tired. I'd like to take this moment of leisure to have a little nap!" So saying, he closed his eyes and appeared to go to sleep, leaning against the branches.

The two mentors just watched the violently agitated wolves, not saying a word.

Wang Liping had no plan of action. Figuring he'd been trapped by the masters, he decided to employ inner power. Working up energy combining inner forces at their source, he raised his right palm.

"Don't kill any of them," the grand master suddenly called.

"Just use thirty percent of your power," quickly added the Wayfarer of Pure Serenity. "Let them live."

With these instructions in mind, Wang Liping thrust his palm out violently. A beam of white light flashed, and several of the wolves collapsed motionless on the ground without a sound.

Liping's heart shuddered. He didn't think he'd used that much force, but after all three wolves had died. Now he'd broken the precept against taking life, a serious misdeed.

What Wang Liping used here was the Five Thunder Palm. This power emerges swift as lightning, with tremendous force. The extraordinary thing about this is that the victim shows no external sign of injury; the power enters inside the body with an explosive force, capable of damaging the internal organs by the shock. Among Taoists, this palm strike has historically been used only for defense, never for aggression.

The Wayfarer of Pure Serenity had practiced this palm strike for years and was highly skilled; he had passed on everything he knew to Wang Liping. The two had practiced together, reaching the most refined levels of attainment. Combined with the Step of Yu, when the hand is suddenly thrust forward in the course of exercise, it has even more of that peerless power.

The grand master had given orders not to take any life by means of this technique. The mentors had followed this rule strictly. Once during practice when the Wayfarer of Pure Serenity inadvertently injured Wang

Liping, he was extremely disturbed by his error. Now that Wang Liping was going to try the technique for the first time, this mentor warned him to use only a little force to avoid taking life.

When several wolves collapsed, that did not scare off the rest of the pack. The remaining wolves became even fiercer; eyes glaring, they leapt up, shrieking hideously. Not daring to use the palm strike again, Wang Liping broke off a branch and tossed it down. Several wolves grabbed at it and tore it to pieces; while the rest scrambled madly. Several put their snouts low to the ground and let out a series of doleful cries. The mountains and valleys echoed with answering calls, and a number of wild wolves came bounding out, adding to the strength of the pack.

Seeing that Wang Liping was at a loss, the Wayfarer of Pure Serenity said to him, "Settle down your energy. We have a method of repelling armies. These wolves are naturally fierce and live in packs; when one is in danger, others come to it. If you keep on this way, more and more wolves will gather, and there will be no way to beat them back even if you try. Wolves have a natural enemy, however. Let a single tiger show up, and a whole pack of wolves will run away."

Having said this, the Wayfarer signaled to the Wayfarer of Pure Emptiness: both men cupped their hands around their mouths, worked up energy from the very bottom of their feet, and all of a sudden produced a blasting roar that sounded like a pride of tigers. Hearing that sound, the wolves were momentarily stunned with fear; then they fled in all directions, without looking back.

This roar was produced by such inner power that it sounded like muffled thunder reverberating in the distance. Wang Liping felt his own insides had been shaken up, such was the ferocity of that "tiger roar." This force was even more powerful than the Five Thunder Palm.

Then the grand master got down from the tree and began to massage the bellies of the three unconscious wolves, saying over and over, "O Creation! Let us hope there is no internal damage, and they are only stunned." Finally, using his inner power, he managed to revive the wolves. As for the cub, Wang Liping found it under a boulder, also half knocked out by the "tiger roar." Liping brought the cub back to its mother and put it at her breast. As the men watched, the four wolves slowly came back to life. Now Wang Liping could finally relax. Observing this scene, the three old masters looked at each other and smiled.

The day was already growing late. The four travelers left this place to go find somewhere to lodge.

The following day, Wang Liping was still thinking about the events of the previous day. He asked his mentors to teach him how to make the tiger roar. Both mentors then transmitted to him the method known as Spewing, also called Spellbinding Sound.

The mentors explained that when humans first began to live on dry land, conditions were extremely negative, and they were often attacked by wild animals. People lived in groups, and when there was danger they would make a kind of sound to call the others. So "spewing" is an inherent human capacity. Even now, when people are in danger, they still cry "O, Mother!" or "O God!" as if seeking help to escape.

Through long observation, people discovered that sound is a very complex power. Even on the lowest level, everything can be made to produce a sound, or can produce a sound. Every sound represents a specific content and the meaning it contains. Speaking in terms of animals, the relationships among their cries include stimulus, harmony, dominance, and control. When a bird calls, for example, that brings on the calls of a multitude of birds; whereas the sound of a cat will make mice run away.

This is the lowest level of understanding the origin of the Spellbinding Sound. Seen on a higher level, the method of Spellbinding Sound is complex and mysterious, containing an invisible power within a special kind of sound. This is hard to understand, but it actually exists, it certainly works, and it does have a function. This is a very high achievement.

The "spellbinding sound" of which we speak here is quite different from mimicry as ordinarily understood. Mimicry is only a simple imitation of a particular sound; it does not contain the "inner power." Spellbinding sound, in contrast, uses sound transmitted through the mouth to release a kind of inner power. Because internal energies are being exercised differently, sounds that are the same or similar can be very different in terms of inner power and function. At an even higher level, even the sound is secondary; sometimes it is possible to dispense with audible sound and just rely on the vibration of the inner organs to spew out a stream of refined energy, which contains an enormous power that can be transmitted to a distance. This stream of refined energy can shake the corresponding internal organs in other people, and it can also cause disturbance in other things. This belongs to the elementary practice of "mental spellbinding."

"Mental spellbinding" requires the cultivation of inner power to a certain degree before it can produce effects; that is why it is an advanced technique of inner work. The issue is one of effective empowerment. The words of a spell will have no power and no effect when you invoke them if you have no foundation of inner work. When the same words are invoked by someone with a sufficient basis of inner work, then the spell is powerful and effective. This is like the principle of drawing talismans.

Why do Taoists emphasize cultivation of essence and development of inner power? Cultivation of essence is setting up the basis correctly; then all exercises and methods are rooted in the Great Way and work for the Great Way. People whose minds are not straight and whose essence is impure cannot enter the gate. The minimum requirements are not taking life and not using Taoist methods for personal gain or for doing bad things. The cultivation of inner power can bring forth countless methods of practice; these methods are stepladders by which to climb to the highest states. To stick with just one method is a kind of attachment, a failure to understand the Great Way.

"Spellbinding sound" is a sort of means of transmitting influence and information between people, between humans and animals, and between human beings and other forces. At the lowest level, it can be used to attract people as well as to repel them; it can be used to summon and also to drive off an animal. Science is now focusing attention on such phenomena, and is starting to study the language of animals. Although considerable research has been done, from the Taoist point of view, it is still on a very low level.

Taoists do not overlook this level of research, but they have transcended it. They seek to load more onto a sound for transmission, so that it can do more things, and more important things. They also seek to produce a soundless sound conveying an even more mysterious power, to accomplish inconceivable things.

Humankind has been through tens of thousands of years of history, without any final conclusion. The only thing that can be affirmed is that in the process of development of humankind there has been both progress and regression.

Since human beings managed to survive under harsh primitive conditions, early humans must have had extraordinary powers of survival and adaptation different from modern man.

The main function of the five senses is to perceive the material world of objects. Does the human body have no other faculties of sense? The phenomenal world is not a simple existence, but a complex entity comprised of many elements, with many facets. If we only used one sense to cognize one facet or one element, we would be far from being able to grasp the world. And the reason that the senses are able to sense is because of the mind or brain. Were there no mind or brain, no judgment would be formed, and there would be feeling without sense. We need not say there is something there beyond the senses to realize there must be a capacity and a method for transcending the senses.

Humankind undoubtedly has the capacity and means of transcending the senses; it is just that these are in a manifest state in some people; while in a dormant or latent state in others.

The reason Taoists value inner work is that their aim is to make dormant or latent powers and abilities become manifest. This is not mythology, but reality. Relying on such means and capacities, Taoists explore a wider, richer, more marvelous world; the work they do is a grand enterprise, one that has extremely important meaning for the present and future of humankind.

While practicing the technique of spellbinding sound to summon animals, Wang Liping deeply felt the intimate communion between humans and animals, and indeed among all living beings, the absence of any barrier or gap between humanity and Nature, the harmonious communion of humanity and Nature, the possibility for humanity to enter into the various domains of Nature, merging into oneness with Nature.

Nature is the mother of humankind; humankind is a child of Nature. Humans are the most intelligent animals, yet all things are teachers of humankind. Master Wang Liping told us, "Although I had orthodox Taoist teachers, in reality I had many more teachers, both known and unknown. Some of these teachers were living people; some were deceased people. Some were animals; some were plants. Some had life; some were inanimate. There were also the sun, moon, stars, and planets, all of them included among my teachers. I had countless teachers, and they taught me countless things. They taught me while I was awake, and they taught me even more while I was asleep dreaming. So I have received instruction from the entire universe." Gazing out the window at a willow tree as he said this, Master Wang Liping added poignantly, "This tree has feelings, just as a human being does." As he spoke of the tree, the feeling was as if he were in the presence of an old friend, or were seeing a venerable elder, a sage, a teacher, or someone likewise worthy of respect.

~~~~~~

Autumn lingers only briefly on Everwhite Mountain before winter comes storming in. It was not long before cold winds were whistling, snow was on the ground, ice was in the air, and the mountain woods were plunged into stillness. On this particular night, the four Taoists passed the night sitting in a mountain cavern, already sensing the clouds spreading densely and quietly scattering huge snowflakes. When Wang Liping took a look outside at dawn, he found the whole world adorned with silver and wrapped in white silk. Snow lay heavy on the green pines; jadelike peaks stood out in rows.

As Wang Liping walked on the virgin snow, he recalled the days of his childhood when he and his playmates would make snowmen. Thinking of those days, he found himself making snowballs and throwing them into the distance.

After playing around like this for a while, Liping thought to himself that his teachers, being so old and so thinly clad, must be having a hard time standing this cold weather. He decided to gather some firewood for them.

Seeing Wang Liping with a bundle of brush, the Wayfarer of Pure Serenity asked, "What's all that stuff for?"

"I'm going to build a fire. Aren't you cold?"

The Wayfarer laughed. "Why make a fire in such warm weather? Aren't you afraid we'll fry?"

Wang Liping had no answer. He thought his mentor was joking. He touched his mentor's hand and found it to be cold as ice. Then he touched the grand master's hand; it too was cold, through and through. "You're about to freeze," he cried, "and yet you say it's warm?"

The Wayfarer of Pure Serenity laughed and said, "If we froze, wouldn't we become even hotter?"

Suddenly Wang Liping understood.

"Come with me," said the Wayfarer, leading Liping out of the cavern into the vast expanse of snow.

The snow was fluffy, over half a foot deep, just right for use as a sitting cushion for practicing exercises. The Wayfarer first asked Liping to sit in a special posture, quickly shut off part of his energy channels, tune his breathing and attention, and rapidly lower his body temperature until it was the same temperature as the outside environment, without, however, allowing the point of true fire in his body to be extinguished.

Wang Liping had already reached the stage in his practice where he could freely close or open any energy channel or sensitive point in his body at will. Now he understood very quickly what he was to do with his teacher's guidance. As he followed instructions, his body temperature actually did fall, and he gradually ceased to feel the snow as cold.

The most remarkable thing was that as he did this there seemed to be a mass of energy surrounding his body; the snow didn't fall right on him, but stopped about a foot above his head and slid down to one side. Even at times when the snow was flying all around there was no snow on his body at all.

There are plenty of examples of this practice in the natural world, not only among plants but also among animals. They all use regulation of body temperature as a means of adapting to climactic changes in order to stay alive. There is a kind of snake on an island north of England that freezes during the winter, then comes out of hibernation when it thaws out in the spring. Most snakes hibernate underground in winter, but this English snake lets itself freeze. How can its tissues freeze without being damaged, how can it freeze without dying, and how can it revive? The reasons are not clear, but at least it can be said that there exists within living beings a kind of capacity to regulate body temperature, a comparatively strong power to adapt to changes in the external environment. Can the human body be frozen and stored, die and revive? This is not impossible. Science is now in the process of researching appropriate conditions and techniques, with certain countries already taking the lead in this quest.

Taoists pursue another approach. They sit in the snow for one or two days, or even longer. While sitting, furthermore, the individual is at all times in a state of clear wakefulness. What Taoists want to do is control themselves and operate themselves deliberately; they seek to watch the subtle changes in the outside world as well as within their own bodies, in order to bring them into mutual harmony. After cultivating refinement to a certain degree, the body temperature may be raised to normal; the difference between body temperature and air temperature is then compensated for by another kind of power.

Humanity follows earth; earth follows heaven; heaven follows the Way; the Way follows Nature.

The mentor required Wang Liping to sit in the snow for eight hours, then conclude the exercise and open up his closed energy channels and apertures one by one in a specific order, using the point of true fire to warm his whole body. Gradually the sensation returned to his skin; only then did he feel the cold engulfing him, as if he were in an ice pit.

Opening his eyes, Wang Liping saw that the snow on the ground was over a foot deep; while all around him it had piled up to form a round tub as high as his shoulders, leaving only his head above the level of the snow walls.

The Wayfarer of Pure Emptiness called the grand master and the other mentor to come take a look at this scene. In a playful mood, the Wayfarer of Pure Serenity threw snow on Liping. As teachers and apprentice played in the snow, the recondite mountain fields echoed with joyful laughter.

～～～～

The four Taoists now continued their journey north. Traveling in snowcovered mountains increased the fun, but it also increased the danger. It was hard to tell whether the footing was solid or not, so everyone had to be exceptionally alert. Although Wang Liping had been born and raised in the northeast, this was the first time he'd ever been in the depths of Everwhite Mountain. It naturally fell to the lot of the Wayfarer of Pure Serenity to take the lead and find the way.

The grand master said to Wang Liping, "You should stay quietly in a snow cave facing a wall and practice exercises while we go roaming around. We'll come back and get you later. How about that?"

Wang Liping replied, "Fine, but how are you going to find me in the trackless snow? It would be better if the three of you went on back home and waited out the winter. When the ice and snow melt and the mountains are flooded with torrential runoff, you can look under the boat you're riding, catch the big fish you see there, and haul it in. I'll be sitting in its belly!"

"Good, good, good!" The three old wizards couldn't help laughing.

One particular day, when the four Taoists had just climbed a mountain ridge, they saw a trail of footprints in the snow. Looking carefully, Wang Liping shuddered; the prints had been made by bare feet! Who could be way out here in the mountains?

The grand master, who had already noticed the footprints, remarked, "Looks like he's getting more and more spiritual the longer he lives."

Wang Liping didn't get his meaning; he just followed the master along the trail of the footprints.

Pursuing the tracks in the snow, the four Taoists skirted a hill, walking over deeply layered snow, and made their way through a wood before they saw an ancient pine on the mountainside, weighted down with snow, like an umbrella or canopy. Under the pine tree was a wooden shack. The shack was simple and rustic yet stood out quite elegantly in the snow.

There was an old man in front of the shack; he was tall and had a massive frame. Simply and thinly clad, he was clearing the snow drifts away from the front of the shack.

The grand master couldn't help intoning the lines,

> *A green pine embraces a little shack;*
> *deep mountains conceal a real human being.*

The old man in front of the shack replied poetically,

> *A thousand mountains tremble at a roar;*
> *one cry, and the hundred beasts shudder.*

Wang Liping felt very strange; he realized that the old man was referring to their encounter with wolves several days earlier. It had already been days now, and the incident had taken place over a hundred miles away. If this old man was able to hear that "tiger roar" and knew what had happened, then he must be a man of high attainment.

The old man in front of the shack came down the mountainside to greet the four travelers. "You've come a long way," he said. "I was just going to melt some snow for you to wash up." The four returned the greetings and followed the barefooted old man into the shack.

As it turned out, this barefooted old man was not an ordinary person after all; he was a successor of the illustrious Great Immortal of Everwhite Mountain. Calling himself the Barefoot Wayfarer, he had lived in seclusion for many years in the depths of Everwhite Mountain and had reached extraordinary attainments. The year these five first met, the Barefoot Wayfarer was seventy-seven years old; at the time of the present writing, he has reached the advanced age of ninety-seven. Following the rules of Taoism, Wang Liping also honored him as a spiritual uncle.

The Barefoot Wayfarer's shack was extremely simple inside, the room fashioned of unfinished wood, with hardly any furnishings, only a long table to put things on, made of natural timber, not even sawed straight, let alone planed, everything done naturally. There was no bed platform, just a pile of straw. The Barefoot Wayfarer took some straw and made four cushions, inviting the four Taoist travelers to sit down. He also took some dried fruit off the table and gave it to them to eat. Wang Liping found the wild fruits delicious.

The Barefoot Wayfarer asked the Wayfarer of the Infinite, "Why have you come so far, making your way here in the snow?"

The Wayfarer of the Infinite explained, "We came to the tail of Everwhite Mountain years ago and stayed there for some time to bring up a new Transmitter to succeed us. Then the country fell into chaos, and all we could do was take our apprentice traveling. In the last three years, we have roamed over half of China, and now we've come back. I came here in the snow looking for you first because of our old friendship."

"You are too kind," said the Barefoot Wayfarer humbly. "I hope you and the other two masters will give me some instruction." The Wayfarer of the Infinite then introduced the Transmitter Wang Liping to the Barefoot Wayfarer. The Wayfarer scrutinized him for some time and was very pleased.

Wang Liping now realized that the Barefoot Wayfarer and his teachers were already in contact and were colleagues in Taoism in spite of the vast distances separating them. At last he understood the meaning of the grand master's remark on seeing the footprints in the snow.

When Taoist colleagues meet, naturally they discuss the Way. The four elders spent the night conversing freely; as Wang Liping listened quietly, he learned quite a few things.

The following day the snow had stopped. The bright sun in the clear sky lit the plain of snow with a shimmering silver light, illuminating a world of complete purity.

The Wayfarer of Pure Serenity and the Barefooted Wayfarer decided to practice Taoist arts together to sharpen their capacities. The two men sat in the snow outside and began to exercise their inner power. Before long, the snow within a radius of several feet around the two had completely melted, exposing green rocks underneath, and even the rocks gradually dried out.

The Wayfarer of the Infinite and the Wayfarer of Pure Emptiness stood by quietly watching. Wang Liping also looked on in silent wonder.

In the blink of an eye, the Wayfarer of Pure Serenity and the Barefoot Wayfarer rose from the ground, sitting in midair. Both remained suspended in midair for about an hour.

As Wang Liping watched his mentor working inwardly with closed eyes, he thought up a scheme. He figured he'd test his own ability by secretly snatching the energy mass from underneath his mentor. The Wayfarer of Pure Serenity had no idea his disciple could do this. Unable to prevent the energy from being drained away from underneath him, he came down from midair at once. Right away he realized what had happened.

Wang Liping was very sharp-witted. Fearing his mentor would pull a trick right back on him, Liping immediately begged him for forgiveness.

The Barefoot Wayfarer already realized what was going on. He kept saying, "You are quite extraordinary, and your young apprentice is a worthy disciple of a distinguished school. I've learned something today!"

Everyone laughed, and the Wayfarer of Pure Serenity pardoned Wang Liping. Now Liping took this opportunity to ask his mentor and his spiritual uncle to teach him how to sit in the air. His spiritual uncle liked this young apprentice more and more.

16

Ever Higher

In early 1970, when the Chinese people, seeking some joy in the midst of hardship and chaos, were busily preparing for the traditional festival of spring, the three Taoist masters and their apprentice quietly returned to Wang Liping's hometown.

Their journey had lasted three springs and four autumns; the grand master was now eighty-nine years old; the mentors were already about eighty. Their apprentice Wang Liping had grown into a refined, free-spirited young man.

The three aged men had set out on this long, grueling journey with their disciple in order to see to it that the Great Way would be transmitted to later generations. Solving all sorts of difficulties with the Taoist spirit, appreciating the mountains and waters of the ten directions, experiencing all kinds of conditions, they had realized many truths. Wang Liping had now seen the world and registered the changes of the universe in his mind.

Three years' journey over thousands of miles is not an easy matter. On the road, all had not been poetic vistas and picturesque scenery; more often it had been desolation and misery. Sometimes the four men saw no human hearths for days on end and had to find caves to sleep in and wild fruits and vegetables to fill their bellies. Sometimes they were caught in storms, soaked to the skin, barely able to get a footing in the mud, yet they pressed on. Sometimes, with fierce sun beating down on their heads, parched earth stretched as far as the eye could see, and not a drop of water could be found, but they still kept going strong.

All four Taoists were men of high attainment, so the hardships of this material world did not faze them. But they were, after all, human beings, made of flesh and blood, so the pains and challenges of the road took a toll on their bodies. The masters were so old that it was no easy matter for them to go through the same hardships that their young disciple did as they trained him. But these were men who had put life and death out of their minds; their concern was to avoid wasting precious time in this limited human life, to pursue the work that had been begun by their spiritual ancestors and continued for generation after generation—searching out the mysteries of the universe and human life. Their mission was to hand on the knowledge they had inherited, enhancing it by their own efforts, fostering further progress. They were not fixed on material hardship or ease; their minds were bent on spiritual investigation and search, enrichment and sublimation.

According to the education Wang Liping received from the three old wizards, action is more important than talk; spiritual inspiration is more important than formal exercises. Over the three years of their journey, the wizards had deposited an enormous treasure of spiritual wealth in the mind of Wang Liping, profoundly influencing his higher development.

Another important gain was made on this journey. Deep in the mountains they had discovered a valuable book personally composed by the Tang-dynasty Taoist adept Lu Dongbin himself. The three wizards knew that before their Ancestor Lu had ascended into the beyond, he had taken a number of books that he had not transmitted to successors and concealed them in caverns on several famous mountains, where they still lie undiscovered. During their travels, the wizards actually found one of these books. Realizing they had discovered a genuine treasure, the wizards were deliriously happy. The text was so old that they had to use slips of bamboo to turn the brittle pages with extreme care. These Taoists are even now in the process of putting this text in order and making an exhaustive study of its contents.

The day the four travelers came back to Liping's hometown, Wang Liping's mother had been uneasy in mind all morning. Thinking her second son must have returned, she rushed to the village outskirts, craning her neck to gaze into the distance. When the four men finally trudged in through the windswept dust, Mother Wang saw that the old "doctors" were sturdy of frame and ruddy of cheek as before; and here was her son, all grown up into a fine young man. Overcome with joy, she wiped tears from the corners of her eyes as she took her son Liping by the hand.

As they walked along together, Mother Wang blurted out that everyone in the family had been having recurrent dreams in recent days, dreams in which they saw the four travelers on their way home. She marveled at how the dreams had actually proven true. While feigning ignorance, the four men smiled to themselves as they listened to Mother Wang, sharing an unspoken secret among themselves. Mother Wang couldn't have known that her son and the old "doctors" had been sending this information by dream transmission.

Now in the China of 1970 class struggle was still raging fiercely, but the Grand Assembly of Representatives had opened, and the power struggle had reached a certain plateau. The peasants were sick and tired of the fighting, and even though factional struggles continued to exert a profound influence, nevertheless many people no longer took them so seriously. For the Taoist masters and their apprentice, the situation was somewhat better than it had been in the early days of the Cultural Revolution.

Now, after more than three years, the three elders would no longer be among the main targets of the "Horizontal Broom" of the Cultural Revolution; now people would pay no attention to them. Since they'd been gone more than three years, what is more, many people had forgotten about them. Now that they were back, the three old wizards concealed themselves more deeply, spending most of the days in the mountain forests, only returning to their old haunt at the smithy by night, bringing some kindling or vegetables. As a result, many people had no idea they were again living there.

The old wizards wanted to find a quiet corner in the midst of all the chaos to complete the final stage of their work of transmitting their knowledge to their apprentice, pushing Wang Liping further on the road of his life journey of ascent. This was the ninth and final stage of Wang Liping's study of Taoism, namely bathing.

Wang Liping had to go through three lives to attain "eternal life." The first life was the Wang Liping of the "lower three realms," the one born of his father and mother. Through fasting, suspended animation, and dying, then being nurtured and restored to life, he became the Wang Liping of the "middle three realms." Again going through gestation in the great "womb" of the universe, only after several years was the "embryo" fully developed, and he was reborn from this "great mother" to fly up into a vaster, unbounded universe. Then Wang Liping was the Wang Liping of the "higher three realms," having now attained to "eternal life."

Bathing in heaven and earth is the final exercise in the middle three realms. This bathing is divided into four types: elixir bathing, earth substance bathing, sky substance bathing, and bathing in the formless and immaterial.

One night, after the three wizards had completed the necessary preparations, the Wayfarer of the Infinite took out a grain of elixir, handed it to Wang Liping, and told him to swallow it.

This was the third time Wang Liping had ingested alchemical elixir. Each time the elixir was different, and the intended purpose was not the same. Taoist elixirs are classified into five types—metal, water, wood, fire, and earth—each type having a different combination of ingredients put through a different process of preparation, resulting in elixirs of different appearances and different effects.

Respectfully receiving the elixir from the grand master, Wang Liping ingested it in the prescribed manner, then sat in a huge tub of hot water prepared beforehand. The hot water had to be maintained at a specific temperature. Wang Liping was supposed to use the power of inner work to dissolve the elixir, diffuse it throughout his body via energy and blood, then use his inner power to eject it from his body. The elixir emerged from the surface of his skin, and on contact with the hot water it came off his skin and floated up to the surface of the water, forming shiny crystalline grains. The impurities inside his body were ejected along with the elixir.

Wang Liping sat completely still inside the tub for two days and two nights. The absorption and ejection of the elixir were both extremely painful processes. There are stories in literature about people experiencing infinite bliss from ingesting Taoist elixirs, but this never happened to Wang Liping.

During this time the three old wizards kept a careful watch, as before. The water had to be kept fairly hot. It couldn't be too cool or too hot. If it were too cool, Liping's pores would shrink, making it impossible for him to eject the elixir smoothly: if it were too hot, it would scald the skin, causing injury and ruining the effect of the exercise. The two mentors took turns adjusting the fire around the tub, maintaining an exhausting vigil. The grand master came by from time to time to see how much elixir was floating on the surface of the water. Taking care of their one apprentice kept all three wizards busy.

Having done very well at elixir bathing, Wang Liping now had an even more extraordinary sensation. One day as he was sitting, Wang Liping suddenly noticed something round pulsating evenly and gently in his lower abdomen. The feeling was like a warm spring breeze, or like a fluffy cloud in the clear sky under the bright moon. Virtually still, and yet moving, it seemed to open and close. Gradually this circle pulsated throughout his whole body, like ripples on a pond, so that every pore of his body opened and closed along with the pulsation. His pores seemed to be like ventilation conduits, with air flowing freely through them.

Wang Liping was intoxicated by this relaxing sensation. He didn't need his mouth and nose to breathe. He felt as if his body had become a fluid, undifferentiated whole, opening and closing within a fluid universe. His own body and the universe seem to have merged into one. There was a very subtle rhythmic contraction, immaculately pure, clean and refreshing, transparently penetrating. Enveloped in a halo of five-colored light, he felt as if he were in flight.

When Wang Liping consciously shuts the pores of his whole body, his umbilicus opens up, turning into a passageway through which energy can enter and exit; the internal organs also tense and relax correspondingly along with the energy flow. If he closes the umbilical pass, then the pores automatically open again, spontaneously inhaling and exhaling. The tacit harmony of these two in concert is an inexpressible marvel; the feeling of relaxation and comfort is far beyond that of breathing through the mouth and nose.

The grand master was very happy to see that Wang Liping had successfully cultivated the state of true womb breathing. Lao-tzu's saying "Return to infancy" seems to refer to this state.

Ancestor Lu also said, "You do not prolong life by absorbing energy; prolonging life requires subduing energy. The embryo is formed within subdued energy; the energy has its own breath in the womb. When energy enters the body, this is called birth; when spirit leaves, this is called death. Knowing spirit and energy can prolong life; keep to emptiness to nurture spirit and energy. When the spirit acts, energy acts; when the spirit leaves, energy leaves. If you want to prolong life, have spirit and energy help each other, not arousing thoughts in the mind; no going, no coming, not exiting, not entering, spontaneously stable. If you practice this diligently, this is the true path."

The grand master explained to Wang Liping that the status of the umbilicus in the human body is very important. The ancients said that the umbilicus in a human being is like the North Star in the sky. It is therefore called the "Pivot of Heaven" and the "Capital of the Spirit." The lair of spirit and energy, it is the root of preserving life, the treasure of outward emptiness restoring positive energy. The umbilicus is connected with the internal organs; when the umbilicus opens, then the internal organs and the womb of heaven and earth can interact directly. The individual has then returned to the beginning of the primordial state; from this point on one must exercise it diligently, not slacking off.

Wang Liping cultivated refinement very carefully according to the methods taught him by the grand master, concentrating his energy and making it supple, continuously there, seeming to be yet not, seeming not to be yet not nonexistent. By long and constant practice, the true breath will always remain.

By this time spring had returned, and all things were sprouting anew. The trees were draped in yellow-green; the fields and meadows were dyed with green—all pulses of a single mechanism of life.

The sun shone with a gentle warmth; a spring breeze brushed lightly by. Wang Liping sat on the bank of a small river beside a green mountain, like a plant newly sprouted from the earth, like a tender bud just opening on a branch, bathing in this light, this breeze, this breath of spring coming from the earth, plants, and trees. Clouds and rain crept up, coming on so lightly they almost seemed to be hesitant to disturb Wang Liping's dream as he bathed in Nature. As the raindrops fell, fine as a young girl's hair, the fields exhaled the fragrance of earth as they grew moist. Wang Liping seemed to sense the delight of the plants in the rain; he seemed to hear the sounds of the buds growing on the branches.

The night sky was clear and calm. There was no wind, just the chilly air of early spring. The new moon hung in space; the stars were dense and bright. The distant mountains lay quietly beneath the starry sky, bathing together with Wang Liping in the mystical colors of the night.

The morning mist enveloped everything as far as the eye could see. The mountains and villages in the distance were invisible. Wrapped in the misty fog, Wang Liping bathed in it.

Cultivating refinement day in and day out, Wang Liping's mind was freed of all rumination, and he was filled with true energy. His skin was like congealed resin, and his bones were like space; his head was surrounded by a halo, and his eyes were full of spirit. When he inwardly viewed his own body, it was as clear as luminescence; when he looked at objects at night, they appeared as distinctly as in the daytime.

The grand master and the mentors instructed Wang Liping not to deliberately seek wonders, but to let them be as they are, allowing them to appear and disappear of their own accord, coming and going by themselves, changing spontaneously. Your mind should always be rooted in clarity and calm; making it peaceful and serene, merging with the Way by means of the spirit, you return to naturalness. At this point, when you observe things in the distance there are no such things in them; when you observe outward form, there is no such form in the form; when you observe mind within, there is no such mind in mind. Not conscious of having a body, you gradually enter the uncontrived Way, into the realm of rare sublimity. If you become obsessed with unusual experiences, your mind will be influenced and attached, and you will enter into a state of bedevilment; your accomplishment will stop at minor tangential techniques, your previous achievement will go to naught, and you will be far from the Great Way.

Now the grand master finally instructed Wang Liping in the methods of the highest level of the *Ultimate Teaching of the Spiritual Jewels*, the three ways of the great vehicle for transcending the ordinary and entering into sagehood, also referred to, in the context of the *Three Immortalist Exercises*, as the exercises for celestial immortality.

As mentioned before, the *Three Immortalist Exercises* are divided into three levels—human immortalism, earth immortalism, and celestial immortalism.

In "human immortalism" exercises, the body is the furnace, energy is the medicine, the heart is the fire, and the genitals are the water. Using the body for the furnace, the body is divided along its equator into upper and lower poles. Using energy for medicine, you refine the energy in the elixir field, so that energy and water interact and turn into gold elixir. Using the heart for fire and the genitals for water, one heaven and one earth, they commune and nurture.

In "earth immortalism" exercises, the spirit is the furnace, energy is the medicine, the sun is the fire, and the moon is the water. Seeking treasure deep in the ocean, traversing the sky gazing at the moon, spirit and energy combine, and the three elixir fields are settled. Reference to the sun and moon means coordinating the sun and moon within your body with the sun and moon in the sky.

In "celestial immortalism" exercises, the spirit is the furnace, essence is the medicine, concentration is the water, insight is the fire; heaven and earth perpetually revolve; Nature and humanity assimilate.

~~~~~~~

Molded by a long tradition of knowledge and wisdom from a profound source, steeped in the omnipresent flow of Nature, bathed in the lights of the sun and moon, nurtured and purified by clear springs of sweet dew, instructed by three teachers of two generations, refined by countless hardships and difficulties over a period of seven years, having exited life and entered death, Wang Liping had arrived at the higher vehicle state of "transcendent liberation and replication of the body."

Wang Liping had certainly changed. His face had become like a peach blossom, and his skin was like fine jade; his mien was kindly, and his body gave off a sublime fragrance. His appearance was delicate, yet within was hidden an indestructible, adamantine body: when still, he was like an expanse of clear water, without waves; in action, he shook the heavens and the earth, his energy swallowing mountains and rivers.

Seeing that Wang Liping had reached this stage, the three old wizards were overjoyed. The Wayfarer of the Infinite recited Ancestor Lu's "Spring Seeping into the Garden":

> *The restorative elixir is in us:*
> *first one must refine the self until the right time.*
> *When one yang first moves,*
> *eternity chimes at midnight.*
> *The lead cauldron warm,*
> *light penetrates the screen.*
> *Creation races;*
> *tiger and dragon mate:*
> *turning up the fire,*
> *overheating's dangerous!*

Over the winding river,
see the moonlight, pure and clear—
there's a lone bird flying.

At that time, you yourself drink from
the medicinal spoon;
and who would have believed,
but in nothingness you've raised a child!
Distinguish purity and pollution at the source,
and the separation of wood and metal;
if not for a teacher's directions,
how can these things be known?
The essence of the Way
is mysterious and subtle;
the mechanism of Nature
is profound and remote;
if you get right to work on practice,
that is still too late.
The road to Penglai, isle of immortals,
needs the fulfillment
of three thousand deeds;
then you return like the clouds,
walking alone.

On this particular day, the sky was blue, and the air was clear. The mountains and rivers stood out clearly; it was a very good day.

The sixteenth-generation Transmitter of the Dragon Gate branch of Complete Reality Taoism, the Wayfarer of the Infinite; the seventeenth-generation Transmitters the Wayfarer of Pure Serenity and the Wayfarer of Pure Emptiness; and the eighteenth-generation Transmitter Wang Liping, the Spiritually Effective One, all purified their bodies, burned incense, and paid obeisance to heaven, to earth, and to their spiritual ancestors.

After this rite, the Wayfarer of the Infinite said to his disciple Wang Liping, "The Way is rooted in nonbeing; whatever is spoken of in terms of being is not the Way. The Way is rooted in emptiness; whatever is spoken of in terms of substantiality is not the Way. Since it has no substance, question and answer about it is impossible; since it has no form, seeing and hearing it is impossible. If you consider mysterious subtlety to be the Way, even mysterious subtlety is not free from the burden of question and answer. If you consider rarefied peacefulness the Way, even rarefied peacefulness does not escape the domain of seeing and hearing. If mysterious subtlety and rarefied peacefulness are still not the Way, then the wherefore of the Way is not known. To call it the Way is forced; it can only be understood spiritually. From now on, whenever you hear sounds or see objects, do not listen as you hear and do not look as you see. Then sounds will dissolve of themselves; objects will disappear of themselves. After you have experienced this, Complete Reality will then become evident. Remember!"

Following the grand master's instructions, Wang Liping sat with his eyes closed. Before long, the grand master and the mentor gradually disappeared; the mountains, rivers, and trees also gradually vanished. All Liping sensed was a feeling of floating into the distance; he had no sense of space or time at all. When, where, who, what—where he came from, where he was going—he knew nothing at all of anything. He seemed to be an infinitesimal particle suspended in a vast universe, and then even this little dot disappeared, leaving empty clarity everywhere.

All of a sudden he felt a chill wind gusting, wave after wave of cold air. In a moment the sky and earth grew dark; black clouds roiling, a wild gale sent sand flying and pebbles rolling, howling like a banshee. Totally unafraid, Wang Liping went straight ahead into the realm of nothing.

Then he heard the sultry voice of a young woman saying, "The road is long—slow up a bit! I have something for you here!" Wang Liping didn't look or listen, and the voice gradually dissolved away.

Now an oaf with a wine jug appeared before Wang Liping. Staggering this way and that, he invited Liping to drink with him. The oaf was a mess and stunk to high heavens. Closing his eyes, Wang Liping sprang past.

Suddenly an enormous tree appeared in the road, so high it reached the sky. In the blink of an eye, the tree changed into a huge serpent of terrifying appearance. Opening its mouth, like a bowl of blood, the serpent lunged toward Wang Liping. Completely unafraid, Wang Liping walked right past. All at once he saw a huge fire, which soon turned into an expanse of radiant light.

Wang Liping felt as if he were flying; he alighted somewhere, but he didn't know where it was. He saw buildings, woods, and bamboo groves, people having fun, horses neighing, drums and music playing. It was like a utopia beyond the mundane, a land of warmth, gentility, abundance, and nobility. Several people came to him and told him that this was a place where Real People dwell, and they asked him to give a talk on the Way. Wang Liping couldn't tell if this was real or unreal; but he sensed a very slight movement in his mind, as if the voices of his teachers were coming to him.

"Inwardly viewing the mind, there is no such mind in mind. Outwardly viewing the body, there is no such body in the body. Viewing things around you, there are no such things in things. When you understand this, there is only one void." This was the voice of the mentor of Pure Emptiness.

"Viewing voidness is also void; voidness voids nothing. Since nothing is voided, nonexistent nothingness is also not there. Since there is no nonexistent nothingness, there is profound, perpetual peace. When there is nothing for peacefulness to pacify, how can desire arise? Since desire does not arise, this is true serenity. Truly always responsive to things, truly you always realize essence. Always responsive yet always serene, you are always pure and serene." This was the voice of the mentor of Pure Serenity.

"Thus pure and serene, you gradually enter the real Way. Having entered the real Way is called having attained the Way. One who can understand this can transmit the Great Way." This was the voice of the grand master of the Infinite.

Wang Liping took the word "serenity" into his heart, and everything was nothing.

When he opened his eyes, it seemed like a dream. When he looked at everything before his eyes, it was all quite real. "When there is water in a thousand rivers, the moon is reflected in the thousand rivers; when there are no clouds for ten thousand miles, there is a ten-thousand-mile sky."

Having gone through this experience, Wang Liping felt a movement in the gate of heaven; a beam of golden light flashed out, and another Wang Liping appeared. Suddenly he heard a voice in the sky telling him, "Please follow us," addressing him as a Real Human.

Looking up, Wang Liping saw three Wayfarers in Taoist garb floating serenely in the sky; he heard them sing out,

> With no mind, no thing, and no body,
> you can understand the primal host.

Here, however, one thing is left;
the pedestal of the spirit gathers red sand.

Flying along, Wang Liping soared into the vastness of the universe. Penetrating beyond the pitch black "emptiness," he saw a great highway of light appear before him.

Part III
A PART IN EVOLUTION

Teachers and Disciple Part

The year 1976 was an unforgettable one for the Chinese people.

Several important events took place in 1976. A number of national leaders passed away one after another. A violent earthquake struck the Tangshan region, killing and injuring several hundred thousand people, and society was also being shaken up. In April hundreds of thousands of people gathered in Tiananmen Square and were immediately suppressed. In October, another tidal wave rose from the upper echelons; the political careers of the "Gang of Four" were over, and the "Great Cultural Revolution" came to an end.

After a decade of calamity and hardship, it is a wonder how the Chinese peasantry was able to bear the impact of these major events all occurring successively in one year.

China's hardship was extremely severe. Life is not easy for a Chinese person.

Political struggle was not confined to the upper echelons; it extended to ordinary families, making the heart of every single individual tremble. The head of state died in bitterness, and many ordinary peasants lost their homes and even their lives. The whole nation was messed up by all these conflicts, affecting a billion people with unutterable misery.

But all this finally came to an end.

Yet in that final year of 1976, the way the troubles came to an end was so pathetic, so tragic, it startled the heavens and shook the earth, causing hearts to tremble and tears to flow.

～～～～～

One deep, dark night late in Autumn of that year, the three aged wizards sat around a lamp in the old abandoned smithy talking about things past and present, lamenting the troubles of the masses and pointing out the changes in worldly affairs. As the lamp flickered, the shadows it cast on the wall waxed and waned, coming and going. The hour grew late, but the three wizards were still engrossed in their conversation.

At one point the wizards talked about the Cloud Roaming Wayfarer, recalling what he had said about the affairs of the land. Two giants who had influenced the development of modern Chinese history had passed away in the last couple of years, but their influence would yet remain for a while. The unification of the nation and the rehabilitation of the people still had a long, long way to go.

The three old wizards had already witnessed and experienced many social upheavals and changes since the ending of the Qing dynasty in the early twentieth century. Although this wave of turbulence had lasted ten years, it was soon to come to an end.

The three old wizards felt a sense of relief that they had managed to dodge disaster and accomplish their task even as the country suffered and both Buddhism and Taoism were subjected to great persecution and plunder. They had completed the great work of transmitting their lore to a successor, so that the secrets of the Dragon Gate, unbroken for a thousand years, could continue uninterrupted. Their disciple, so carefully raised, had learned all the practices; fourteen years of training had produced splendid results, and the dissemination of the Great Way throughout the land only awaited a future change in conditions.

And the three old wizards were preparing for things to come.

Wang Liping is a key Transmitter, and a special Transmitter, in the history of the Dragon Gate sect. There are a number of things for him to do.

Wang Liping's study of the Way was not on a mountaintop; it was in the mountains, yet out of the mountains. He was never apart from his teachers, yet never apart from his parents and family. He was a Taoist, yet a man of the world; inwardly Taoist, outwardly worldly.

When he returned from traveling, Wang Liping again appeared to be an ordinary member of society. His parents' income was very small, and they had a lot of trouble feeding everyone in such a large family. Before long, Wang Liping himself got a job as an apprentice worker to support himself and reduce the burden on his parents.

Wang Liping had two sets of parents: the father and mother who gave birth to him and raised him, and the teachers who enabled him to be "reborn." He owed a great debt to both sets of parents, but since his "rebirth" parents, his Taoist teachers, were over eighty years old, they were deserving of preferential treatment.

Wang Liping's monthly salary was very small, and his livelihood was quite austere; he was already used to this. The first thing he'd do when he got his salary was buy things for his teachers, everyday necessities, and deliver them to the old wizards in the abandoned ironworks in the hills. His parents supported him in this practice and even encouraged it. In those days all necessities of life, including food and fuel, were strictly rationed; Mother and Father Wang both spared some of their ration for Liping to send to his teachers in the hills. The Wangs knew they couldn't do much, but their gratitude to the old wizards was boundless. Their hearts were in the right place; everyone was suffering so miserably.

The three old wizards, for their part, were so used to cave dwelling that they were quite accustomed to austerity. While they were traveling around, they did not make a habit of accepting money or food from people for their own convenience; they didn't even ask any recompense for their healing and relief work. Now, living in the highlands, they still grew their own food and gathered their own fuel to support themselves by their own labor. Each time Wang Liping brought them some food and supplies, the old wizards would always thank him, but they would also scold him, fearing to burden the Wang family. Liping would always laugh and say, "We have enough at home. You should also have something from human hearths—this too is one of the pleasures of life."

Wang Liping wore the same work clothes no matter whether it was spring or summer; but his overalls were always clean and neat, not dirty and oily like others'. His diet was simple, consisting mostly of vegetables. He got along easily with other people, not speaking much. His mind was free from pollution, not veiled by material desires. Melting into Nature, he reverted to purity and quietude, and his face shone with a rosy glow.

Soon winter came to an end, and the earth greeted a new spring. Having survived untold hardships, the people once again saw the blue sky, the green earth, the light of hope. There is a constancy in the movements and changes of energy between heaven and earth; true goodness and beauty can never be completely destroyed in the human world.

The old ironworks shed in the hills also returned to the way it had been before, when the wizards were living there in the past. The old Taoists no longer had to hide out; every day people came to ask the "old doctors" to treat their ailments. The old wizards had also replanted flower and vegetable gardens around the building.

Wang Liping went to work by day; then in the evenings he went to his teachers' place to continue his Taoist practice as before.

The spring rain would pour one night, then the next day the wind would disperse the clouds, and the weather would become exceptionally clear.

Wang Liping went to work cheerfully. His fellow workers were much more relaxed nowadays, and there was more conversation. Finally he heard a worker talking about Buddhism and Taoism, saying that temple monks had been invited back, and that the government had designated personnel to be "monks." These "monks" held jobs, going to work by day and returning home by night.

Hearing this, Wang Liping remained calm outwardly, but in his heart he was excited. After work, he hurried to bring this news to his teachers, so the old wizards could share his joy.

Liping headed for the hills with quickened steps. The distant mountains brushed the horizon; the crimson sunset lit up the misty earth. A yellow ox stood by the river, gazing into the clear current. A formation of geese came from the south, gradually disappearing into the northern skies.

As Wang Liping enjoyed the picturesque spring scenery, a couplet of an ancient verse unexpectedly occurred to him:

> *Going, going, a thousand miles a day;*
> *boundless, vast, a corner of the sky.*

He couldn't remember who wrote these lines; the odd thing was why they should have occurred to him.

The grand master knew a lot of old poems by heart, and he had taught Wang Liping quite a few. A more cheerful poem about spring would have been more appropriate:

> *The flowering of April's ended in the world;*
> *the peach blossoms at the mountain temple*
> *are just blooming full.*
> *We always lament when spring's gone back,*

> *no place to look for it,*
> *not realizing it has come in here.*

Spring entering a mountain temple—spring had come for Buddhism and Taoism.

> *Before, the snow was like flowers; now,*
> *the flowers are like snow.*

Fine. Spring means flowers, flowers mean spring: the hundred flowers bloom; spring fills sky and earth. Whose verse is this? How could it be so perfect? Liping thought it was the work of Fan Yun, a poet of the southern dynasties. The title was "Parting Poem"—how could such beautiful verse have such a title?

Wang Liping no longer thought it strange that this verse should have occurred to him. He simply figured that his teachers were again greeting the springtime of their work, and this was stirring him up.

The old wizards had done but one thing all their lives, diligently cultivating their practices in hopes that the Great Way would be continued by a successor and be spread throughout the land. Their only quest was to have all humanity know of the truth pervading the universe, realize how humankind has its place and value in the universe, and understand that there is a road of light leading to our own ultimate destiny. But how many people can understand the truth and practice it in their own bodies? Particularly when humanity is afflicted with internal warfare, the living spirit is polluted, we freely destroy the natural environment, and technology and intelligence have in some senses become instruments of the destruction of the human race; who is there to ask after the great knowledge and great wisdom to expound Buddhism or Taoism?

The transformations of springtime seem to give people new hope.

Lost in thought, before he knew it Wang Liping was nearing the ironworks shed where the old wizards were staying. Collecting his mind a bit, he went on with a laugh.

At that time, the Wayfarer of Pure Serenity was pruning the plants by the door. Seeing Liping coming, he turned and called to the other wizards.

The grand master came out, still holding an article of clothing he had been mending. The other mentor, the Wayfarer of Pure Emptiness, emerged from the vegetable patch in the back, his hands covered with soil, saying, "The grand master was just thinking about you. He told me to pick some vegetables to get ready, and now here you are!"

Wang Liping shook a bowl he was holding in his hands. "I've prepared something tasty for you today," he said to his teachers, "salted peanut rice. Live it up a little!"

The grand master invited Liping inside, while the mentors hurriedly prepared a meal. Wang Liping took the garment from the old master, saying he would mend it for him.

The Wayfarer of Pure Serenity said, "When did you teach Liping how to do this?"

The Wayfarer of Pure Emptiness said, "That's what is meant by the saying 'Such a father must have such a son.'"

"This is what is meant by 'Mastering it on one's own, without a teacher,'" rejoined Wang Liping, watching the needle carefully.

Closely observing this clever, lively disciple, the grand master said, "Why didn't you come over yesterday?"

Wang Liping bent over double with laughter. "Master, you're so old you're getting senile! Last night I went walking in the mountains with you, and sat with you when we came back, listening to the spring shower. Have you forgotten already?"

The two mentors glanced at the grand master, not saying a word.

"I had been thinking this was happening, and yet it has also seemed as if it weren't. I can't distinguish between yesterday and today. I must really be senile!" As he spoke, the grand master's eyes never left Wang Liping.

"How about if I buy you a notebook tomorrow," suggested Liping, in evident earnestness, "so you can jot things down?"

"No need," replied the master. "Besides, it'll cost money to buy a notebook, and you need to save your pennies, because you have other things to do with your money." The master seemed a bit dispirited.

Wang Liping didn't catch the grand master's mood. He simply remarked as he sewed, "Money is an external thing. What do I need to save it for?"

The mentor of Pure Serenity hurriedly interjected, "What the master means is that you still have to take care of your family. What will you do if you have no money after you're married?"

Wang Liping stopped sewing and looked up, blushing. "You must be teasing me," he exclaimed.

Everyone laughed. The mentor of Pure Emptiness turned away, brushing the corner of his eye with his hand.

"Soup's on!" cried the mentor of Pure Serenity, setting out utensils and a few simple dishes.

As they ate, the grand master said, "The vegetable garden is doing quite well. We won't have to buy vegetables anymore, just beg some rice." The two mentors told Liping, "After we eat, go tell your parents not to wait up for you." Wang Liping agreed. After the meal was done and the utensils washed, he solemnly announced to the three old wizards that he had some news for them. The grand master hurriedly stopped him, saying, "There's no need to say anything. We already know. The three of us are people outside of conventional society. All we have to do is keep the Great Way with integrity. It's still early.

Go look in on your parents, so they won't worry."

So Liping left right away. As he was going, the old master told him, "When you come each day, leave early and go home early."

Thus for a number of days in a row Liping rushed to the wizards' abode right after work. The old teachers always cleaned up and waited for him to come back. Once he got there, the wizards again burst into a flurry of activity, as though there was something they had to do, yet nothing they could do. There was something to be said, but it was impossible to say anything.

Wang Liping sensed that something was going to happen, but he didn't know what it was. Ever since the grand master began to show signs of "senility," Liping had been having such inexplicable feelings. The lines of verse that had mysteriously popped into his head days ago were also manifestations of these feelings.

What was going to happen? Perhaps the wizards wanted to return to their cavern headquarters, now that times had changed. Why did the mentor of Pure Serenity joke around like that, suggesting Liping should get married? Maybe his teachers were going to leave, abandoning him here alone.

Wang Liping understood that intuitive feelings are quite accurate when his stage of development has been reached. He couldn't hide anything from his teachers, and they couldn't hide anything from him. But all of them were human after all, flesh and blood, with human emotions; and theirs were very genuine, rich, and profound feelings. Were they to part?

Wang Liping did not believe, did not hope, did not wish this would actually happen. That would be too hard to bear. The spiritual pain in these feelings was much worse than the pains of training. Wang Liping was now undergoing another kind of ordeal.

For their part, the old wizards were experiencing much the same thing. Already in the evening of life, they had no families, no children, but their feelings for humankind were most profound, rich, and genuine. This was particularly true when it came to their apprentice and successor Wang Liping, on whom they had lavished their attention for nearly fifteen years, watching him grow from childhood into manhood, bringing him along step by step in his development. Their feelings could hardly be expressed; now that the teachers and their disciple were going to part, how could it not hurt?

But the matter was already decided, and preparations had quietly been made. No one had said anything about it; everyone kept their feelings strictly in check.

On this particular day, Wang Liping finished up his work early. On leaving the factory, he went shopping. He bought two pairs of sturdy cloth shoes for his mentors, and a suit of clothes for the grand master. Wrapping them up, he headed for the hills.

The western sky was tinged with crimson by the evening sun; the mountain air was exceptionally clear and fresh.

The three old wizards were standing outside the door, waiting for Wang Liping to come by after work. As he approached, he saw the elders' shadows. He also saw the willows they'd planted in front of the door years ago, trees he'd grown up with, now with fresh heaps of earth around them. All four men gazed absentmindedly at these trees, no one saying a word. It was as if all of them were remembering how it had been when they had planted the trees more than a decade earlier. Time flies, and the trees had already grown large and luxuriant. At the same time, Wang Liping had grown up into a man, and his teachers had become venerable Taoist ancients.

Package in hand, Liping walked up to the old wizards and silently knelt before them. The mentor of Pure Serenity quickly pulled him to his feet and said, "Why are you coming here again? And why did you go to such expense, in spite of what the master said?"

"Please accept these trifling gifts," pleaded Liping, his voice choking. "Come inside," said the mentor, and all four went into the shed.

As they sat there, the four continued to regard one another in silence. Everyone knew that what had to happen was about to take place.

The grand master clasped Wang Liping's hand, lightly brushed his hair, and said in a low voice, "You've had a busy day. Go home and rest."

The three elders rose as one. Liping also got up, saluted his teachers, and said farewell in a subdued tone. In a daze as he left, Liping turned and saw his three teachers still standing there. Finally he headed down from the hills.

The sky was pitch black; Wang Liping couldn't tell where he was going. Suddenly he heard a song in the whistling of the willows:

> *Outside the inn,*
> *by the ancient road,*
> *the blue-green of fragrant grasses*
> *reaches to the sky.*
> *As the evening breeze brushes the willows*
> *a whistling sound remains;*
> *in the setting sun, there are*
> *mountains beyond the mountains.*
> *At the edge of the sky,*
> *the corner of the sea,*
> *companions half disappeared,*
> *a gourd of unfiltered wine*
> *is all the joy I have;*
> *tonight, dreams of separation are cold.*

Wang Liping realized that this song was composed by Li Shutong, who later became the Buddhist priest Hongyi. Only the Wayfarer of Pure Serenity could sing this song; it had been out of general circulation for a long time. Hearing a song of parting at this time certainly saddened Liping.

Eyes brimming with tears, Wang Liping could no longer control his feet; he might as well let them walk on and on to "the edge of the sky, the corner of the sea"! But his legs became too heavy to move—the edge of the sky was right here; this was the corner of the sea. Before him was an endless expanse of darkness.

Collapsing on the ground, Wang Liping fell into a deep sleep.

He had no idea how much time had passed, or where he was; all Wang

Liping felt was an extraordinary lightness. All around was quietude, the air fresh and clear. Before him was a dark, verdant mountain. Wang Liping climbed the mountain, following an ancient pathway; it seemed to require no effort at all. Not far from where he was, he saw a pine tree, under which there sat three people with an ethereal air. Taking them to be Taoist adepts, Wang Liping went forward to pay his respects.

The three men made no answer to Wang Liping's salutations; they behaved as if no one had come. Now Liping took a close look and was overjoyed to realize that they were none other than his own mentors and their grand master! Hurriedly Liping asked the old wizards what they were doing sitting there quietly in that place.

The grand master bade him sit down, then slowly explained, "We came down from the mountains on a mission, to teach you to become the eighteenth-generation Transmitter of the Dragon Gate branch of Complete Reality Taoism. We have been doing that for fifteen years now, following the traditions of our spiritual ancestors to teach you all the rules, principles of practice, methods of practice, and secret arts. Your learning of the Way has been successful, so our mission is complete. Now that our work is done and the land is finally at peace, we are going to return to our cavern headquarters. You stay at home for now. When your attainments and virtues are complete, then you can go up in the mountains again and gather people. This is the teacher's command, which you must not disobey. Although there are a lot of feelings between us, all we can do for now is endure the pain and detach from sentimentality."

At this point, when the talk touched upon what was causing him such distress, Wang Liping involuntarily began to choke back tears. "My gratitude to you is monumental. How can I bear to part! You three are so old. Furthermore, you've gotten to the age where you should have an attendant. I could never, ever repay even the minutest fraction of the debt I owe you for fostering my rebirth and development. I cannot bear to part. Please let me go with you."

By this time, the three elders were crying too.

Wiping away his tears and putting on a stern face, the mentor of Pure Serenity said, "We've been through plenty of trouble and hardship, yet here we are acting like a bunch of sissies! Liping, you're not the same as us—you have parents and brothers and sisters. Even though you've given yourself up to enter the Way, nevertheless human social norms are not to be neglected. The burden on you is greater than the burden on us. How can you bear it if you're going to be so sorrowful? Don't worry about us—let this parting also be a model of heroism."

The four men's tears stopped. The mentor of Pure Emptiness said, "In reality, it is unbearable for us to leave you out here in the world all alone. But this is a serious matter, which depends entirely on you; no one can take your place or do it for you. Inside the teaching and outside the teaching, leaving the world and entering the world, every sort of investigation and experiment is your sole individual responsibility. It is all up to you to carry it out to completion. You will have to have unbreakable spirit and strength to accomplish your task." The grand master rose, beckoning Wang Liping to come with them; all four then went roaming around the mountaintop. All of a sudden a red-crested white crane flew up out of an ancient pine tree, soaring into the sky with a long cry. Then they saw streaming light brimming with color and heard the sublime sounds of immortal music; all four of them were now in a totally different state of mind. The Wayfarer of the Infinite began to recite from "Spring Seeping into the Garden" by their spiritual ancestor Qiu Chuji:

> *Great wisdom is at ease,*
> *free and clear, unconstrained;*
> *letting it be natural, as is,*
> *to it I entrust*
> *my finest feelings and mystic joy.*
> *Among the pines, on the rocks,*
> *I sing aloud and drink till drunk;*
> *under the moon, before the breeze,*
> *a jade girl plays pan pipes,*
> *a golden boy does a dance,*
> *sending one intoxicated into the great mystery.*
> *The principles within the mystery*
> *all bob in a flow*
> *that comes from its own continuity.*
>
> *Wondrous, this sublime scene*
> *is hard to express in words;*
> *perhaps it is a special heaven*

for the human world.
Unbending, solid,
the mountain is polished by time;
enduring people's slights,
a sea can turn to a garden.
Spirit and energy harmonized,
yin and yang rise and descend.
Having attained the wizardry
to wander free on earth,
I have no more afflictions;
so I open my heart and write,
crazily penning poetry.

An auspicious cloud then floated down and took the three old wizards away.

Wang Liping joined his hands in a gesture of respect, seeing them off.

When Liping woke up, he was back at home. He remembered everything in his dream with crystal clarity. Realizing that everything was already arranged, and all he had to do was go along with the natural course, he felt quite a bit better. But he was still concerned about his teachers making the long trip back to Mount Lao at their advanced age. Finally he went over to the railway station and bought train tickets. Purchasing some fruit as well, he raced to the wizards' encampment in the hills. The three old men had already cleaned everything up, inside and out; they were leaving the place as empty as it had been when they came.

Wang Liping said, "Why not take in another new experience on your way back this time—how about going by train?" He handed the tickets to the Wayfarer of Pure Serenity.

The three old wizards laughed. "All right," said the grand master, "let's go along with our disciple's arrangements. We're old rustics, let's have a taste of what the Cloud Roaming Wayfarer called those round iron legs!"

It was still early, so Wang Liping went home and asked his mother to bake some biscuits. When she found out that the three elders were about to leave, Mother Wang couldn't help crying too.

When he got back to the mountain, Liping found the three old wizards standing in from of the door, all packed and ready to go. The grand master handed the spiritual turtle over to Wang Liping, instructing him to take good care of it at home. Taking the turtle, which remained utterly still, Liping held it close to his face, then put it in his palm so it could say good-bye to the three old wizards.

Finally all four turned their gaze once more to the old ironworks shed, the flowers, plants, and trees, the recondite highland quiet. Joining their hands in a gesture of respect, with deep feeling they bade farewell to this place and made their way down from the hills.

When the four men arrived at the train station, the whole Wang family was already there, quietly waiting for them. The three old wizards followed Wang Liping into the train. After briefly explaining the procedures for changing trains, Liping then got off and stood on the platform. Mother Wang handed the old men the biscuits she'd made, all the while unable to keep from crying.

As the train pulled slowly away from the station, the three old wizards waved farewell, their eyes brimming with tears. Mother Wang, supported by her daughters, was still weeping. The girls too began to cry. As the train moved off into the distance, Wang Liping stood there frozen, like a wooden statue; he said nothing and shed no tears—his brain was a total void.

For some fifteen years the three teachers and their disciple had been together every day; their feelings for each other were deep as the sea. Now on the train without their apprentice, the three old men felt the roaring of the train increase the oppressive mood. None of them felt like enjoying the scenery along the way; looking at each other without a word, they sat silently as the train hurtled onward.

The going was easy all the way. Whenever there happened to be some difficulty, someone helped them out right away. The three old men paid no mind to whoever it was helping them. They were intent only on getting to where they were going, without further ado.

Very soon they arrived at Tsingtao. From there they took the road east. They could already see Mount Lao.

It had been fifteen long years since they had left their ancestral ground here. The brief stopover while on the journey with their apprentice was already seven years in the past. Now that they were back, their feelings tossed and turned like the ocean tide. But without their apprentice, the three old wizards felt alone even though they were traveling together.

The three old men headed right for the Cavern of Eternal Spring; they didn't feel like taking in the scenery along the way. Although the path was familiar, their footsteps felt heavy. As soon as they got to the entrance of the cavern, suddenly the Wayfarer of the Infinite called out, "There's someone inside!"

Just as the grand master spoke, someone emerged from the cave. Taking a good look at him, the three elders were amazed and delighted to see that it was none other than their disciple, Wang Liping! At first they thought it might be a projection of his yang spirit. When he came forward and took their baggage from them, they then knew it was the real Liping standing before them. They greeted him warmly. Even though it had been only a day, it felt like they hadn't seen him for three autumns!

The Wayfarer of the Infinite asked, "We came by train. How could you have gotten here ahead of us?"

Ushering the three elders into the cavern, Liping explained, "I was accompanying you all the way, watching out for you. Didn't you see me?"

The three old men woke up as if from a dream. Now they realized that someone had indeed been looking after them along the way; only they were so immersed in their own thoughts that they had never really paid enough attention to notice who it was. The three old wizards looked at each other and laughed.

Then they looked around. Everything in the cavern was clean, and all the utensils were in order. Even their sitting cushions were set out neatly. Evidently Wang Liping had already been there for quite a while.

The grand master then got serious and said, "We have already parted ways.

Why did you come back here?"

Wang Liping first asked the elders to sit down and rest after their trip. Then he explained, "I will naturally go along with the way things have been arranged, but there's one thing I don't quite understand, and I've come to ask you to explain."

All four sat down. The grand master then asked Liping, "What isn't clear?" Wang Liping said, "Ever since I've been studying Taoism, you have all been guiding me in the Great Way, teaching me pure serenity and emptiness, getting rid of material desires, cutting off false thoughts, having done with mundane affairs, coming with nothing and going with nothing. I went through many trials, studying the Way for years, before realizing its principle. So why have you instructed me to live at home and fulfill the way of humanity even as I keep the Great Way? I can't figure this out."

The three old wizards looked at each other. They smiled and nodded.

Speaking slowly, the Wayfarer of the Infinite explained, "You're sure not woolly-headed! Now think: aside from our Dragon Gate sect, where in the world are there two generations of elderly teachers with one disciple? Here's another thing to think about: during those ten years of chaos throughout the land, when no one could be sure in the morning of being alive at night, how many people would have wished to enter our school but could not? You studied the Way for many years; we took this opportunity to take you into the mountains and cut off mundane entanglements—that's perfectly natural, isn't it? And why did we take you traveling around for several years, and then bring you back home and have you experience the trials of ordinary life again? As far as our feelings and sense of duty are concerned, there is more to the relationship between teacher and disciple than between parent and child. We're already in our eighties and nineties; its almost as if we ourselves cannot bear the pain of this separation. We haven't been so sad in decades! Leaving you in the mundane world to fulfill the way of humanity is actually not our arrangement. This is simply the way things have to be."

The Wayfarer of the Infinite spoke with feeling and with reason; everyone listened in silence as he continued: "The workings of heaven and earth have their patterns and equations. The mechanisms are so subtle that they are not thoroughly explicable. It has now been over eight hundred years since the founding of our school. Although it has flourished and declined in that interval, nevertheless it has continued uninterrupted. The Way acts throughout the universe, circulating throughout cosmic space; it is vast, comprehensive, and deep, subtle and mysteriously pervasive. Through various circumstances we came to leave the mundane world, living secluded in mountain forests, cultivating the ability to hold to the Way and seeking to understand it. Everything we have done in life has all been for the Way alone. And yet none of us has made much of a contribution to the widespread dissemination of the Great Way. It's not that we didn't do anything about it, but that the time was not right. We have practiced Taoism for decades, doing this one thing for all our lives. So we've taken fifteen years to transmit the Way to you. The time is now right for you to spread the Great Way. This grave responsibility rests on you."

Regarding Wang Liping with the profound gaze of the aged, the grand master continued in a hopeful tone: "After a few years, the religious consciousness of humanity will reawaken, and the relationship between heaven and humankind will become a central focus of investigation. Chinese civilization has a deep store of knowledge about this. Taoist culture is replete with functional profundities, which will be rediscovered when the time comes, releasing great enlightenment. One who would spread Taoist culture must first have authentic transmission of Taoist culture and must then also have personal experience of worldly affairs. Without these two conditions, no one can accomplish the task. Do you hear me?"

Wang Liping felt as if he were waking up from a dream. He said politely, "Your words have been like a breeze sweeping away remaining traces of clouds. Now I understand."

With great kindness, the grand master added, "Now, when you go back this time, you must conceal your light and nurture it unobtrusively. Harmonize illumination with the world, acting as an ordinary man, honoring your parents and being kind to your brothers and sisters, getting along with the neighbors, being flexible and modest, not being argumentative, taking care of your household economically with diligence and frugality, doing good for others, building up breadth of hidden virtue. Be truly sincere with others; be faithful and cordial in dealing with people. Be broad-minded and free-spirited; be aloof and develop your will. Return to innocence, revert to purity, and enjoy natural reality. Simply put, do your work well, be a decent human being; after you have a family, live your life well, save the dying and help the injured, carry out the Way in behalf of heaven. If you think of us, come up the mountain to visit. This is your home too."

Nodding repeatedly, Wang Liping said, "I'll remember."

The Wayfarer of Pure Emptiness then spoke up, addressing Wang Liping: "When the grand master first began to teach me and my spiritual brother here, your other mentor, he always used to say that it is hard to be clever, hard to be foolish, and harder yet to go from cleverness to foolishness. Let the first move go, take a step back, and only then will you gain peace of mind. You now know too much, too many things that ordinary people have no way to accept and are not able to understand. You're young and full of energy and should avoid arguing with ordinary people. This is a process of polishing the mind, learning to be natural in the company of all sorts of people. As Lao-tzu says, 'The way of enlightenment seems dark.' Leaving you to carry out the Way at home is also precisely this principle of going along with what is natural. To let you gradually realize this in the course of daily life, without giving you an explanation of your grave responsibilities, also retains the basic sense of naturalness. Originally we were going to leave this matter without comment, so it could be inferred. It's better not to explain it too clearly. But you are so sharp! How can you rise to a higher level unless you are ignorant?"

Wang Liping laughed and said, "With this guidance of yours, I'll be even less ignorant!" All three old wizards began to laugh.

The Wayfarer of Pure Serenity said, "You will be very lonesome, left all by yourself in the world, so how about if we name you the Lone Layman?" The other three clapped their hands and expressed their approval.

Now the four men left the cavern and went outside. All they saw were the jutting mountain silhouettes, green pines and emerald cedars, clouds and sea extending into infinity. They heard the waves breaking on the cliffs, the gusting of the mountain winds, the chattering of the birds. The Wayfarer of the Infinite recalled another poem by the Master of Eternal Spring, entitled "No Mundane Thoughts," which he recited for Wang Liping's benefit:

> When the wheel of teaching begins to turn,
> the wind of wisdom arises;
> suddenly you feel an infinite clear cool.
> White light congeals in the void;
> auspicious energies gather,
> sweeping clean your heart,
> formerly clogged with dust.
> The five brigands run away;
> the three parasites flee:
> inside and out, there's not a trace;
> mind and thought are calm, at peace,
> tranquil, serene, unembattled.
> Strolling in the red dust of the Capital,
> eating when hungry, drinking when thirsty,
> every day I seek according to conditions
> in the freedom outside of things
> the treasures of heaven and earth;
> time and again I play them like chimes.

If you're late, call on a guide;
what lies ahead is the road to home.
There is, of itself, real information;
a crane's letter comes with a call
to mount it and rise
and travel through the skies.

The four Taoists went back into the cavern to pay respects to their spiritual ancestors. Wang Liping then paid respects to each of the three teachers and then left, descending the mountain.

18

Transcending Sagehood to Enter the Ordinary

During several long conversations with us, Master Wang Liping never said a single word about his separation from his teachers. Finally, after repeated urging, in a slow, low tone of voice he told us what it had really been like. At that time, he fell to a low point in his life, as he had after having undergone suspended animation, death, and revival. When he was accompanying his teachers back to Mount Lao, no one said a single word or shed a single tear; but after he got back home, he became sadder and sadder as he reminisced. People usually don't weep when they're saddest; that comes later. After Wang Liping returned home from Mount Lao, he became very ill, so ill that the severity of his ailment did not abate for more than twenty days. At the same time, the old Taoist masters up on Mount Lao also fell ill.

As he related this to us, Master Wang Liping's eyes reddened.

People reading this may think that the detachment of the old Taoists might be in question. But those who have attended Master Wang Liping's classes cannot forget how a sort of emotional influence takes place after teacher and students have been taking meals together, living together, and practicing exercises together. Whether the students are feeble elderly people, or middle-aged people with chronic ailments, or young people with psychological troubles, all of them feel as if they have been brushed by a gentle spring breeze blowing away all pain, sorrow, confusion, and disappointment, so that everyone is inexplicably joyful and happy, like a bunch of children, all renewed. What is even more interesting, between teacher and students there seems to take place a synchronization of "biological clocks," such that if Master Wang Liping does not sleep, the students have no hope of getting a good night's rest; and if the students do not sleep, Master Wang Liping does not sleep peacefully either. This started to produce some antagonism until Master Wang Liping exercised some real influence and treated the students so that they were able to get to sleep.

According to Master Wang Liping, Taoism expounds the merging of the microcosm and the macrocosm; in terms of the human race, this means the merging of humankind and the universe. From the standpoint of the individual, this is not only communion with Nature; it also requires communion with other people. Collective cultivation of refinement is a kind of unspoken interpersonal communication, a coactivation of thought, a silent meshing of spirits, a communion of feelings. Cultivating refinement tunes interpersonal relationships and is a good method of bringing people closer together as friends and companions relying on one another.

Master Wang Liping practiced refinement with his three teachers for a decade and a half. Their communion was not merely emotional and intellectual; it was a communion of the totality of life. When they parted, therefore, it meant a reorganization of life for all concerned, so the suffering they went through at the time should be understood in this sense.

This may be a kind of philosophy about people.

In the course of our education at school, especially in primary and middle school, the teachers and students are together all day, yet this does not necessarily produce the effect of Master Wang Liping's presence at a seminar lasting only twenty days. Why is this? Because Master Wang Liping not only communicates with students verbally and in writing; he also seeks communion of heart and of life. If our school education could gain some useful inspiration from this, hopefully we could also find a "formless, immaterial" route in our educational methods. This sort of method would be extremely beneficial in developing affections in young children.

⁓⁓⁓

The science of refinement by inner work takes a very serious view of character development. Some practitioners interpret the relationship between inner work and virtue in this way: if you do many good deeds and accumulate a lot of virtue, there will then be more and more people silently encouraging you in their hearts, wishing for your welfare; and when you practice cultivation in the midst of this formless mental field created by a multitude of people, then your accomplishment will naturally grow quickly. In reality, this only deals with a very small part of the issue;

the cultivation of refinement by inner work is a matter of polishing the mind, nurturing the natural disposition, and purifying the heart. In daily sitting, the totality of body and mind gradually enters into a state of peace, harmony, balance, clarity, purity, and selfless communion with all things. All commotion, conflict, destructiveness, defilement, and selfishness are washed away. When body and mind are constantly steeped in this feeling, in this state, then that which is good, fine, and genuine will silently emerge in a natural way, unaffected by worldly things.

When Master Wang Liping talked about his impressions from long years of practice, he said that what made the deepest impression on him was the way his heart unconsciously became more and more gentle, such that he could not bear to see the existence of evil and unhappiness.

The five thousand characters of Lao-tzu's Tao Te Ching speak of the Way and of virtue. The Way is the primordial root, the source of the universe. From the Way are produced all things and all beings. As for the basic nature of the Way, Taoists of later ages summed it up in terms of ten major characteristics: nonresistant, pure, natural, pristine, simple, easy, clear, nonartificial, yielding, and noncontentious.

When they are manifest in the human body, these characteristics are higher virtue. Higher virtue is a humanization of the Way, in which it is expressed as ethics. The concrete manifestation of the Way in people is called virtue.

Lao-tzu says, "Higher virtue is not ingratiating; this is why it is potent." Also, "For the countenance of great virtue, only the Way is to be followed." What this means is that the highest virtue is spontaneous, formless, invisible, imperceptible; it is internal, stored within, not revealed obviously. It is not intentional but natural.

Whatever is artificial, deliberate, obvious, or formal is lower virtue. "Lower virtue is not mindless of reward, so it lacks potency." Showing off everywhere as very virtuous really doesn't amount to virtue.

"Higher virtue is uncontrived, yet there is nothing it does not accomplish."

The grand master always used to tell Wang Liping that doing good deeds hoping for reward isn't virtuous action. Doing good deeds without concern for reward, and yet remembering it yourself is called evident virtue. Doing good deeds without being self-conscious of it is called hidden virtue.

We wanted to take some moving anecdotes from Master Wang Liping's nine years of household life to illustrate how he carried out the Way in behalf of Heaven, helping society and helping people, but when we brought this up the master gave us a funny look, as if to say, "Is it necessary to bring this up? All this is quite natural."

Later we came to understand that the finer things such as kindness, compassion, affection, and helpfulness are completely subconscious in people of higher virtue, even to the point where it could be said that these qualities are for them a kind of instinct.

Lao-tzu says, "The Way gives birth, virtue nurtures, things lend form, momentum completes. Therefore all beings honor the Way and value its virtue. The honor of the Way and the value of virtue are not granted by anyone, but are forever naturally so. Thus the Way gives birth and virtue nurtures, growing and developing, completing and maturing, building up and breaking down, producing but not possessing, acting without presumption, fostering without domineering; this is called hidden virtue."

Lao-tzu also says, "Sages have no fixed mind; they make the mind of the people their mind."

Those imbued with higher virtue are sages. To go through ordinary life with the virtue of a sage, mixing in with the mundane world, is an even higher level of life, referred to as "transcending sagehood to enter the ordinary."

As a Buddhist said, "Having understood the Beyond, come back to act in the here-and-now."

Full of love for all people in the world and all life, intoxicated with Nature, seeking the inner secrets of the universe, society, and human life, Master Wang Liping began his daily life in the ordinary world in a state of naturalness and simplicity.

At home, Master Wang Liping was extremely respectful toward his parents, with deep and genuine feeling. When sitting quietly practicing refinement, his thoughts frequently went back in time to the loving spirit of his mother as she nursed him; scenes of her toil bringing up six children would appear before him. These visions were so clear and so real that they could not but affect Wang Liping. When children are bathed in the love of their parents, they think it completely normal, totally natural, like when bathing in the sunlight; nothing can shake their emotional attachment. When people recall their parents' care after they have grown up, how could they not be moved by parental love? Because of the fact that Wang Liping was able to recollect infancy, actually witnessing true visions of his childhood, he felt even deeper affection for his parents than do ordinary people.

Since Wang Liping's three teachers had devoted so much attention and care to his development, he wanted to repay them by doing something more than living up to their expectations, but after they had finished their task of transmitting their teaching, the old masters had left and gone away.

The grand master used to tell Liping, "Respecting your parents is respecting your teachers." Liping thus put his expression of affection for his old teachers into his affection for his parents and for all elderly people in the world. He looked upon the life of his parents as part of his own life. The present life is temporal, but primal life in its most proximate stage depends directly on nurturing by the parents. Even though people are independent of their parent's bodies after birth, nevertheless their roots are still there, and their destiny is still there, so respecting one's parents is in reality also strengthening the foundation of one's own life.

Therefore, when Taoists speak of respect for elders, this does not have only a humanistic, ethical meaning; it contains an even deeper meaning connected with life itself. From a Taoist point of view, the life of an individual comes into being through the agency of Nature and the evolution of numerous elements in time and space; that life is not an independent, isolated entity, but one stage in a long line of causes and effects, a single point in a network or globe of myriad interrelated elements.

Wang Liping lived with several elderly people, including his parents and parents-in-law. He often used to tell stories to amuse the older folks, and sometimes when he was tired out he'd nap with his head on his mother's lap, just like when he was little.

~~~~~~~

When he was twenty-nine years old, Wang Liping married a young woman, a coworker named Dong Bin. The marriage was quite old-fashioned.

Wang Liping's mother and Dong Bin's mother had grown up together and were as close as sisters. From early on they had a private promise that they would be real relatives in the future. And Heaven did indeed fulfill their wish, for ten years later the Wang family had a boy, and the Dong family had a girl. Thus the two children grew up together and were very close. When Wang Liping began to study Taoism later on, Dong Bin simply thought he was learning manual arts from the old "doctors." She didn't know that the little sprite she used to play hide-and-seek with had already entered the gate of the Way; she loved him as an ordinary person.

When Wang Liping returned to the ordinary world in obedience to his teacher's directions, he wanted to marry and have a family like ordinary people. He also knew the young woman's thoughts, yet he found it hard to talk about the matter plainly. As a result, he became somewhat frantic, but fortunately the will of Heaven cooperated, and the lovers finally became a couple. On the wedding day, the old wizards who had taught Wang Liping naturally came to offer felicitations, but they didn't show themselves, for fear of startling the crowd. Only Wang Liping could see them. After the ceremony, the wizards took leave to go back into the mountains, but before they left the grand master whispered to Liping that he would have a son the following year.

During the honeymoon, Wang Liping was the perfect husband, warm and attentive. The lifestyle formed by fifteen years of Taoist training, however, was hard to change. Every night very late he quietly rose and sat facing a wall until daybreak.

Eventually his wife found out about this. At first, she paid no mind, but when it continued day in and day out, she could not but worry. All she could do was lie there with her head on the pillow night after night, gazing at Wang Liping. Wang Liping neither argued nor explained, but gladly listened. Happy at heart, his wife would fall asleep peacefully.

One particular night, the two were sleeping sweetly. Deep in the night, his wife sound asleep, Wang Liping again rose quietly to sit and practice inner work. At some point his wife awoke, finding her husband was not beside her. Turning on the light, she saw him sitting immobile as before. Seeing him so still, eyes closed, she reached out to feel his breath. Apparently he was not breathing at all! Totally nonplussed, she involuntarily began to wail.

Wang Liping opened his eyes and laughed as if nothing had happened. "What are you crying about? Isn't this all right?"

Now at this time Wang Liping was rather at a loss for words. How was he to explain to her? This was not something that could be explained all that easily! Everyone knew he had been hanging around with the "doctors" who had come from the heartland fleeing famine, but he had been a mere teenager then, and not even his parents knew the secrets he had learned. Other people were totally unaware of his inner attainments. When his teachers had left, the grand master had admonished him not to reveal anything until the right time. When his wife asked him something about Taoist study, he would be vague, figuring she'd stop asking questions when she got used to his way of life.

But his wife's bewilderment increased. Since her husband wouldn't explain clearly, she got ideas. During the day she would rest up as much as possible on the job so that she could keep an eye on her husband by night, to see what he'd do.

On one particular occasion, Wang Liping slept soundly till dawn. His wife was delighted. She began to blame herself for having slept like a log in the past and crowded her husband out of space in bed. But just as she was rejoicing to herself, the door opened and Wang Liping walked in. She hurriedly looked back at the bed—it was empty! Then she looked again at her husband standing before her; his slippers were muddy, and his legs were soaked with dew.

Seeing his wife so bewildered, Wang Liping involuntarily laughed. As he removed his slippers he explained that he'd just been out to relieve himself. "The dew is really heavy," he said. His wife couldn't tell what was real and what was illusion. Quite perplexed, she wondered about her husband and started to get suspicious again.

"This man is really strange!" his wife used to say to herself. She noticed that he read very little, but often wrote in a notebook. Since a husband should have no secrets from his wife, it was reasonable to see what he was writing. He never made a secret of it; the notebook was openly placed in a drawer in a little cupboard. But neither she nor anyone else in the family had ever given a thought to looking through this notebook. When he finished one notebook, he'd start writing in a new one. In his wife's mind, he appeared to be a very studious man. He ordinarily never asked anyone for information, yet it seemed that nothing escaped him. Whenever he happened to remark on matters at work, at home, related to his friends, or even related to affairs of state, he always hit the mark. His statements on future events, in particular, were always accurate. When visitors were coming to the house, Liping always knew beforehand; he would tell his wife that they should buy more food, and then when they got home it would turn out that guests had in fact appeared.

One afternoon when the couple was going to market to buy something, Wang Liping suddenly stopped. Urging his wife to hurry home, he told her her mother had been taken seriously ill and was being rushed to the hospital. His wife was very displeased on hearing this. She had just had lunch with her mother, and the old lady had been fine. How could she have gotten seriously ill in the short time since then? She saw her husband was in earnest, however, and he himself turned around and hurried back home, so she followed along, half believing and half doubting.

As they reached the door of their home, they heard a commotion inside; the family was just then taking Dong Bin's mother to the hospital. Seeing this scene, Dong Bin was so flustered she could only cry. Wang Liping, in contrast, remained calm throughout. Clasping his mother-in-law's hand, he called her "Mom," and the old woman's tightly shut eyes slowly opened, and her breathing became easier. Wang Liping then said, "Feel better? Why not get up and try to walk?"

The old lady actually sat up, holding onto Wang Liping's hand for support. She then stood up and walked a few paces. Her steps were steady. She looked a lot better too. Her eyes had their spirit back, even seeming more vital than before.

At first everyone was startled; then everyone rejoiced. They all said that the old lady had a robust constitution and really shouldn't be getting sick. Only Dong Bin stood there in a daze. Wang Liping smiled at her and said, "What's the matter? Don't you understand? Your mama got sick because she missed you. Didn't she get well as soon as you arrived?" Dong Bin could neither cry nor laugh.

The second year of their marriage, the couple had a son, just as the ancient master had predicted. After the birth of their beloved child, extraordinary things happened one after another. When his little son was in day care, Wang Liping always knew at once when the boy was crying or fussing. He would immediately tell his wife, who worked on the same line, to go look in on the child. At first Dong Bin thought the caretakers were informing her husband on these occasions, but on inquiring she learned that they had never done any such thing. Yet her husband had been right every single time he had told her to go look in on their son.

Dong Bin finally decided to ask her husband how he did this. Ironically, this time Wang Liping replied quite candidly, "I really can't say how I know. It's like when we used to play hide-and-seek as children—I'd find you somehow or other. When people grow up, their capacities are naturally greater than in childhood, and, besides, there's a blood relation between father and child."

Thinking back, Dong Bin realized it was true; no matter how carefully their playmates would hide, Wang Liping had an uncanny knack for finding them. He had already been clever even as a child. Once she thought about things this way, it all seemed perfectly reasonable. And yet there still seemed to be some sort of indefinable sense of mystery there. Her husband was a good person at heart, honest and upright, punctilious and dutiful, a fine upstanding man glad to lend others a hand. But there was something she just couldn't put her finger on.

~~~~~

Even in the midst of human feelings and worldly affairs, it is possible to transcend them and be unaffected, not lingering over them, being calm and clear, so that spiritual truth is always operative. And yet one does not appear puritanical, but is like ice in the sunlight, melting without a trace. When the mixed up world and the clear open Way are unified, it is like fish in water, like water with fish, forming a natural completeness, reflecting each other in a total reality.

Taoist practice at home is quite different from Taoist practice in the mountains. When practicing in the mountains, most days are spent in company with heaven and earth, the sun and moon; whereas when practicing in the midst of the ordinary world one mostly associates with people at large. Taoism has lofty views on managing relationships with others; this is the subject of Taoist "Chamber Arts."

Chamber Arts are Taoist sociology, the study of human life, a systematic doctrine and praxis regulating interpersonal relationships.

Chamber Arts are divided into twelve sections, among which the main ones deal with such topics as the Way and virtue, spaciousness, infinity, the relation between heaven, earth, and humankind, human life, parents, husbands and wives, and brothers and sisters. Chamber Arts mainly deal with the systematics and rhythms of the universe of the human body, with changes in life, with hygiene, and with the structuring of life. These principle ingredients interpenetrate, forming a complete system of Taoist life philosophy. This is an important part of Taoist culture.

The Chamber Arts of which we speak here do not refer to the "bedroom art" in the narrow sense that people think of it today. In this narrow sense, bedroom art simply refers to sexual relations between men and women, but this is just one part of the section on husband and wife in Chamber Arts.

The theory of life systematics delves into the whole process of human life from birth to death. It is divided into three sections: on pregnancy, on growth and development, and on aging. The section on pregnancy deals with conception and gestation, and what the man and woman should practice during each month of the process. The section on growth and development distinguishes different physical stages, each of which requires different methods of cultivation. The section on aging covers the causes of deterioration and methods of postponing it.

The theory of life rhythmics delves into the rules governing natural changes in the human body, and variations in the process of inner work cultivated to adapt to these changes. Taoists have come up with a rule of five kinds of periodic wave. Here for the moment we will present three kinds: the line of life, the line of emotion, and the line of sexuality.

The Great Way is infinite; the line of life has no beginning and no end. In terms of an individual, however, since there is birth and there is death, there is a beginning and an end in the line of life, demarcating the lifetime of the individual. As long as people have not died, the line of life continues unceasing, and the lines of sexuality and emotion also operate along with the line of life. Once the line of life stops, the lines of sexuality and emotion also stop along with it. Outside these three lines are two more lines, which are operative while people are alive and are still operative after people have died. This is the Taoist theory. The beginning of the line of life, according to Taoist reckoning, is the moment the umbilical cord is severed. At this point a person enters from the primal into the temporal. The state before the cutting of the cord is half primal and half temporal.

The two lines besides the lines of life, sex, and emotion continue to be active even after a person's death, reaching understanding of human existence and mode of action in the universe, and attaining to recognition of the fundamental nature of life.

The line of sexuality reflects a person's sexual desire and procreative capacity; it also reflects a person's intelligence. Aging and rejuvenation both take place along this line. When the element of sexual arousal is no longer there, old age has set in. According to the Chamber Arts, refinement work first cultivates the line of sexuality, to stimulate the element of sexual arousal, thus prolonging life. For a woman, the onset of the menstrual period is the lowest point of sexual desire. The twelfth or fifteenth day after that, just on the verge of ovulation, is the highest point of sexual desire. For a man, the determination must be made by observation.

The line of emotion indicates the periodicity of people's emotional waves. Taoists have found that emotions vary along with sexual desire, with but a slight time lag between them. Right after the low point of sexual desire, the emotional low point appears; and the emotional high point follows upon the peak of sexual desire.

The lines of life, sexuality, and emotion each have regular periodic up and down waves. This fluctuation can be observed in the context of a whole lifetime, and it can also be observed in terms of months of the year and days of the month. When calculated according to a uniform standard, the periodicity and wavelength of each line differ according to the individual, and must be determined by the practitioner through keeping a continuous record.

If we draw out the lines of life, sexuality, and emotion using a month of life for a sample, we see that each of the three lines has extremes, and they also intersect. Times when the three lines all intersect at once are the most unstable times for an individual.

After finding out the rhythms of variation in the three lines in the human body, Taoists came up with different methods of cultivation at the peaks, valleys, and intersections; this is a kind of "firing process," or process of refinement.

For example, at the peak of sexual desire, a person is most easily stirred and incapable of self-control. At this time, in practice it is necessary to work strongly with the "martial fire" to cull and refine energy. The male performs the external five-element channel opening exercise, the eight-trigram mental sphere, and mind-nurturing bathing. The female does active exercise to open the energy channels, and does the second step of "feminine alchemy work" in stillness.

At the low points of the line of emotion, people are most susceptible to indescribable depression. In young people, this may become so severe that it produces feelings of despair. At such times, it is necessary to use warm, gentle nurturing methods, gathering the mind and nurturing essential nature, performing the "immortal induction technique."

Through appropriately timed cultivation, the regularity of natural variation in the human body is strengthened, so all sorts of contradictions and conflicts within your own body can be resolved in a timely manner, allowing you to maintain internal equilibrium to the maximum degree, so it is natural to be optimistic, intelligent, healthy, and long-lived.

In harmonizing personal relationships it is also very helpful to grasp the rhythms of natural fluctuations in the people around you. In Master Wang Liping's own words, this is something most useful in everyday life, in family life. For example, at times of peak sexual desire, males should actively find some work to do; while females should take elderly folks for walks out of doors. In children, this time is when quarrels and fights are most likely to occur, so adults need to pay added attention to avoid mishaps.

When tending the ill, of course, it is even more imperative to consider the periodicity of the fluctuations in their lives. In general, it is necessary to determine four stages of a cycle: the stage of yang rising, the stage of yang descending, the stage of accumulating yin, and the stage of producing yang. This facilitates the adoption of different healing methods.

In the 1950s and 1960s Western researchers discovered biorhythms, periodic waves in the human body; they came up with three lines—physical strength, emotional feeling, and mental power. They even applied this discovery to prevention of air and sea accidents. In the last few years, this theory has become popular in China, even to the point where it has been introduced into calculating machines, which is something of a novelty. Taoist Chamber Arts, however, had already formulated a complete system in the time of the Seven Real People of the North. The Chamber Arts section on the rhythms of human life deals with five kinds of rhythm; this represents a much deeper inquiry into the nature of life. Unfortunately, this brilliant doctrine has been inaccessible to society for eleven centuries.

After having studied the systems and rhythms of human life, Taoists focused on the future, coming up with theories of changes in human life, predicting harmful or beneficial changes that could occur in people's future natural life, social relations, relations between human and natural worlds, and so on, also offering ways of averting trouble, heading for good fortune, and avoiding ill fortune. This also touches upon divination, though divination is in itself a complete, independent doctrine. In the context of the doctrine of life changes, divination mainly studies what Taoists call changes in form, meaning changes that can be predicted by way of ordinary experience and knowledge. For example, according to a work on the sixty-year cycle, the year 1989 is a yin year belonging to "great forest wood," and yin "wood" corresponds to the human gall bladder. 1990 is a yang year belonging to "earth by the road," and yang "earth" corresponds to the stomach. This tells the Taoist practitioner to attend to the specific body part in cultivation, and to prevent ailments that may occur. Based on a foundation of recognition of the system, rules, and variations of life, Taoists practice regulated, purposeful hygiene. Cultivation is then like what Chinese physicians call dialectic treatment, practicing different methods according to differing conditions, mastering differing firing processes. This is why the doctrine of hygiene is very practical and precise.

Finally, Chamber Arts elucidate a theory of the structuring of human life. Through long-time cultivation, the structure and capacities of one's body must undergo an enormous change, with more and more temporal and spatial elements becoming involved in one's life activities. For example, when Wang Liping began to cultivate refinement, he only merged with the natural environment of the immediate surroundings; then he gradually communed with the sun and moon; and later he practiced interaction with the solar system and twenty-eight constellations. So his life activities unfolded in a vaster and vaster universe. At the last stage of cultivation, one must transcend time and space, entering into a more multidimensional universe. Thus the elements that participate in and exert effects upon a person's life activities are undergoing a fundamental change, requiring a conscious restructuring of the various life forces and capacities, so that life continues an uninterrupted process of sublimation.

The contents of the foregoing five facets of Chamber Arts are interconnected, forming a Taoist doctrine of human life that has not been disseminated these thousand years.

In the last couple of years, there have from time to time been people or books in the marketplace hawking what they call bedroom arts, claiming that Chamber Arts are "paired refinement of male and female." Thus a dignified cultural tradition has had its reputation marred by a few indecent people.

In reality, the paired refinement of male and female is merely part of the section on husband and wife in Chamber Arts, and this section on husband and wife, furthermore, is but one part of the greater topic of "male and female, yin and yang." The first step deals with how to cultivate good feelings between husband and wife, so they can get along in spontaneous harmony. It is only at the second step that the paired cultivation of male and female is discussed, comprising altogether one hundred and eight techniques. The mutual tuning of husband and wife can strengthen the body and heal a variety of ailments. The best natural contraception method is also included. The whole system of practice was brought to perfection by two of the Seven Real People of the North, Master Danyang and Sun Bu-er, who were husband and wife.

Because of restrictions in traditional thinking, Master Wang Liping has refrained from lecturing on this topic for the time being. He once expounded a bit to some foreign friends, who excitedly surrounded him, nagging him to write out the whole thing for publication abroad. Master Wang Liping dismissed the idea with a laugh. As he confided to us, "Don't think I'm being petty. My sense of national pride is very strong."

In Chamber Arts, the sections on parents, spouses, and siblings deal with methods of cultivating refinement in the home and among relatives and friends. Taoists regard the use of blood relationships as of utmost importance. Many people may have had experiences where they have an inexplicable strange feeling or sensation right at the very moment when someone close to them is involved in a serious emergency far away. This sort of experience illustrates the existence of an uncanny sensitivity between people who are very close, a sensitivity not affected by time or distance. Scientists have just begun to pay attention to such phenomena, but Chinese Taoists have long been consciously employing this kind of sensitivity. Although they have never indicated what sort of "wave" it is, they have investigated this phenomenon in great detail. Even though they are from the same mother, practical cultivation of relationships between brothers and between sisters are not the same. Through mutual cultivation with people closely related, feelings are deepened and enriched, enhancing all aspects of communication. As Master Wang Liping says, "Life is practice: cultivating refinement of disposition, cultivating refinement of harmony in the home, with mirth, attentiveness, and heart-to-heart connection."

At first Master Wang Liping kept his lips sealed about all this, just managing it inconspicuously. Later the grand master told him he could test it out on a small scale, so he gradually taught some of it to his household and to elderly neighbors. These old folks practiced quite well, to the point where some of them could even sit in the snow.

~~~~~~~

Master Wang Liping's parents and parents-in-law, all elderly people in their seventies and eighties, practice sitting and do exercise every day; they are all healthy, clear of eye and ear, cheerful and open, nimble and able to get about easily. From time to time they go out looking for some good deed to do. At home, they do not remain idle either, but do various chores.

Master Wang Liping and his wife lived an austere life, supporting five elderly people on both sides of the family, as well as their son. Master Wang Liping's everyday dress is plain and simple, while his work clothes were big and baggy, showing his real refinement. If he wore fancy clothing, it would on the contrary be excess and would look awkward on him.

Master Wang Liping's diet is even simpler. He never partook of meat, tobacco, wine, or tea; later on, emulating his teachers, he also gave up piquant things such as onions, garlic, ginger, and leeks. He eats plain food, plain vegetables, and then only a little as if he didn't care about eating at all. Once when we were at a meal with Master Wang Liping where the host presented a sumptuous table including chicken, duck, fish, and prawns, Master Wang Liping only drank a cup of water and ate some strips of bean curd and some bean sprouts. After the meal we asked Master Wang Liping if he really never even thought of eating meat. He replied, "It's not that I never ever think of it. Sometimes I think of tasting something delicious, but I erase the thought, on account of a kind of belief."

Universal love, compassion, the spirit of altruism and self-sacrifice—are these not precisely the greatest needs of present-day society, filled with material desires but emotionally desensitized? If everyone lived with a loving heart, our world would have less loneliness, injustice, and murder. Then even if our material livelihood were not everything we might wish, we would still feel as if we were enveloped in a warm spring breeze. In public pronouncements, it is more effective to emphasize love and justice than enmity. The former nourishes a loving heart; while the latter fosters hostility. We should be sympathetic to all beings; surely the world would be a better place with universal human love!

One quiet afternoon, we went to Master Wang Liping's house. Master

Wang's mother-in-law cordially invited us to have a seat, then hurriedly set about preparing some tea. In the meantime, we took the opportunity to look around Master Wang's living room. It is a more than ordinary house, with two adjoining rooms, rather worn with age. The large room is about fifteen or sixteen square meters. With the door of the small room open, one can see half of a large bed. There is also a big bed in the large room, with a television set up next to the wall, and an old 1970s-type radio beside the TV. There is also an old-fashioned chest for clothes. Other than these items, there is nothing at all in the living room; if the television set weren't there, it would seem like a household of the 1950s.

Master Wang Liping took a folding chair from the corner and sat down. His mother-in-law brought tea. We drank from porcelain cups, while Master Wang used a glass jar that had once contained some drink. Such were the utensils he normally used at home!

"So this is your house?"

"Isn't it great?" Master Wang Liping surveyed his house with satisfaction. "Two of the elders live in the big front room; while my wife and I live in the small inside room."

We took a look in the small room. It was about nine square meters in size, with much of it occupied by a bed. At the head of the bed was a shelf with a Taoist canon on it. At the foot of the bed, against the wall, was a dressing table, its top covered with small articles. A square mirror hung on the wall. That was all there was in the whole room.

"Where does your son live?"

Inviting us to take tea, Master Wang Liping replied, "My son lives in his grandmother's house. The house has two rooms, like this one. My parents live in the outer room; my younger sister lives with my son in the inner room. If we want to go over there, they both have to wait on the sofa bed outside."

"Where do you write?" Nowhere was there a desk where one could write freely. We wondered where he composed the writings he plans to leave to later generations to amend the gaps in the Taoist canon.

Master Wang Liping pointed to the big bed in the little bedroom and said, "I write on the bed. There's plenty of room on a 'desk' that big!" He spoke in a very light, relaxed manner.

Readers may well wonder if the situation is really this extreme. Today, in the 1990s, the average home is likely to be half "modernized"—how could an internationally known Taoist Transmitter live in such humble circumstances?

Had we not visited the master's house ourselves, we would not have dared to write this, even though he had mentioned his home situation to us before. At that time he had said, "Compared to most people's houses, I have very little furniture, even though I have a color TV. When too many people come over, I even have to borrow benches from the neighbors."

Commenting on his home situation, the master had told us, "After all, material comfort is secondary and superficial; essentially it depends on the person. If the person is in a good state of mind, everything is fine. When I went traveling with my teachers at the time of the Cultural Revolution, even when we had nothing to eat and nothing to drink, and our clothes were in tatters, we were still merry all day long. Even when it rained so much we were slipping and sliding and absolutely covered with mud, we still sang as we went along."

Whenever he mentioned his teachers, Master Wang Liping's face brightened with cheer. "Those years were really the happiest time of my life." Having said this, Master Wang remarked, as if to conclude, "People's aims are different, so their lives are different. Their wishes are different, so they seek in different directions. Their aspirations are different, so they travel different roads."

As we were sunk in reflection, Master Wang Liping brought a couple of stamp albums from the back room and invited us to share his hobby. He and his son both enjoy collecting stamps. As we looked them over, we noticed there was not a single specially valuable stamp; most were recent issues. The inclusion of quite a few foreign stamps, however, made it a novel collection. With all the pictures of landscapes, people, and animals, of all colors and varieties, looking at the stamps is like seeing vignettes from children's stories through a small window. And Master Wang Liping was very charming as he forgot himself while pointing out this stamp and that. It seemed he must have been getting a lot of mail at the time and couldn't bear to throw away those pretty pictures, so he carefully kept them.

We never imagined that this Complete Reality Taoist had such a hobby. We had known that he is very fond of children, and he'll be somewhat out of sorts if too many days pass without having the chance to play with children. If people bring children when they come to visit, often the master will unconsciously disregard the adults and take to the children first.

He loves innocence, and he is most grieved by things that hurt children.

Once as he was riding his bicycle through town, Master Wang Liping came upon a scene where a group of primary school children were sweeping the streets and cleaning storefronts, while the adults stood by watching. A frown crept over the master's face, and he slowed down. At the next corner, there were children pumping air for the bicycle tires of passersby, many of whom had stopped for the service even though they had no need of it. Seeing the children huffing and puffing as the adults stood by gesticulating, Master Wang Liping stopped and made his way through the crowd. Taking out a hand cloth to wipe the sweat off one child's forehead, he said to her, "Here, little girl, you're tired. Why don't you go rest while uncle takes your place for a while." Losing interest, the adults dispersed, pushing along their bicycles, which had never really needed air anyway.

We believe that the impression made on the child by Master Wang Liping that day was greater, truer, finer, and more beautiful than the impression made on her by the work assignment.

Let us only hope the innocent heart remains in this world forever!

19

Emerging on a Mission

In recent years, China has seen an unprecedented surge of interest in traditional culture, with the popularization of traditional martial arts and all sorts of practices for the benefit of the people.

While this boom was taking place all over the country, Master Wang Liping remained concealed. He still went to work every day, just like anyone else. He spoke little and always had a kindly smile on his face. As far as his coworkers were concerned, he was an ordinary, diligent worker. When he got home, he'd look in on the older folks, do some household chores, and occasionally take his son on his shoulders and go out to do a little shopping. To his neighbors, he appeared to be a fine young man, content with his lot and always happy, respectful to the old and kind to the young.

Sometimes, when a serious illness or minor disaster occurred in the neighborhood, or when a fellow worker had some problem, Master Wang Liping would invariably show up with words of comfort. The strange thing was that those illnesses, troubles, problems, and whatnot would then dissolve in some unknown way. Eventually people began to wonder about this, and they'd ask Master Wang Liping, but he would dissemble, so no one knew for sure whether or not there was any "medicine in the gourd."

But this Complete Reality Wayfarer was keeping a close eye on the popularization of traditional Chinese culture, observing the direction of the trend. Sometimes Qigong energetics teachers would give classes nearby, and Master Wang would attend, paying the fees out of his meager salary and sitting silently in the audience. Never once did any of these Qigong teachers discern the presence of a genuine adept in the audience.

Master Wang Liping was carrying out an examination and study of actualities. Through interaction with other members of these audiences, he came to understand more about prevailing conditions and what people today are thinking. A master plan was forming in his chest. His communications with his teachers far away now became more frequent. These communications were not written. Even as he did his work, in his chest he was taking in spiritual communications from a distance and was also constantly sending back his own thoughts.

Now a critical moment had arrived.

A number of traditional methods of physical training have been popularized under the name of Qigong or energetics, so Qigong has gradually become a socially accepted form.

The conditions were ripe for introducing people to yet higher levels.

The time had come for revealing the advanced methods held secret for a thousand years in the Dragon Gate sect of Complete Reality Taoism.

By the year 1985, confusion and crisis lay concealed in the popularization of Qigong. With fish and dragons mixed, it was hard to tell what was true and what was false. In some places, there were even bold impostors claiming to represent the Dragon Gate school, stealing the name to fool the world.

Master Wang Liping quietly awaited his teachers' command, preparing to emerge from concealment. The Wayfarer of the Infinite, now one hundred and five years old, sent the message to Wang Liping: emerge to carry out the Way, based correctly on its pure source. Disseminate the classical methods of inner work handed on in the Dragon Gate sect of Complete Reality Taoism, spreading the Great Way throughout the land.

Now the eighteenth-generation Transmitter of the Dragon Gate Sect, inheritor of the classical Spiritual Jewel arts of inner work for developing mental capacities, having studied and practiced for fifteen years and guarded the Way for eight springs and autumns, having silently lived in obscurity for twenty-three years altogether—Wang Liping finally appeared in the world as he really was.

In the southwest corner of Beijing, the magnificent capital of China, is White Cloud Observatory, the largest Taoist establishment in northern China. White Cloud Observatory is one of the three great seats of the Dragon Gate sect of Complete Reality Taoism. Around the end of the Song dynasty and the beginning of the Yuan, the Master of Eternal Spring, Qiu Chuji, founder of the Dragon Gate sect, began to preach the Way here, popularizing the Complete Reality teaching. Eight centuries later, the eighteenth-generation successor of the Master of Eternal Spring,

Wang Liping, came to this place, paid respects to his spiritual ancestor, then went to the eight great places in the western hills, where he wanted to organize large-scale classes on the classic Spiritual Jewels arts of inner work for development of mental capacities.

A place to practice was set up at the Fragrant World Temple, one of the eight great places. Surrounded by green mountains on all four sides, encircled by clouds and mist, the Fragrant World Temple emerges from the fog in the dawn light. The temple had long been without an abbot to keep it clean, so it was full of cobwebs and dust. Master Wang Liping went there, cleaned out the rooms, and then sat all night in each one of the buildings, examining them thoroughly, getting rid of years of accumulated dankness, so the temple could welcome the more than one hundred students who were to participate in the class. Transmitting stillness exercises to such a large group of diverse people, male and female, old and young, each individually different mentally and physically, was an undertaking without precedent. Facing students from all different regions of China, Master Wang Liping first wanted to clarify certain muddled perceptions, introducing the basic source to the people. Briefly raising doubts about popularized Qigong, the master followed up by defining three states of energy:

"The most important thing in Taoist hygienic arts is to understand Nature and obey natural laws. People are born in Nature and exist between heaven and earth, so we have an inseparable relationship with Nature. The principal modality of this relationship is energy. Thus Lao-tzu deduced this formula: humanity emulates earth, earth emulates heaven, heaven emulates the Way, the Way emulates Nature.

"Nowadays everyone talks about energetics, but in olden times there was no such term. There are differences, furthermore, in the usage of the word 'energy.' In concrete terms, there are three kinds of energy.

"The first kind is the energy of breath, the energy in the natural atmosphere. This has no form, no governing rules, no set course. This is energy that exists in the human body as well as in Nature, communing and circulating internally and externally.

"The second kind of energy is a subtle substance intrinsic to the human body; it is the flow of power within the body. Although it is imperceptible and intangible, it nevertheless has mass and contains particles, which can be mechanically measured. This is substantial yet formless matter. This energy is the so-called true energy of which we commonly speak.

"The third kind of energy is luminous energy, which is also a particle-containing flow of power within the body. This luminous energy has radiance and gives off heat; it is perceptible to others when it emanates, and can be used to broadcast electromagnetic waves forming a 'magnetic field' that is employed in curing illnesses.

"These three types of energy, representing different levels of practical attainment, can also be made to change into one another and interact with one another. The practice begins by training natural energy, coming to perceive the reality of the human body in the context of the laws of Nature. When the power of your inner work reaches a certain level, the first kind of energy transmutes into the second kind. With continued practice, the second kind of energy transmutes into the third. Then the practice has reached an advanced level.

"When the second type of energy transmutes into the third type, some reactions may occur, such as abstention from grain, meat, tobacco, alcohol, tea, and so on. At such a time, careful management is necessary; otherwise it is easy to waste the effort you have made and give up halfway along. In sum, if you want to actually transmute the second type of energy into the third type, you need to practice quiescent exercises, because there is no way to accomplish this by active exercise.

"In practicing quiescent exercise, the main thing is to cultivate the 'four directions' of the human body—front, back, left, and right. The outer coming in is the combining of spirit, intent, and the first type of energy. The inner going out is the combining of spirit, intent, and the second type of energy. Emanating energy outward is the combining of spirit, intent, and the third type of energy.

"To sum up the foregoing points, the first type of energy is the natural breath in the body of Nature. The second type of energy is the mystery of the universe in the human body. The third type of energy is the secret of cultivating reality and attaining wizardry.

"The wonders of Taoist hygiene are in the infinitely wondrous energies of the first, second, and third level."

Hearing these words, the minds of the students were opened. Master Wang Liping knew that Taoist theories come from long-term praxis using both body and mind, discovered through minute observation and direct understanding. Just listening to principle is still shilly-shallying outside the gate; if you want to go in the gate and go on to ascend into the hall and enter into the room, realizing the deep meaning in the shallow words, there is no way to go but to cultivate refinement intensely.

In the mornings Master Wang Liping lectured; then in the afternoons and evenings he led the students in practice. As far as possible, he taught the students using the methods he had learned from his own teachers. Generally speaking, in quiescent exercise, which is work on essence, sitting cross-legged is most difficult and painful. It is necessary to maintain a relaxed body, relaxed form, relaxed bones, relaxed thinking, relaxed attention, and relaxed perspective even in the midst of the most intense pain; certainly not an easy thing. When they began this practice, some of the students did not understand the inner subtlety of it; before they had been sitting very long, they were in such pain that they could not stabilize their will. As he encouraged everyone to persevere and not give up the posture, Master Wang Liping gave them an explanation in the following terms:

Sitting cross-legged to practice inner work is most painful; sitting until you pass out is the limit. *Essentials of Attainment* says that even iron men find it hard to endure, for it is more painful than any other pain. The pain doesn't kill you, and yet it doesn't let you live. So what is the advantage of undergoing such pain? It is to let people know that beyond this world of persons, events, and things, which we first come painfully through, there is the world of heaven, earth, and humanity, which must also be painfully crossed. We should experience this pain once. If we can take this pain, then we can stand any pain. People can in fact endure it. When they cannot, it means that their will is faltering, and they need to use thought to control their will. When beginning cross-legged sitting, it is essential to cultivate the bones and marrow, and change the quality of the blood, in preparation for the exercises of refining the inner five elements and opening the marrow. After sitting for a year or two, sweetness emerges from the bitterness, and it really seems as if you've entered another world.

These words are easy enough to understand on the surface, but according to Master Wang Liping, the principles behind them can only be mastered by going through hardship time and again, dying and being reborn several times over. He taught according to his own personal experience, so it sounded exceptionally intimate and unusually simple. As he spoke and laughed, he led people into the gate of mysterious wonder.

Cultivating refinement is very painful, and it cannot be done in one day. Based on the experiential methodology transmitted over eleven centuries, Master Wang Liping taught in an appropriately measured way, starting with the fundamentals, unlike the self-proclaimed "Qigong Masters" who claim to teach some sort of rapid methods of energetics. Wang Liping was also concerned that new students might be overeager and unable to stand the pain of solitariness, so from time to time he performed some minor arts for the students' benefit, adding some amusement to the life of practice, and providing an opportunity for the alert to come to an understanding of certain principles.

~~~~~

Beijing in June is oppressively hot, so one runs with perspiration even without walking or moving around. The place of practice was a room in the temple about as large as a classroom, packed with over one hundred and fifty people sitting. The doors and windows were shut tight, too, so the room was closed to any air circulation, like the pit in the earth where Master Wang Liping sat and practiced as a youth. The students were all soaked with sweat, as if they had gotten into a steamer. Even their sitting cushions grew moist. Everyone felt hard put as they gasped and panted.

Master Wang Liping had everyone open their hands and place them palm upward on their knees, paying attention to changes in the temperature surrounding the universe of their own bodies. As he spoke, he crouched slightly and waved his hands lightly back and forth like small fans, mumbling something under his breath.

After about one or two minutes, a current of air started up in the room. Very shortly, it felt as if all the doors and windows had been thrown wide open and cool breezes were passing through the room, each gust colder than the last. After seven or eight minutes, the terrible heat had dispersed, and the perspiration on the faces and bodies of the students gradually dried cold. In the blink of an eye, a steaming hot room had become cool as a mountain cave with a running spring. Some of the students couldn't believe this was really happening; surreptitiously opening their eyes and taking a look around, they saw that the doors and windows were still shut tight as before; not a breath of air had gotten in. All the other students were sitting with their eyes closed, smiles of comfort on their faces.

One of us was among those who peeked. At the time we couldn't imagine how one individual could lower the temperature in such a large room in so short a time. Later, on learning equilibrium exercises, we discovered that when one can practice with a pure yin being, like a snake, to the point of attaining equilibrium, and only then can it be theoretically plausible that one could take the pure yin energy of snakes and radiate it, or that a human could emulate the capacity of snakes to emit yin energy and cool the air.

As more and more extraordinary happenings occurred, the perspectives of the students were greatly expanded. But it was all quite ungraspable and incomprehensible. Quite a few people had dreams, mostly of Master Wang Liping. The strange thing was that when the subject of dreams came up in conversation the following day, it turned out that a number of people had had the same dream. Sometimes for several nights in a row there would be dreams like a serial novel, one chapter following on another. When asked about this, Master Wang laughingly said, "Maybe everyone's doing sleep work together. When thought is exercised in unison, the chance of people having the same dream is somewhat increased."

Most of the students only came with the aim of improving their physical well-being and did not look very deeply into this phenomenon, thus ignoring an experience of great scientific value. In reality, using dreams to transmit awareness is one of the higher vehicle arts of the Dragon Gate sect. Master Wang Liping took the opportunity afforded by this class to perform an experiment, causing a number of people to have the same dream at the same time. Earlier he had carried on such experiments only with his own teachers; since both the old masters and their successor were at a high level of attainment, they could exchange thoughts in dreams and carry on soundless conversation. But none of his predecessors had ever made a concrete experiment in simultaneous control of a number of people's thinking; this responsibility fell on the shoulders of Master Wang Liping. Even today he is still involved in researching and investigating this.

We encountered such situations more than once; evidently Master Wang Liping entered our dreams, acting and speaking with great clarity. We could remember what he did and said, and found everything in the dreams subsequently proved true; so we suspected Master Wang was transmitting awareness in dreaming. When we confronted him and asked him, he said he knew nothing about it.

We believe that anyone who has a comparatively great deal of contact with Master Wang Liping may have had such experiences. These phenomena illustrate how highly accomplished people can do things consciously while in an unconscious state. How should we classify such spiritual phenomena? It looks like Western psychological concepts such as conscious and subconscious are insufficient for analyzing the levels of consciousness of the brain of cultivated people.

After half a month of practice in the mountain temple, Master Wang Liping told the students that a lot of small animals would be showing up. He instructed the students not to fear the little creatures; he said to be kind to the animals and not hurt them in any way. After a few days, he added, the animals would go away on their own. The students half believed and half doubted; but by the next day the temple had become like a menagerie. One by one rats and weasels appeared, as if from nowhere, frolicking fearlessly in broad daylight. They also invaded the practice room; after the class had spent a short time of quiet sitting, a bunch of rodents scurried in, running around in between the sitting cushions, some of them finally lying inside shoes, as if they had found something delicious in the shoes. Snakes slithered over the window frames, some of them poking their bodies probingly into the chinks at the corners of the room, as if they were absorbed in sniffing something. An amazing number of badgers also appeared, suspicious and nervous. Some students who were practicing standing meditation under the trees that evening found badgers standing in front of them when they concluded the exercise and opened their eyes.

Master Wang Liping explained to the students that the practice of inner work can attract small animals. This is not superstition; there is a scientific principle to the phenomenon. Everything in the realms of "persons, events, and things" and "heaven, earth, and humanity" has its own "field," which can radiate "waves" of a specific frequency that enter into relationships with the environment. These countless different fields are one totality, and yet they are also individually independent. Because of their oneness, the entire universe is a whole; because of their independent individuality, all things and beings are distinct. When a group of practitioners has been cultivating refinement together for many days, the constitution and capacities of the human body undergo changes, and so does the frequency of the energy waves it emanates. When the frequency of these energy waves matches that of the energy emitted by small animals, then the animals will spontaneously gather around, as if they smelled attractive food.

In reality, there are principles of chemistry, physics, and biology involved here. Extending the principle, if people pay attention to the minute and subtle changes inside the body while sitting cross-legged, this enables people to sense the subtle changes in vibration frequencies on the surface of the earth. Equilibrium exercise standing with your back to a tree bathing in its energy is seeking to assimilate your "field" to the "field" of the tree; if small animals also actually practice cultivation in the presence of humans, that means that they too are tuning their energy "field."

So people in ancient times consciously used both variability and consistency of energy fields to stimulate capacities latent in human beings.

As a modern Complete Reality Taoist, a master who has attained a profound realization of the marrow of Taoist thought, Wang Liping uses acceptable modern language to express the thinking of the Way. In the process of absorbing modern scientific theory, and at a time when Eastern and Western civilization have been converging, he came to feel all the more keenly the limitations of modern science, and precisely herein lies the impetus behind his dedication to the dissemination of Taoist culture.

After the conclusion of the class at the Fragrant World Temple in Beijing, Master Wang Liping slipped away back to the Cavern of Eternal Spring on Mount Lao, where he told his teachers about this experience, about his new impressions and understanding. He also asked for instructions regarding some problematic illnesses he had encountered. The old masters were delighted to see how their disciple had matured and how well he was bearing his great responsibility on his own.

Wang Liping stayed with the old teachers for some days. During the class, he had been leading exercises, healing ailments, and giving lectures, expending a great deal of energy. After a few days, he had recovered. As he was leaving, he handed over all the money he had received as class tuition to the grand master, for the eventual realization of the master's wish to reconstruct a place to disseminate the Way.

The grand master admonished him, "Although you have attained the Way, you still have not left ordinary society. You live in the ordinary world, and you have an extended family with material needs. After this debut, furthermore, you will have to deal with an increasing number of guests, requiring you to go to considerable expense. Our work is already beyond the world; we live in the world of the Way. Heaven and earth provide adequate support. What do we need with money?" The grand master wanted Wang Liping to take the money back, but Wang Liping refused.

After that, at the conclusion of each class, the communist work brigade in charge took most of the income, and Wang Liping took what little of the painfully won earnings was left after expenses and took it to the mountain to hand over personally to the grand master. Unable to make him change his mind, the grand master could only accept; he was touched by Wang Liping's character in respecting his teachers and serving the Way.

Shouldering the heavy responsibility of disseminating Taoist culture, mindful of the expectations his teachers have of him, once he got started Master Wang Liping couldn't be stopped. For years he has traveled north and south, giving many classes and seminars in Wushun, Shenyang, Beijing, Shijiazhuang, Sian, Wuhan, Guangzhou, Nanjing, Jinhua, Shanghai, and other places, offering the marrow of the traditional culture he learned through untold hardships twenty years earlier on the road with his teachers, and working diligently for the revival of traditional Chinese culture in the world.

Having a deep feeling for his own hometown, soon after coming back from Mount Lao, Master Wang Liping organized the second class in the Spiritual Jewels inner arts of mental development. This time, with over four hundred local elders in attendance, Master Wang Liping exerted all his strength to set up an energy field for all of them and bring them along with him in inner exercises by hooking them into his inner power. In the final stage of the class, varying degrees of latent capacity had emerged in a quarter of the students, with the opening of the eye to heaven having a comparatively sensitive reaction. Later Master Wang Liping took these students to a scenic spot where he had them sit quietly around the top of a hill with an open view. Then he told them to shut their eyes, look straight ahead, and remember what they saw. After a couple of hours, Master Wang Liping instructed them to conclude the exercise; not allowing them to talk, he had them write down their visions. After a while, the more than one hundred students handed in their reports. As it turned out, most of them had seen a battle scene. More than thirty of them gave detailed descriptions of people, uniforms, banners, battle formations, and changes in the course of the fighting, just as if they had experienced it all themselves. These thirty-odd accounts, furthermore, basically described the same scenes; without any discussion beforehand, many people wrote in similar terms, saying it had been like a nightmare, a scene of horrifying slaughter.

Such an event has been recorded in the history books. In the year 1618, the Manchu Nurhachi attacked three Chinese citadels on the grounds of "seven major complaints" held against the Ming Chinese government. That April, the Chinese president of the ministry of defense led an army against Nurhachi's troops, engaging them in a bloody battle. The Ming army was routed so badly that "more than ten thousand died, with no more than one or two of ten surviving." The three citadels and surrounding territory were lost, and the power of the Ming dynasty went into a steep decline.

There is a relatively detailed record of this battle, and comparison of the recorded descriptions of uniforms and banners with those seen by the students in their visions would indicate that the students' visions were actually scenes of part of this battle.

Master Wang Liping spoke to us of this incident in these terms: "The reappearance of an ancient battleground has three possibilities. One is that with my guidance the students reversed the flow of time, straddling over three hundred and seventy years to witness a scene of battle from that era. Another is that the scenes of past wars still remain in the universe in some way, which we can grasp through a special modality. The third is that I used a Taoist art to project a scene before the students, just as if I had caused them to have a dream. What I want to say is that I certainly did not project a scene; and even if I had, where did the scene I projected come from? Therefore you can eliminate the third possibility, and write about concepts of time and space and modalities of material existence."

In May of 1986, at the invitation of the Association for Scientific Research of Energetics in China, Master Wang Liping once again held a workshop in the mountains west of Beijing, attended by more than three hundred people from all over the country. Over the course of forty days of lecturing and teaching exercises, Master Wang Liping took his meals along with the students and stayed with the students throughout. The students brought him all their problems, great and small, from chronic illnesses to household matters. There was a very profound sensitivity and feeling between the teacher and the students. With his compassion, cheer, wisdom, and truthfulness, and his lofty Taoist character, Master Wang planted a firm belief in the hearts of the students that it is good to learn the Way.

Later, speaking of what he came to understand from his years of teaching experience, Master Wang Liping said that to be a teacher it is necessary to become one with students; one must teach from sensitivity of feeling.

One day during the workshop several people came up the mountain bringing an old woman who had suffered from paralysis for several years. Over eighty years old, the silver-haired woman called to Master Wang Liping the moment she saw him, crying, "Save me, Bodhisattva!"

This old lady had always believed in Buddhism and respected Taoism. She was a pious and goodly woman, but in 1982 she had suffered a blood clot in the brain that had left her completely paralyzed. After going to many major clinics for treatment, she had improved a little, but she was still paralyzed on one side.

Opening his celestial eye, Master Wang Liping found that her condition was not terribly serious, but she had not been treated in time and had not been treated with the correct method. He told the woman's relatives that he still had to look after several hundred students, so he couldn't go to her house to treat her; but if they could bring her there once every day, her treatment would take a week. Her relatives agreed immediately.

So it was that the elderly woman came every day when Master Wang Liping was lecturing, and sat near the dais. As Master Wang lectured, he invisibly released inner power to treat the old woman. Absorbed in listening, without realizing what was happening the old lady was able to get up and walk after two days with the support of her family. After three days, she could make her own way slowly with the help of a cane. After five days she could get around on her own. After seven days she was completely well, able to walk around on the temple grounds.

At the conclusion of the workshop, the old woman came with the whole family, nearly a dozen people, to express her thanks. Taking Master Wang Liping's hand, she said, "This affliction of mine could not be cured by an ordinary person. The day I saw you, it seemed I was seeing the light of Buddha; then I knew I was saved. When I was young I also suffered an illness that was cured right here in this very temple by a Buddhist abbot who gave me some spiritual energy. Now that I've received spiritual energy from you, these old bones can stand up again!" Even as she spoke, she had her family kneel down in respect. Somewhat flustered, Master Wang himself hurriedly kneeled down to help the old woman up, repeatedly saying, "That's too much, Granny, that's too much!"

The three hundred or so students sat cross-legged in two large rooms adjoining in a T shape, with Master Wang Liping at the juncture, leading them along with his inner power.

"Everyone loosen your clothing and belt; with your whole body relaxed, adjust your posture properly. Your back should be straight, but not stiff; relaxed, but not slumping. Let the tongue rest on the upper palate. Having made your sitting base steady, shut the lower three yins. All right! Now raise your heads and look in front of you, the further the better. See if there is a point of brightness, and of what color. OK! Gradually gather the spiritual light in, gathering it back into the point between the eyebrows, which is the 'opening' of the 'opening of the eye to heaven.' Then bring it further in. "

The students sat up straight, not moving at all, so the place was peaceful and quiet, without a sound. Now Master Wang Liping extended his palms, lightly raised them once, then shook them once to the left and the right. All of a sudden these three hundred students starting swaying uncontrollably, as if they were sitting in coracles on a stormy sea. Then, as Master Wang made as if he were turning over two coins in his hands, the students shook even more intensely. Some swayed forward and backward, some tossed their hands out with rapid movements, some beat their chests, some made graceful dance gestures, some made rapid series of gestures with their hands, like experts at sign language. All of a sudden, some began to wail sorrowfully; while others began to laugh crazily. Both rooms were in an uproar.

Master Wang Liping stood in the middle, watching the strange goings-on all around him with a childlike smile on his face. After a while, he raised his right hand toward the room facing east to west, while pushing his other hand lightly downward. Then he turned around to the room facing north to south, appearing to manipulate a couple of coins while uttering some sounds.

Now the people in the west half of the east-to-west room went crazy, crying and wailing madly. Those in the east half, meanwhile, seemed to have been exhausted by the upheaval, their movements becoming feebler and feebler, their sharp cries turning into panting, then quieting down, until they were sitting stably. In the north-to-south room, it was already calm, the more than one hundred students like docile sheep. Some were snoozing, some lightly snoring, sleeping without paying any attention at all to the wailing and laughter in the other room.

After thirty minutes, Master Wang Liping calmed down the people who had been wailing and making noise, then muttered a spell upon which those who had fallen asleep began to awaken. Master Wang told everyone to rub their hands, massage their faces, unlock their legs, and conclude the exercise.

When they were done, the students clamored to have Master Wang Liping explain what had happened. Happy as a child, the master told the students surrounding him about the phenomena: the process of constructing an energy field, laying out an arrangement, and effecting empowerment, developed from ancient Taoist and Buddhist teachings. There are three vehicles.

The first vehicle is called the random array. This means that at the time of empowerment there is no restriction regarding the people involved. There are no rules, and there is no arrangement; the power is allowed to flow spontaneously. Wild wailing and laughing, gesticulating and dancing, all sorts of strange behavior may come out in those affected. The main purpose behind this is for the one doing the empowering to use this format to observe the nature, character, mentality, and flaws of the affected individuals; so one deliberately avoids interference.

But it does not take a highly developed person to produce the effect of the random array. External forces such as fame, prestige, status, and profit can also cause people to lose their basic nature, forget what they are doing, and lose control over themselves. This has mixed up the subjective psychological elements of many people. Modern pop singers, for example, or the performances of movie stars or athletes intoxicate many young people, putting them in a kind of stupor. So people should not think that the induction of spontaneous actions on a large scale is a good thing; when there are highly developed people doing the empowering, in reality this is a low-level phenomenon.

The second vehicle is called laying out an arrangement. Here the one who does the empowering delineates different sectors, locations, and angles, all according to the different natures and temperaments of the individuals involved; only then is the technique employed, sending the people in different sectors into different states. Some are made to move, some cry, some laugh, some sleep, some sit quietly, each acting individually and not interfering with others. The one who does the empowerment is the actor; the members of the audience are the ones acted upon. It is also possible to make one spot cold and one spot warm within the same room, or to make some people's timepieces run a little faster while others' run a little slower. All these effects are derived from the same principle.

The realm of the highest vehicle of empowerment is called "mind taking in spiritual understanding." Speech and action are both unnecessary; the subtlety of the operation lies in mind alone. At this juncture there is a transition from external movement to internal movement, from internal movement to movement of the spirit; both sides communicate mentally by means of spirit, combining in unspoken communion.

Finally, Master Wang Liping explained that when spontaneous movements of the body occur during practice, this means energy is in front and spirit is behind; spirit goes along with energy, so one's body has no master. The practitioner should make the self the ruler, turning external movement into internal movement, examining the minute, extremely subtle changes within the body in the midst of clear quietude.

The Scripture of Clarity and Calm says, "Always using intent to observe the opening is movement; always using dispassion to observe the subtlety in the opening is stillness. Gathering medicine is movement; obtaining medicine is stillness." It also says, "This heaven and earth in the body respond sensitively to the heaven and earth outside the body, so the heaven and earth outside the body thereby respond to the heaven and earth inside the body; thus when the heaven and earth inside the body have a master, then the energy of the heaven and earth outside the body wind up inside. If there is no master, the energy of the heaven and earth inside the body winds up outside, resulting in inability to attain the Way; instead there is loss on the Way." Taoists say, "My fate is up to me, not Heaven," but it is essential to accord with the Way in all aspects of life, whether in terms of individual personality, livelihood, self-cultivation, or work. What is important is that "the heaven and earth in the body have a master," that one is able to master oneself, earning progress and enlightenment by one's own effort and reflection, not losing sight of intrinsic essential nature by indulging in blind worship.

~~~~~~~

Master Wang Liping's teaching activities attracted more and more people, until the Fragrant World Temple could not hold them all and they overflowed into other habitable temples on the mountain. When the mountain accommodations were full, there were also day students who came up the mountain in the mornings, then went back down the mountain to rest after lectures and practice. Seekers of the Way from Hong Kong also came, and physiological researchers from Japan also got in touch with the Association for Scientific Research of Chinese Energetics in hopes of doing field research.

20

Shouldering a Heavy Responsibility

One of the most important tasks the three old wizards gave to Wang Liping is to supplement and edit the Taoist Canon. Master Wang Liping says that the Taoist Canon is like a documentation of Chinese culture; it is also an encyclopedia of ancient Chinese culture.

The Taoist Canon is not a history book recording the ups and downs of dynasties and eras. Its concern is the relationship between humanity and Nature: how the universe is formed, how it changes, how it operates, how humankind develops, what the source of humanity is, and what its destiny is, what the position of humanity is in the universe. In short, the Taoist Canon is concerned with the inner secrets of the universe and human life. It investigates these great questions by means of a special way of thinking, forming a special cultural form, arriving at some unique conclusions, which became the contribution of knowledge and wisdom made to the whole of humankind by the Chinese people, or by the East. It is in this sense that the Taoist Canon may be called a documentation of Chinese culture or an encyclopedia of ancient Chinese culture.

The scope of the Taoist Canon is enormous. In ancient times it was already said that "Taoist arts are complex and manifold." Whoever said this didn't understand Taoist culture; people without understanding of Taoist culture would also say the same thing in later times.

And yet, considering the breadth and detail of the issues with which Taoism is concerned, its historical literature could hardly avoid being multifold and complex. But the enormous richness of the historical literature preserved in the Taoist Canon makes it an enormous cultural treasury for people of later times.

The history of the compilation and organization of the Taoist Canon spans over a thousand years, with numerous episodes. Professor Chen

Guofu wrote *Study of the Sources of the Taoist Canon*, for which Professor Luo Changbei wrote the following preface to the first edition,

"The compilation of the Taoist Canon went through three phases. First it was noted in the records of literature in *Documents of the Han Dynasty*; subsequently people such as Ge Hong, Lu Sinjing, Meng Fashi, Dao Hongjing, Yuan Siaozhu, Wang Yang, and Yi Wencao augmented, edited, and organized it. But even though the table of contents was complete, the actual compilation was not. This was the first phase.

"The Taoist Canon was first named when it was edited and organized in the Kaiyuan era of the Tang dynasty, between 713 and 742. Called 'Precious Collection of the Three Open Channels,' it comprised 3,744 scrolls. This was burned and scattered in the wars at the end of the Tang dynasty and in the succeeding era of the Five Dynasties. During the Song dynasty, in the times of the emperors Taizong (976–997) and Zhenzong (998–1022), Xu Xuan, Wang Jing, and others made comparative studies by imperial command, and sent selected titles to court. The overall structure of the collection was disorganized, however, and there were discrepancies, so time passed without a thoroughgoing organization of the Canon into subjects. Then Zhang Junfang compared a variety of texts, evaluated the variants, and in several years of labor organized the canon into a collection of works in 4,565 scrolls. This was called the 'Treasury of the Celestial Palace of Great Song,' where the expression 'Celestial Palace' refers to numbers from the *Thousand Character Classic* enumeration system. Zhang Junfang also made extracts of the essentials of the Canon, which comprise the *Seven Bamboo Strips in a Cloud Satchel*. Then, in the Chongning era of the reign of emperor Huizong (1102–1106), an imperial edict was sent out seeking lost books of Taoism, of which the government board of culture then had critical editions made by Taoists, increasing the Canon to 5,387 scrolls. This was the second phase.

"The oldest known critical edition of the Taoist canon is the one printed in the time of emperor Huizong, known as the Wangshou Taoist Canon of the Zhengho era. During the Zhengho era (1111–1118), lost Taoist books were collected and compared by imperial command, then printed and circulated in a collection contained in 540 cases. The woodblocks still existed in the time of emperor Zhangzong of the Jin dynasty (1190–1208), but they were defective. So a search for missing texts was made by imperial order to amend the collection, bringing it to a total of

6,455. This was printed under the title *Treasury of the Mystic Capital of the Great Jin Dynasty*. The carving of the woodblocks began in 1190 and was finished two years later.

"In the Yuan dynasty, Song Degang, following the will of his teacher Qiu Chuji, searched out lost books, bringing the canon to more than 7,800 scrolls. The carving of the blocks and the collating of parallel texts took eight years. The resulting book was also called *Treasury of the Mystic Capital*. Then in the reigns of emperors Xianzong (1251–1260) and Shizong (1260–1295), debates between Buddhist and Taoists on the question of the authenticity of the *Hua-hu jing* or 'Scripture on Conversion of the Barbarians' led to the dissemination of an imperial directive to burn the Taoist Canon. This far-reaching disaster led to considerable loss.

"A complete Canon was reconstituted in 1445, and a continuation of the Canon was added in 1607. Altogether there are 5,485 scrolls in 512 cases. This was published, and is still current. There were also some books in private hands, seen by few people. This was the third period." (*Study of the Sources of the Taoist Canon*, Zhonghua Publishing Co., 1963)

Professor Luo's writing is simple and short, but it gives an overview of the thousand-year history of the compilation of the Taoist Canon. Now let us pursue this a little further, expanding somewhat upon the details.

Ge Hong was a famous Taoist theoretician of the Eastern Jin dynasty (317–419), and author of *The Simpleton*. According to that book, there were 670 scrolls of Taoist texts, as well as over 500 scrolls of talismanic charms, amounting to some 1,200 scrolls in all.

During the Liu Song dynasty (420–479) there was a famous Taoist named Lu Xiujing who made an extensive collection of Taoist books, which he classified into Three Open Channels, creating the foundation for the Taoist Canon of later generations. According to Professor Li Yang-zheng's *Outline of Taoism*, (Zhonghua Publishing Co., 1989), Lu Xiujing obtained the Supreme Purity scriptural teachings of Yang Xi and Xu Mi from Shu Qizhen of Mount Mao in Jurong Prefecture, he obtained the Spiritual Jewel scriptural teachings from Ge Cen of Jurong, and also got the Three August Ones scriptural teachings. He published critical editions of the Taoist books of the Wei and Jin dynasties, identifying therein the guidance and admonitions, prescriptions and medicines, and charms and spells, enumerating 1,218 scrolls, although the actual number is 1,090. He divided the Taoist scriptures into three sections, the Open Channel to

Reality, the Open Channel to Mysteries, and the Open Channel to Spirits. The Open Channel to Reality is centered on the Supreme Purity scriptures, the Open Channel to Mysteries is centered on the Spiritual Jewels scriptures, and the Open Channel to Spirits is centered on the Three August Ones literature. In the year 471 Lu Xiujing compiled a table of contents, this being the oldest table of contents for the Taoist Canon.

In his work *Study of the Sources of the Taoist Canon*, Professor Chen Guofu cites the *Scripture of the Original Situation* as follows: "The Open Channel to Reality means nonadulteration, the Open Channel to Mysteries is named for nonobstruction, and the Open Channel to Spirits functions inconceivably. Thus 'open' means communing; the Three Open Channels, higher and lower, commune in their esoteric meaning. The Open Channel to Reality is about the secret of spirituality without adulteration; hence the term 'reality.' The Open Channel to Mysteries is about creating the heavens and establishing the earth, effective function unobstructed; hence the term 'mystery.' The Open Channel to Spirits is about summoning and controlling ghosts and spirits; the effects being inconceivable, they are called spiritual. These three teachings can all lead through the ordinary into the sacred, merging with the Great Vehicle; hence the name Open Channel."

The Three Open Channels are also called the three vehicles: higher, middle, and lower. The Three Open Channels are each divided into twelve sections, making a total of thirty-six parts. The twelve sections are as follows:

1. main texts
2. spirit talismans
3. secret teachings
4. spiritual diagrams
5. records
6. precepts and rules
7. manners and rites
8. methodology
9. arts
10. histories
11. eulogies and hymns
12. manifestos and declarations

These form the skeleton of the later Taoist Canon.

Meng Fushi was a man of the southern dynasty of Liang (552–556). He wrote *Index of Books in the Seven-Part Scriptures of Esoteric Learning*, adding Four Auxiliaries to the Three Open Channels for a total of seven parts. The Four Auxiliaries are called Absolute Purity, Absolute Peace, Absolute Mystery, and Correct Unification; these expound and amplify the Three Open Channels. Absolute Mystery is auxiliary to the Open Channel to Reality, Absolute Peace is auxiliary to the Open Channel to Mysteries, and Absolute Purity is auxiliary to the Open Channel to Spirits. Correct Unification pervades the Three Open Channels and Three Absolutes.

Professor Chen Guofu writes (p. 102), "Taoist books were produced in profusion from the end of the Han dynasty through the Three States, Two Jins, and Northern and Southern Dynasties (ca. 180–580). But since Taoists treasured their books and kept them hidden, most Taoists of those times did not have very many books in their collections. Some, however, willingly undertook long and difficult journeys in quest of different or unusual books; while some purchased books for their collections. Thus one Zhang Yin of the Eastern Jin dynasty (317–419) collected 670 scrolls, while a Wang Daoyi of the Later Wei (220–264) accumulated over 10,000 scrolls. During the Tang dynasty these were arranged in an orderly way for the purposes of making a Canon."

In the imagery of Professor Li Yanzheng, "If Taoism was seeded in the Warring States Era, it sprouted in the Eastern Han, sent up shoots in the Wei, Jin, and Northern and Southern Dynasties, then flowered and fruited in the Sui, Tang, and Five Dynasties."

The Kaiyuan Taoist Canon is so called because it was compiled in the Kaiyuan era (713–742); in the year 748, copies were made by imperial command for the purpose of dissemination. This was a major event in the history of Taoist culture.

Subsequently, however, through the rebellions of An Lushan (755–757) and Shi Siming (758–761), the collections of Taoist books in the two capitals were mostly destroyed. Later, after further disturbances at the end of the T'ang and during the Five Dynasties, a man named Du Guangding and others reassembled the Canon, but they managed to preserve only 30 to 40 percent of the Taoist texts extant in the earlier Six Dynasties era. Compilations of the Taoist Canon were also made later in the Song (907–1278), Jin (1115–1234), and Ming (1368–1644) dynasties; these too were destroyed.

When Qiu Chuji had succeeded in learning the Way, he was summoned by imperial ambassadors of the Jin and Song dynasties, but he did not go to court. Then in 1121, when he was summoned by the order of Genghis Khan, he traveled west. Meeting the Khan, he talked to him about stopping the killing, saving countless lives. From this point on, the Complete Reality path flourished.

Qiu Chuji had a disciple named Song Defang who was also the teacher of an age. Song once spoke to Qiu about the disappearance of the Taoist Canon and how it should be restored. Qiu told Song, "The Canon is important, but I don't have time. You should take care of it some day." Following his teacher's will, Song began the printing of the Taoist Canon in 1237, putting his disciple Qin Zhi-an in charge of the work. After eight years, during which gaps were filled and missing texts searched out, the task was completed in 1244. (cf. Professor Guo's study, pp. 161–62)

The last major compilation of the Taoist Canon was published in the Ming dynasty, in 1444, after forty years of compiling and editing; then a continuation of the Canon was published in 1601. Altogether, the Ming Canon and Continued Canon consist of 5,485 scrolls in 512 cases. This is the only historical printed version of the Canon still extant in its entirety.

The Ming Canon disintegrated during the Qing dynasty; then when the armies of eight allied nations invaded Beijing in 1900, the Canon was finally completely destroyed. Both Ming and Qing courts had distributed many copies of the Canon to Taoist sanctuaries and observatories, but very few survived the fires of warfare.

From 1923 to 1926, a certain publishing company made a photographically reproduced version of the Canon and Continued Canon kept in Beijing's White Cloud Observatory. From 1957 to 1977, the Chinese Taoist Association of Taiwan reprinted this version. Because the White Cloud Observatory's text was missing a number of pages, however, neither of the editions based on it is complete. Then in 1988 a complete photographic version of the Ming Canon was published with the missing pages replaced.

The complete Taoist Canon that people see today is a collection of texts existing before 1601, so there are some missing works. For example, there are numerous texts written after 1601. One hundred and ten of these works, in two hundred and eighty-eight scrolls, were included in the "Collected Essentials of the Taoist Canon" during the Kangxi era (1662–1722). There are also texts missing from the earlier canonical collections, and there were many important texts discovered in the caves of Dunhuang in 1899, which were stolen by English and French explorers. A number of important texts on silk were also discovered at Mawangdui in 1973. Some texts are also preserved in what remains of the Ming dynasty Yongluo Encyclopedia.

There are some problems regarding the classification of texts within the Canon. As Professor Chen Guofu explains, over the ages there were Taoist books that did not fall within the categories of the Three Open Channels and Four Auxiliaries, but in the Tang dynasty collection all Taoist books were put into these categories, even though not all of them were connected with the texts in these seven groups. Commentaries on the Supreme Purity scriptures and writings based on them, for example, all go in the Open Channel to Reality section; but it is very hard to decide where to assign the writings of Taoists of Tang, Song, and later dynasties, like the books of the Taoists of the Southern and Northern Schools.

The Taoist Canon was recompiled several times after the Tang dynasty, but it was destroyed over and over in wars and by the book burning of the Yuan dynasty. The Ming dynasty version of the Canon we have now is partly of the Three Open Channels and Four Auxiliaries, but the Six Dynasties Taoist scriptures have been mixed up, so they are not like they originally were in the Tang dynasty. Other Taoist books are similarly misplaced.

There are some outstanding examples of confusion in the Ming Canon. The Supreme Purity scriptures should be in the Open Channel to Reality section, but now many have been mistakenly put in the Correct Unification section. Commentaries on the Liberating Humanity scriptures should be in the Open Channel to Mysteries section, but now they have been mistakenly put in the Open Channel to Reality section. Commentaries on the works of classical Taoist masters should be in the Absolute Mystery section, but they too have been misassigned to the Open Channel to Reality section of the Canon.

These problems are the shortcoming of the Taoist Canon as it currently exists. Scholars are studying these issues, and so are Taoist Transmitters, who take them even more seriously and are working to amend these shortcomings. The first imperative is augmentation, second is reorganization, third is indexing. From the point of view of Taoists, this is part of their job; it is a major event in Taoist culture, and at the same time also a major event in human culture.

Shouldering such a heavy responsibility, Master Wang Liping and his teachers have correspondingly great spirit and courage. They have already begun working tirelessly on this task.

During their travels, they discovered part of one of the hidden works of Lu Dongbin in a cavern; this is one that should be included in the Canon.

As Professor Chen Guofu writes, Taoists used to keep their books secret and did not hand them on readily; though some searched all over for different books, they still relied on the explanations of masters. That is why transmission was also important. This was characteristic of culture in feudal times; it was also one of the major obstacles to cultural development. But there is another way of looking at it. Under the severity of feudal dictatorships, whole collections of books could be burned on command; and there was also wastage and loss through war and natural disasters. Under these conditions, hiding books in the mountains, or handing them on between teacher and disciple or father and son under the strictest of covenants was a kind of emergency method of preserving culture.

At present, methods of disseminating culture are readily available, the culture-destroying "Great Cultural Revolution" has passed, and people have a little more recognition of human culture. Under these conditions, it now must be considered extremely important to make a great effort to seek, collect, and disinter cultural treasures, including Taoist cultural treasures hidden in the mountains, underground, among the people, and within hearts.

Master Wang Liping and his teachers are now in the process of carrying out this task for the benefit of humanity. They want to fill in the blanks in the Taoist Canon.

Their work has already borne fruit. Following his teachers' instructions, Master Wang Liping has already composed a book on Taoist practice for women. The first draft was 170,000 characters in length; after condensation and streamlining, the final draft was 120,000 characters long. It will soon be ready for market.

Taoist methods of practice over the ages have been for males, without reference to females. In olden times there were women who attained the Way, but they have been relatively few in number, and works of the Taoist Canon specializing in women's practice are missing. In recent years women all over, both in China and abroad, have taken an interest in Taoist practice, but there are no books on feminine practice for them to use. Sometimes old books on female practice can be found in the marketplace, but they are vague in their explanations, and one cannot rely on them for concrete exercises. This is a problem that Master Wang Liping and his teachers have perceived, and one of the issues they want to address.

The Complete Reality Path developed a system of Taoist practice for women, taking into account the biological differences between men and women, and the experiences of earlier female practitioners. Lu Dongbin transmitted the system to Wang Chongyang, and he taught it to Sun Bu-er, who accomplished the practice and became one of the Seven Real People of the North.

Organizing feminine Taoist practice into a book in accord with his teachers' instructions, Wang Liping wrote in easily understood vernacular, explaining the principles and methods clearly for the convenience of female practitioners.

The conditions under which Wang Liping wrote the book on female Taoist practice were such as people could hardly imagine. The Wang household lived an austere and simple life, with nothing but a few pieces of the simplest furniture; there was not even a desk. Master Wang is an internationally known individual, and a holder of knowledge to a rare degree; but who hasn't even got an ordinary desk, outside the poorest and most backward areas? We can hardly avoid feeling deep emotion as we write this, and we think people of good conscience would feel the same way on reading this. But there may also be people who might wonder if we are not creating a modern myth. They don't believe that these are true facts.

Actually, the truth of the matter is simple. Master Wang Liping wrote the text on female Taoism page by page while lying on his bed, or resting the book on his knees. In the future, if those who are fortunate enough to read the book and actually apply it in practice will keep in mind the conditions under which it was written, that will surely be a big help in practice.

Master Wang Liping, the grand master, and his mentor (the other mentor of Pure Serenity having passed on, his body preserved intact) are all carrying out experiments, keeping records, and accumulating material, reorganizing and augmenting the Taoist Canon.

Under a number of conditions, the grand master and the Wayfarer of Pure Emptiness propose a theme for Wang Liping to carry out in an experiment in society, then they make a record of the results achieved.

For example, giving seminars to large classes and carrying on large-scale meditation exercises with so many students, like Wang Liping does, is something the grand master and the Wayfarer of Pure Emptiness have never experienced, and there are no such records in the Taoist Canon, so it is a matter of accumulating experience through experimentation, seeking verifications. Master Wang Liping's classes are held under different conditions, the purpose being thereby to obtain different resource material. Every time he lectures, he always sets out different exercises, and says he himself has no experience in such matters and does not know if it will be possible to succeed or not. It is not entirely out of modesty that he says this; in reality there is another principle involved.

Once when Master Wang Liping was in Sian, he ran into a case of a rare illness. He asked his teachers about it, but they had never encountered it either, so they were unable to teach Wang Liping a concrete method of treatment. Wang Liping then received instructions in a dream from a high master; and when he applied the indicated method, the illness was banished. Later Wang Liping made an extensive textual search, but he was unable to find the name of the high master who instructed him in the dream. Anyway, he made a detailed record of the symptoms and treatment of the illness, thus producing valuable reference material.

The Wayfarer of the Infinite and the Wayfarer of Pure Emptiness are very advanced in age, yet they still persevere steadily in practice, making records of their experiential findings on Taoist practice in old age. These records are also a valuable resource that does not exist in the Taoist Canon.

There are already some university students and researchers who have become very interested in Master Wang Liping's thinking and pragmatic methodology. Together with Master Wang, they have been looking into new problems coming up in the development of philosophy and technology.

When Master Wang Liping conversed with us, one thing that made an unforgettably profound impression on us was the monumental task of reorganizing the Taoist Canon, a task given him by his teachers. He laments being inescapably immersed in everyday occupations. There are layers upon layers of fetters and chains on him. He has been assigned an important responsibility at work, as a factory security officer. People come to him from all over, far and near, with sickness, with difficulties of one kind or another, with this problem or that. They come looking for him day in and day out, constantly bothering him, such that he can neither avoid them nor hide from them. His precious time is thus preoccupied in this way. He does, however, laugh at himself and say, "The mountain Taoists are people outside convention, who have not experienced a life so restricted by other people. Perhaps in the future what I am going through now might also be recorded in the Taoist Canon."

When we first visited Master Wang Liping, it happened to be lunchtime. Master Wang took us to an ordinary diner. This diner was a single room, set up facing the street, with a few round folding tables. Run by two people, it was one of those private eateries that have sprung up in recent years. Master Wang was quite gallant: "I have guests today," he called, "Let's have some food!" He handed one of us a menu. After we ordered, he then ordered some bean curd for himself, and asked for some beer. Bean curd is Master Wang's main diet; the beer was for his guests. He was very happy at having some visitors from afar who did not talk about mundane matters but only asked about the Way. He said, "To this day I have never learned to order food—please feel free to get whatever you want, without hesitation." He ate less than the others, and more quickly; when he finished, he went to pay the bill. When he came back, he told us with a smile, "Today a hundred dollars came in from a magazine in payment for an article, so I have money and don't need to borrow any. Otherwise I'd have to borrow some money to treat you today."

From that moment we realized how truly plain and unaffected Master Wang Liping is. This is one facet of his daily life. He also has to go to Mount Lao to see his teachers every year, and he has to go see his spiritual uncles, the Cloud Roaming Wayfarer and the Barefoot Wayfarer, every two or three years. He has to take care of his parents and parents-in-law, and he has to help his younger brothers and sisters and raise his son; he has to fulfill all of his personal human responsibilities. With himself, however, he is extremely frugal; he is beyond material desires. What is on Master Wang Liping's mind is how he can fulfill the critical task that lies so heavy on his shoulders. People have been seeking out Master Wang Liping, and there will be others seeking him out in the future; Master Wang is dedicated to them. There are even more people who have not found Master Wang Liping and will never have a chance to meet him; Master Wang is dedicated to them as well. The responsibility weighing heavily on the shoulders of Master Wang Liping should also be our responsibility as well. We have the power to add a handful of earth to a mountain.

21

Returning to the Source

O nce again we sat down in Master Wang Liping's simple house. His father, a mellow old man keen on the Way, also sat there, happily listening to us conversing freely about Taoism. Summer vacation hadn't started yet; outside, there was a group of children playing. Drawn by the atmosphere of their innocent liveliness, Master Wang would turn and glance at them from time to time, then enthusiastically continue the conversation.

Facing Master Wang Liping, with his ever-beaming smile, we felt none of the gravity, tension, wariness, and oppressively stuffy atmosphere of speculation characteristic of deep philosophical inquiry. Instead, we felt as if we were lying at ease in the green grass gazing at the white clouds in the blue sky, thoroughly untrammeled, perfectly clear, enveloped in a spirituality in which we unconsciously dissolve with a feeling of relaxation, freedom, and clarity. At such times, it is as if everything has already opened up and we can see into the universe, and yet we still want to silently ask the blue sky: why are heaven and earth like this, and what is there beyond?

The inner quality and spiritual light of an individual who has cultivated realization successfully will spontaneously manifest outwardly, creating a "magnetic field" around that person's life, influencing and affecting the surrounding world. In the process of examining Taoist culture, we could sense, subtly yet strongly, that Taoist culture, which is an essential part of the structure of traditional Chinese culture, has a value that goes even beyond self-cultivation and the art of living, seeking harmony, peace, and transcendence. When body and mind are placed in a state of profound stillness, people can become keenly aware of standing at the door of human wisdom, feeling the fascination of its antiquity and its magnitude.

Master Wang Liping says that in the near future Eastern cultures, including Taoist culture, will attract more serious attention in the world, and Chinese culture will have a chance to revive. In studying Taoist culture, there is the question of what the essence is, and what the function is. In the process of interviewing Master Wang Liping, our sole aim was to clarify what the richest power of life in Taoist wisdom is. Is it the dialectic of simplicity everyone recognizes in the Tao Te Ching? Is it the great body of training methodology known as Taoist hygiene? These certainly have a perennial fascination, but what we consider most essential is Taoism's effort to develop and employ the thinking capacity of the human brain to the maximum possible degree. The ocean of the brain is as vast and deep as the universe itself; whoever can travel freely in that heaven and earth can lead the tide of human intelligence.

From the very first day they began teaching Wang Liping, the three old wizards made the first step of the work a thorough liberation from fetters of thought, restoring human thought in its original state. In order to take the thinking mode of a thirteen-year-old youth and return it from a routine, linear mode of thinking to a nonroutine, nonlinear primordial state, the three old wizards exerted themselves to the utmost, while Wang Liping for his part also "sailed against the current, right up to the source."

When young Wang Liping practiced "gathering the mind and nurturing essential nature" for two years, the grand master spoke only of reining in his wildness; the principles of the exercise are "returning to the source" and "building the foundation." But after long practice, Wang Liping finally realized that cultivating exercises is secondary; training thought is what is basic. In order to merge with the Way, it is a matter of attaining sensitivity and effectiveness within profound stillness.

There is a well-developed theory of this in the Lao-tzu. Chapter 16 says,

> *Attain the climax of emptiness,*
> *preserve the utmost quiet:*
> *as myriad things act in concert,*
> *I thereby observe the return.*
> *Things flourish,*
> *then each returns to its root.*
> *Returning to the root is called stillness;*
> *this is called return to Life.*
> *Return to Life is called the constant;*

knowing the constant is called enlightenment.
Random acts in ignorance bode ill.

Chapter 52 says,

The world has a beginning,
that is the mother of the world.
Once you've found the mother,
you thereby know the child.
Once you know the child,
you return to preserve the mother,
unperishing though the body die.

These passages clearly depict the pattern of placing thought in its original state and thus being able to see into the subtle hidden designs of the universe. "The climax of emptiness" is the essence of the Great Way of the infinite merged with the elemental, the root of heaven and earth and all things. Embracing oneness and preserving utmost quiet, profoundly still, one can then observe the return of heaven and earth and all things. Although the universe and all things transmute in many ways, yet they return to the beginning in quiescence and nothingness. When thought has mastered this fundamental basis, then it can understand the myriad things and beings produced from it.

This is what ancients spoke of as "finding out the principle and penetrating the source, knowing the mind and getting to the root." A river has a source; a tree has a root. People think about everything in the world; then what is the root source of human thought? Is this root source of thought a pond of stagnant water, or a pivotal mechanism containing Creativity itself? Is it merely passive reaction, or does it have capacities of penetrating observation and panoramic awareness? The great intelligence and wisdom of Eastern civilization are to be found in investigating and answering these questions.

Taoism says, "For learning you gain daily, for the Way you lose daily. Losing and losing even that, you thereby reach effortlessness, effortlessness that nonetheless can accomplish anything." It is also said, "Clear the mystic mirror." Buddhism talks about "breaking through the barrier of habit," meaning to clear away the feelings and desires that obscure and pollute mind and thought, to clear away the ash and dust of the ages obscuring our thinking, and remove the various formless obstructions between the true mind and the outside world, making the mind like a clear mirror hung high, like the autumn moon in mid sky, so lucid it can directly perceive the original face of the universe, spontaneously arriving at the truth of all things. It is a matter of getting rid of stickiness, removing bondage, comprehending directly without complications or hangups.

When we were with Master Wang Liping, we were often astounded by the keenness and swiftness with which his thinking responds. When people would ask about concerns or about illnesses, he would answer clearly at once, seemingly without having to reflect or ponder. According to Master Wang himself, in Taoist training of thought the key lies in training intuition. Intuition is a higher mode of thought, but it is not learned from experience or knowledge; it must be strengthened gradually in the course of refinement before it can be used deliberately. Taoist learning comes mostly from actual experience in practical cultivation, so if you want to enter the gate you must cultivate refinement. Direct awareness, sudden realizations, and intuitions are real experiences that almost everyone has had, so no one can deny their existence. These latent capacities of thought are what Taoist practitioners deem important. Stillness can produce insight; many people with years of practice in sitting and cultivating refinement have had this kind of experience. Embracing unity, keeping still, tranquil, and unstirring, does not refer to dead sitting with a blank mind like a rock or a piece of wood. Emptiness does not mean nothing exists; stabilization does not mean everything is lifeless. On the contrary, within the climax of emptiness and utmost quiet are contained the elemental ingredients of all things, the potentiality of creation; this is the original state of the mind, the root of essence. Because of its unadulterated purity, calm serenity, pure tranquility, and high degree of unification, the mind does not wander in confusion, does not cling to attachments; spontaneous and effortless, this is therefore the finest state for the human brain to be in, where all functions are mobilized. Sometimes a thought will flit across the calm ocean of the brain—it may be of a person, or of a thing, or an event—but it arises spontaneously and disappears spontaneously, without lingering or remaining. After the exercise, before long you can find, quite amazingly, that the thoughts that crossed your mind in quiet sitting have appeared in actual reality. Sometimes it may be that a person you happened to think of actually comes calling, or something that occurred to you really happens, or you may arrive at an answer to a question you had been pondering for a long time without resolution. As things like this happen again and again, even the slower people will begin to wake up and polish their hearts. As for people well-grounded in practical refinement, even when they are not sitting, indeed even in the midst of tense and busy work, as long as they maintain a transcendent, serene, calm state of mind, intuitions can occur in their brains without interruption.

We have had many conversations with older students who study the Way with Master Wang Liping, and everyone has a tacit understanding of this, even though they cannot exactly spell out what they know at heart. For now, at least we can share this much of a common understanding: "attain the climax of emptiness, preserve the utmost quiet" is a kind of high-level state of thought in the brain from which human intuitions emerge. Intuitive thought is not impossible to master, for it can be cultivated. When the ancients spoke of being profoundly still in the silence of eternity while being sensitive and effective, this was in fact an advanced summary of intuitive thought.

One of the methods in the Dragon Gate exercises for development of mental capacities is recollection back to infancy, which involves remembering back in deep quiet sitting, recalling the experiences of a lifetime as if showing a movie, bringing them up before your eyes. When Master Wang Liping taught this method at the Fragrant World Temple outside Beijing, quite a few people resurrected forgotten experiences; some of the elderly folks even cried out like babies. Where does this recollection ultimately come to an end? Master Wang Liping says that, depending on the level of cultivation and the depth of stillness, there seems to be virtually no limit to this recollection. People can even get to know all sorts of things that happened before they were born. With each step one rises in one's level of cultivation, furthermore, one will shed a shell, (the authors do not yet understand precisely what Master Wang means by shedding a shell; they simply report what he said) whereupon one can see a certain period of time past; then one sheds another shell, and looks even further into the past. This may mean that the human unconscious is divided into many levels, with each level containing a certain amount of content, the various levels arranged in a certain order. The human subconscious is orderly.

Master Wang Liping says that the capacity he normally uses most is thinking in dreaming. Sometimes he may come across a puzzling ailment that he doesn't know how to treat, or he may be asked a question about something he has never studied or encountered, or he may want to conceive and compose an article he is writing, or he may want to organize the contents of a lesson he is going to give the following day: he never sits there in front of a desk racking his brains; instead, he goes to bed, sets up the topic in his brain, and then dozes off, whereupon his brain seems to work by itself. When he wakes up, he notes the thoughts that occurred in dreaming; this is the answer to the question.

A scientist once said that what blocks people's perceptions of the world is often not what they don't know, but what they do know. The immense knowledge that people have accumulated over hundreds and thousands of years has also gradually given rise to comparatively rigid forms of thought. Things that can be understood by these modes of thought will be included and accepted; anything else is repudiated and rejected. Forms of thought have gradually become walls of thought. This has changed the fluid, lively brain rich in latent capacities into a calculating machine operating according to a fixed program. Buddhists call this "obstruction caused by knowledge." Speculation and logic have their particular ways of cognizing the world, but the human brain also has higher and more perfect modes of thought. Taoists endeavor to break through fetters of thought, so that thinking becomes tremendously free and liberated, like traveling clouds and flowing water, a celestial horse galloping through the sky, radiating beams of light in ecstatic abundance.

As we talked with Master Wang Liping, we forgot all about the time, and didn't notice the sultry heat. The sounds of the street outside the window gradually faded away, and a cup of tea dispersed the remaining heat.

Master Wang invited us to drink some water, and called outside to his son Boyang to bring three pieces of fruit. The boy soon brought the fruit in a tray. He was still a little childish and shy around strangers. Seeing four people, he said, "Pa, there's four people, but you only told me to bring three pieces of fruit. There's not enough."

Master Wang said, "There's enough. Think of a way to divide them up."

Boyang crouched on the ground, staring intently at the fruit.

Master Wang watched his son with a smile. "See how his thinking has gone in one direction: he is thinking that one person will eat one fruit; he hasn't considered that four people can also eat one fruit."

With this hint, Boyang realized the solution right away. Surreptitiously fixing his eyes on his father, the boy picked up a fruit knife from the table and cut each fruit into four pieces. Finally, he pointed to the smallest three pieces and said, "Pa, these are for you!"

Master Wang patted the boy on the head and laughingly spoke words of approval. Having distributed the fruit, the boy ran back outside to play.

As we were eating the fruit, Master Wang asked us, "How many corners does this room have?"

"Four."

Master Wang smiled and said, "Don't the ones on the bottom count?"

"Oh! Eight."

Master Wang shook his head. "Many more. Why only eight? In my youth, I spent quite a time trying to figure the number of corners in a room."

This topic aroused our curiosity, and we requested that he continue.

Master Wang said, "Our usual thinking forms a fixed framework, which is centered in the self. As it emerges from the self to examine and contemplate the surroundings, the flow of thought is unilateral. The universe, however, is omnidirectional and omnilateral; or it may be said that it basically has no directions. My teachers thought up quite a few ways of changing my directional sense of thinking."

In the beginning, the three old wizards first told Wang Liping to learn to stand on his head. We usually look at the world right side up; what are things like when we look at them upside down? Once he could stand on his head for a few minutes at a time, he calmly and quietly observed the surrounding mountains, trees, houses, crops, utility poles. At first it seemed like everything was upside down, but this illusion gradually disappeared and everything returned to its original state. From this simple exercise Wang Liping realized that it is thought that changes, not external things. He always says that things are inert, and it is human thought that has life. This comes into play when there is intuitive feeling.

Later his mentor locked him in a room and told him to work out how many corners it had. Fourteen or fifteen years old at the time, Wang Liping sat in the middle of the room and began to count. First he looked the room over again and again; no matter how he looked, there were eight corners. His mentor laughed at him and told him to count again. With an extremely determined effort, Wang Liping continued to work on the problem, not budging in the slightest. In those days his thinking was unidirectional, and it only occurred to him to view his surroundings from where he was sitting. The grand master, who was standing outside the window, stroked his whiskers and said to Liping with a laugh, "Am I looking at you, or are you looking at me?" And with that he walked away.

Wang Liping was bright and got the hint right away. He immediately realized that there is also a corner on the outside of each corner of a room. The corner of a room being three-dimensional, from inside looking outward he could see only the inside corners. At last he got out of simplistic unidirectional thinking and was able to reverse directions and look from outside in.

What was best about the way the three wizards developed Wang Liping's thinking was that they skipped all sermonizing and transfusion, letting their apprentice arrive at his own experiences and understanding. Then, at appropriate times, they would give a hint to guide him. Thus they trained his thinking to operate in any way that the universe could be described.

Later on, the three wizards enclosed Wang Liping in a globe constructed of tree branches, sealing the globe tightly with a coating of mud, so it was pitch dark inside, with no way to discern direction. Then they suspended the globe in the air. Next one of his mentors poked a little hole in the globe, allowing a ray of light through, and asked Wang Liping to identify the direction. Based on ordinary ideas, Liping said, "Above." The mentor rotated the globe, made another hole, and asked, "What direction is this?" Again relying on ordinary conceptions, Liping replied, "Below." Then with each hole the mentor made in the globe, he had Wang Liping name the direction. Finally he spun the globe so that Liping became dizzy and disoriented and his answers became confused. After repeated spinning, Wang Liping no longer had any sense of direction. In the end he realized a certain principle: the universe originally has no directions, no above or below, no left or right, no inside or outside, no front or back. The directions later defined by people have only relative meaning.

The three old Taoists' training of their apprentice was not only in the form of special exercises, but was integrated with daily life, as the four of them worked on each other and engaged in contests of wits. Under these conditions, Wang Liping's thinking never became stultified or rigid, but was kept very sharp, effective, and active.

One morning, the grand master looked in the water container, then looked at Wang Liping and said, drawing out his words, "Oh! Why the water in the container . . . ," leaving the thought unfinished. Puzzled, Wang Liping looked in the container and saw there was no water in it. "The water is all gone," he said. "Then go get some more!" retorted the grand master at once. Wang Liping had no way to refuse; he had to go draw some water.

Things like this happened quite often before Wang Liping realized the grand master was deliberately tuning him, seeing how he responded, observing whether or not he was on the alert.

Wang Liping also learned how to keep his teachers on their toes. Once when their rice was ready but the grand master was still sitting on the earthen platform, Wang Liping quickly said, "There's no need for you to stir, master, I'll bring you some rice." Heaping a bowl with rice, Liping mischievously placed it in front of the old master just out of reach and walked away. The grand master called him, but he pretended not to hear. After all the old wizard had no choice but to unlock his legs and break his posture to get his own rice.

We listened with great interest as Master Wang Liping recalled his times with the three old wizards. Right then, however, the old lady from next door came over, with Wang Liping's son in tow. With a smile she said, "Liping, your boy Boyang was over there digging at the base of the wall of my house!"

Boyang came over, all sweaty, with a little trowel in his hand. Master Wang Liping hurriedly apologized to the old lady and invited her to come in and sit down. Seeing there were guests, however, she smilingly took her leave. It looked like their neighborhood relations were as close as family.

When your own child digs at the base of the wall of a neighbor's house, how do you admonish an uncomprehending child? An ordinary parent might give a lecture, take away the trowel, and warn the child not to do any more digging. A somewhat stricter parent might spank the child, as a warning and a lesson. Master Wang Liping was more interested in taking a look. Going out to the half-room kitchen, he set aside a basket of greens, pointed to the white limed wall, and said to his son, "Come, dig here!" The boy knelt down and began to dig.

We were surprised at this scene, not knowing what Master Wang's intention was.

Boyang stopped when he had managed to scrape off some of the surfacing of the wall. Speckled with dirt, he happily exclaimed, "I found out, Pa! I found out!"

Master Wang asked him, "What did you find out?"

"Inside the wall is red brick, and between the bricks is sand."

Boyang had found out what he wanted to know; at this point we suddenly understood Master Wang's approach. He was using Taoist methodology to educate his own son.

Master Wang Liping explained that his eldest teacher, the grand master, always used to say, "Playing with children is my teacher." He embodied the Taoist spirit of reverence for Nature. The whole secret of Taoist cultivation is to return the temporal in human beings back to the primal; this is what people call "rejuvenation," referred to by Lao-tzu as the ability to be like an infant. But it is not simply a reversion or a return; it is a remanifestation of the state of childlike genuineness on an even higher level. This is not only true physically, but also spiritually.

The thinking of innocent children is "natural" thinking, which is the realest and freest, unpolluted by artificiality, unstained by society. What it presents to us is pure, unadulterated natural reality. In bringing up children, therefore, we should establish a means of preserving and also further developing this sort of untrammeled thinking, along with a spirit of courageous investigation and fearlessness of the future. We cannot suppress it or constrict it, and we cannot force our own fixed habits of thought on the thinking of children, or raise children according to our own personal likes and dislikes. On the contrary, we adults, who are so sophisticated about the reasons of things, ought to learn from children what we have lost in the process of temporal conditioning.

Regarding the education of children, Master Wang Liping respects their natural spontaneity and protects their natural genuineness, stimulating wholesome development of their natural faculties. Precisely because of this, his own son's thinking is quite different from the thinking of other children. Frequently he comes up with some very extraordinary thoughts.

At school, for example, in the lesson on "Common Knowledge," when the teacher read that the sun comes up every day in the east and a new day begins, the other children read along with the teacher, but Boyang stood up and asked why the sun doesn't rise in the west. The teacher couldn't answer this question, and neither can the greatest modern scientists.

One day Boyang came home from school with an unhappy look on his face. Master Wang Liping asked him what the matter was. Boyang said that when the class lined up by height, the teacher always told them to even up on the right. Why not even up on the left? The child's natural genuineness and innocence delighted the whole household. Master Wang knew that it is precisely this sort of mind that contains the seeds of wisdom.

Once when the school held a field day, the parents all went to watch. Seeing their fathers and mothers in the distance, the children were shouting "Papa! Mama!" One child alone was calling, "Wang Liping! Wang Liping!" Master Wang Liping recognized his boy at once in the midst of the crowd of children. The other parents and children thought this strange. On the way back home later, Master Wang asked his son why he had called "Wang Liping" when the others were calling "Papa" and "Mama." The boy explained, "Everybody was wearing the same uniform, and everybody was shouting 'Papa' and 'Mama.' So how could anyone tell them apart? As soon as I called your name, you found me in the crowd." Master Wang Liping was delighted to see how his son kept his own original thinking.

Yet Master Wang also says, not without concern, that he's been so busy over the last few years, and away from home so much, that he hasn't been able to look after his son's education as closely as he would like; school education is already gradually making his son's thinking routine and linear. Human life itself, however, is basically nondirectional; if you're going to go forward, which way is forward? Turn around, and it becomes backward!

This topic led Master Wang to a discussion of the trouble with modern education: the range of thinking activity of those who receive education becomes narrower and narrower the more schooling they have. In primary and middle school, children all learn some astronomy, geography, history, math, physics, chemistry, fine arts, music, zoology, botany, biology, and so on. When they get to high school, though, they are divided into departments of humanities and sciences, reducing their perspective, making it directional and limited. In college, furthermore, there is specialization, where one concentrates on one particular field of knowledge. When it comes to reading for the master's and doctorate degrees, study becomes even more highly specialized, focusing on one branch or one point. The structure of knowledge and the flow of thought are then like a pyramid, becoming smaller in compass the higher up you go.

Taoist development of human thought patterns is precisely the opposite. As one ascends from the lower three realms to the middle three realms and then on to the higher three realms, with each leap the individual's thinking activity becomes broader, vaster, and deeper in both time and space. At first one studies all the phenomena and principles in the world of "persons, events, and things" in which ordinary people live. After that one must transcend this to study the world of "heaven, earth, and humanity." Heaven, earth, and humanity encompass persons, events, and things, but are much vaster and much deeper. Finally one transcends time and space to study "time, space, and the universe." Thinking is now liberated and radiant. And one does not investigate only the external universe; the higher one's state, the greater the need to attend to examination and investigation of one's own inner world, that is, the brain.

Finally, Master Wang Liping explained that the problem of education is not a question of breadth or narrowness of curriculum. The three worlds are three different levels of the same thing. The key is in having "three world" thinking, which requires a new philosophy.

Here we interjected a saying from a Buddhist scripture: "See the lands of the ten directions on the tip of a hair; turn the wheel of true teaching sitting in an atom."

Master Wang Liping smiled and nodded.

The Tuttle Story

"Books to Span the East and West"

Our core mission at Tuttle Publishing is to create books which bring people together one page at a time. Tuttle was founded in 1832 in the small New England town of Rutland, Vermont (USA). Our fundamental values remain as strong today as they were then—to publish best-in-class books informing the English-speaking world about the countries and peoples of Asia. The world has become a smaller place today and Asia's economic, cultural and political influence has expanded, yet the need for meaningful dialogue and information about this diverse region has never been greater. Since 1948, Tuttle has been a leader in publishing books on the cultures, arts, cuisines, languages and literatures of Asia. Our authors and photographers have won numerous awards and Tuttle has published thousands of books on subjects ranging from martial arts to paper crafts. We welcome you to explore the wealth of information available on Asia at **www.tuttlepublishing.com.**